The
IDEA MAGAZINE FOR TEACHERS®
MAILBOX®

2004–2005 YEARBOOK

The Education Center, Inc.
Greensboro, North Carolina

The Mailbox® 2004–2005 Grades 2–3 Yearbook

Managing Editors, *The Mailbox* Magazine: Diane Badden, Lauren E. Cox

Editorial Team: Becky S. Andrews, Kimberley Bruck, Karen P. Shelton, Diane Badden, Thad H. McLaurin, Debra Liverman, Karen A. Brudnak, Sarah Hamblet, Hope Rodgers, Dorothy C. McKinney

Production Team: Lisa K. Pitts, Margaret Freed (COVER ARTIST), Pam Crane, Rebecca Saunders, Jennifer Tipton Cappoen, Chris Curry, Sarah Foreman, Theresa Lewis Goode, Clint Moore, Greg D. Rieves, Barry Slate, Donna K. Teal, Zane Williard, Tazmen Carlisle, Irene Harvley-Felder, Amy Kirtley-Hill, Kristy Parton, Cathy Edwards Simrell, Lynette Dickerson, Mark Rainey

ISBN 1-56234-661-X
ISSN 1088-5544

Printed in the United States of America.

The Education Center, Inc.
P.O. Box 9753
Greensboro, NC 27429-0753

Contents

Arts & Crafts

Arts & Crafts

Slices of Summer

A scrumptious patch of summertime memories is just a few steps away! To showcase a memory, trace two large circle shapes on white construction paper. Squeeze a dollop of red tempera paint on one circle. Then, using a crumpled wad of plastic wrap, repeatedly dab the paint until the circle is covered. On the second circle, illustrate a favorite memory from the past summer.

When the paint dries, cut out both circles. Glue the painted circle onto a slightly larger piece of green construction paper and trim the green paper to make a rindlike border. Next, turn the project over. Glue (or tape) a jumbo craft stick handle to the project and then glue the illustration on the green paper. When the glue dries, fold the project in half, keeping the illustration to the inside. Add a few seed cutouts and initial the handle. Invite students to share their memories with the class and then display the slices of melon in florist foam (available at craft stores) for all to see.

adapted from an idea by Darcy Brown
Ward Elementary, Winston-Salem, NC

Designer Desktags

These student-designed desktags are sure to earn rave reviews during open house! For the base, make three lengthwise accordion folds in a 6" x 18" strip of construction paper. Unfold the paper, squeeze a trail of glue along the center crease, and fold the paper in half. Then display the paper as shown, with the fold at the top. Next, trace letter stencils or cutouts onto colorful construction paper to personalize the desktag. Decorate and cut out the letters and then glue them to the base. Trim the ends of the base as desired. Very vogue!

Pam Temerowski—Grs. 1–3 Multiage
Green Acres Elementary, Warren, MI

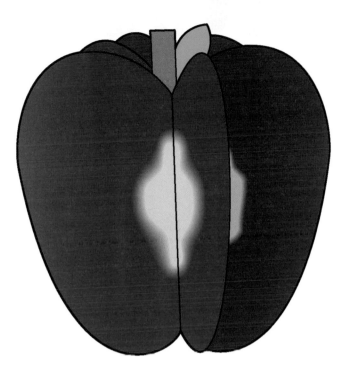

Autumn's Apples

When it's apple pickin' time, pick this project! Prepare a half-apple template similar to the one shown. Trace the template onto folded construction paper six times, each time aligning the straight edge of the template with the fold. Cut out the tracings. Also cut a stem and a leaf from construction paper.

To assemble the apple, spread glue on the top surface of a folded cutout. Align a second folded cutout atop the glue and then spread glue on the top surface of this cutout. Repeat the process with each cutout. On top of the final cutout, lay the stem near the fold. Then pick up the project and press the top and bottom surfaces together. Next, lay the project on its side. Working around the apple, place a drop of white tempera paint in the crease of every (or every other) apple section, fold the section closed, and rub the paper to spread the paint. Add the leaf and this "apple-lutely" gorgeous fruit is ready to display!

Darcy Brown
Ward Elementary
Winston-Salem, NC

Red, White, and Blue

Get to the heart of your students' patriotism and creativity! Provide an assortment of red, white, and blue craft supplies, such as construction paper, curling ribbon, pom-poms, and star stickers. Begin by cutting a heart shape from construction paper. Then use the provided supplies to decorate the cutout in a patriotic way. As students work, invite them to explain why they feel proud to live in the United States. If desired, write the students' thoughts on a length of bulletin board paper titled "We Love the USA!" Then display the list and use the students' artwork to create a star-spangled border around it. Hooray for the USA!

Arts & Crafts

Creature of the Night

Heads will turn when students make these clever paper bag owls. To make the owl's body, carefully stuff one brown paper lunch bag three-quarters full with pieces of crumbled newspaper or scrap paper. Use a pipe cleaner to securely tie the top of the bag. To make the owl's head, position another lunch bag flat with the opening toward you. Cut off the bottom four inches of the bag (the base) using a wavy cut, and discard the remainder of the bag. Next, trim a 3" x 5" piece of brown construction paper into a face shape as shown. Then glue the cutout onto the head so that the bottom of the bag is now the top of the owl's head. Add details using construction paper scraps. Finally, place the owl's head on the body. Show students that their paper owls display an adaptation similar to one that many real owls have—their heads turn so the owls can look in all directions. What a hoot!

adapted from an idea by VaReane Gray Heese—Gr. 2
Springfield Elementary
Springfield, NE

Friendly Monsters

Grrr! Create these child-size monsters to set the scene for Halloween. In advance, tape a child-size sheet of butcher paper to the wall so it just touches the floor. Have each student, in turn, stand in front of the paper and strike a scary pose. Shine the overhead projector so the student's shadow is on the paper and outline the child's shadow. To complete his monster, a student cuts out the shape and decorates it with crayons, construction paper, and wiggle eyes. Post these spooky, kooky characters in the hallway outside your classroom with the title "Welcome to [Ms. Heese's] Monstrously Fun [Second] Grade. Enter If You Dare!"

VaReane Gray Heese—Gr. 2

Better Than Mother Nature?

Invite your youngsters to play the part of Mother Nature by creating beautiful and unique fall leaves! Enlist your students' help in gathering a supply of fallen leaves (or pictures of fall leaves), and have children study them. Place a small amount of blue tempera paint and larger amounts of yellow and red tempera paint on disposable foam plates. Place a clean nylon bath puff on each plate. A student uses the bath puff to blot the paint onto white construction paper, using two or three colors to cover the page. Discuss how the colors combine to create other colors. When the paint is dry, fold the paper in half and draw a leaf shape on the unpainted side. Cut along the resulting outline through both thicknesses of paper. Place a length of monofilament line between the two cutouts and glue the two unpainted sides together. Finally, invite students to write a story from the leaf's perspective about gently floating from the tree to the ground. Suspend the leaves and stories together.

adapted from an idea by Cindy Barber, Fredonia, WI

Happy Thanksgiving Wreath

Create a festive wreath to celebrate the special day for giving thanks!

Materials for one wreath:

wooden ice-cream spoon	raffia
brown construction paper	glue
construction paper in assorted colors	tape
paper plate	scissors
brown crepe paper	markers
hole puncher	pencil

1. Trace the ice-cream spoon onto brown construction paper to make the turkey's body and then multiple times onto other colors of construction paper to make the turkey's feathers. Cut out the shapes.
2. Stack the feathers; then fan them out and glue them to the back of the turkey's body. Use markers and construction paper scraps to add eyes, a beak, and a wattle.
3. Cut out and discard the center of the paper plate. Wrap the crepe paper around the rim of the plate, overlapping the edges. Tape the crepe paper in place.
4. Punch two holes side by side, ½-inch apart, in the plate. Loop one piece of raffia through the holes with the loose ends in the front. Use the ends to attach a raffia bow.
5. Tape the turkey to the wreath, under the bow.

adapted from an idea by Debby Dula—Grs. K–3, Drexel Primary, Drexel, NC

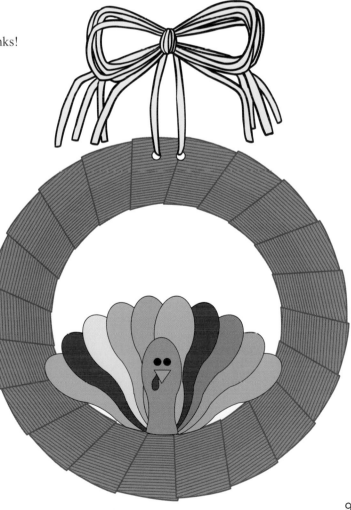

Arts & Crafts

Handmade Holiday Bags

Are your students ready to wrap up the holidays, literally? Pick and choose from this collection of gift bag ideas. Each project begins with a paper lunch bag. First, fold back the top of the bag, punch two side-by-side holes through all four thicknesses, and then unfold the top. Starting at the front of the bag, thread each end of a two-foot length of ribbon through a different hole in the lower set of holes. Pull the ends taut. Next, use markers, glue, construction paper, gift wrap, pom-poms, cotton balls, and other assorted supplies to decorate the bag to your liking. When finished, carefully open the bag and tuck inside a holiday gift wrapped in tissue paper. Close the bag, fold back the top, thread the ribbon ends through the second set of holes, and tie a bow. Attach a gift tag and deliver. Happy holidays!

inspired by an idea by Kathleen McCarthy
Marymount School of New York
New York, NY

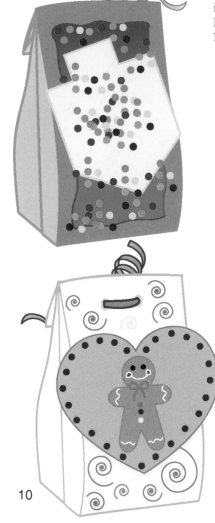

To: Daddy
From: Kate

Yum Yum!

10

Sled riding is so much fun.
It's my favorite thing to do!
Maddie

Candy Cane Sled

Hold on tight! You're about to take a ride on a peppermint sled! Plan to purchase candy canes at an after-Christmas sale. To make this clever wintertime project, use white tempera paint to sponge-paint a snowbank on blue construction paper. Allow the paint to dry. Next, use construction paper scraps, crayons, markers, pom-poms, and so forth to make a miniature self-likeness in a sledding position. Glue the self-likeness on the painted paper so that it is flush with the snowbank. Then use craft glue to fasten a wrapped candy cane sled in place. Add a personalized caption and the project is ready for display. Whee! What a fun ride!

Melissa Gatchel
East Palestine Elementary
East Palestine, OH

Smiling Snowflake

It's a fact that no two snowflakes are alike. The same holds true for these smiling versions! Cut a snowflake body from a nine-inch square of white construction paper. To make the snowflake's head, decorate a six-inch construction paper circle. Next, cut a pair of mittens from a half sheet of construction paper and a hat from another half sheet of construction paper. Decorate the hat and mittens as desired. Then assemble the project. Display the snowflake personality on a bulletin board covered with bright paper. Or glue the snowflake on colorful paper and trim as shown. Either way, with these smiling snowflakes all around, you'll be content to just let it snow!

Barbara Marks
St. John La Lande School
Blue Springs, MO

Arts & Crafts

Love Bug Box

When the buzz of Valentine's Day swarms your classroom, "bee" prepared! Have a class supply of empty tissue boxes on hand. To transform a tissue box into a love bug, mix red tempera paint with a small amount of glue. Use a small foam paint roller to apply the prepared paint to the top and sides of a box. To make painting easy, hold the box by the plastic liner inside the box's opening. When the paint is dry, cut away the plastic liner. Then decorate the box using a variety of materials, such as construction paper scraps, waxed paper (wings), pipe cleaners (antennae), pom-poms (nose and stinger), and sequins. Remember to add a nametag too. What did one love bug say to the other? "Please 'bee' mine!"

Sign of Love

This hand-crafted valentine greeting comes straight from the heart! To make one, cut a large heart from 12" x 18" red construction paper. Then, on writing paper sized to fit the heart cutout, write and sign a valentine greeting that includes the provided poem. Glue the greeting to the heart. Next, trace your hand on pink construction paper. Cut out the shape and glue it to the blank side of the card, keeping the ring and middle fingers free. Then bend the fingers forward, as shown, to create the sign language symbol that means "I love you" and glue the fingers in place. Add a stem and leaves cut from green construction paper. Last, use construction paper scraps and crayons to further decorate both sides of the greeting. How lovely!

Lisa Ratliff, Bayou Woods Elementary, Slidell, LA

Dear Mom,
It's not a rose of red.
It's not a violet of blue.
It's a pretty paper flower,
And it means "I love you!"
Love,

Nicholas

March Masterpieces

Keep these reminders of St. Patrick's Day close by, and the luck of the Irish may follow! Cut a large shamrock shape from green construction paper. Cut two squares from white construction paper, each sized to fit inside the shamrock. Lay the squares on a covered work surface and squeeze individual dollops of green, yellow, and white tempera (or acrylic) paint near the center of each. Then cover one square with waxed paper. Press down gently on the waxed paper, pushing the paint toward the edges of the white square. Then lift the waxed paper, reposition it, and press together the new color combinations. Repeat this step one more time. Use a fresh piece of waxed paper to paint the second square in a similar manner. When the painted squares are dry, glue them on opposite sides of the shamrock. If desired, suspend the dazzling foliage to create a festive field of green!

Carol Stillings, Bill Metz Elementary
Monte Vista, CO

Handsome Hares

Easter in March? Just by a whisker! Top off your springtime festivities by tucking a few treats inside these student-made bunny baskets.

Materials for one bunny:

empty Pringles potato crisps can
9" x 12" sheet of white construction paper
two 2" x 6" pieces of pink construction paper
two 2" x 6" pieces of white construction paper
12" pipe cleaner
scrap paper or newspaper
handful of Easter grass

construction paper scraps
tape
glue
scissors
markers
pushpin (for supervised use)

Steps:

1. Wrap the sheet of white construction paper around the can. Tape it in place.
2. For the bunny's ears, stack the white paper strips and cut an ear shape from both. Also stack the pink paper strips and cut a smaller inner-ear shape from both. Glue each pink cutout onto a white cutout. Then tape the ears to the back of the can, near the paper seam.
3. For the basket handle, use a pushpin to carefully poke a cluster of two or three small holes on opposite sides of the can, about one inch from the top. Push one end of the pipe cleaner through a cluster of holes and then knot the end of the pipe cleaner. In a similar manner, secure the opposite end of the handle to the opposite side of the can.
4. Use construction paper scraps and markers to add facial features and other desired decorations to the can.
5. Partially fill the bunny basket with scrap paper or newspaper and then lay a handful of Easter grass on top. Hippity hop!

Rita Arnold, Alden-Hebron School, Hebron, IL

Arts & Crafts

Fancy Flyers

It takes just a flit and a flutter to make these shimmering showstoppers! Using templates like those shown, trace a butterfly body onto construction paper. Then trace the wing shapes onto folded construction paper, being sure to align the straight edge of each template with the fold. Cut out the tracings and unfold each set of wings. Spread glue in the center area of each wing, sprinkle foil confetti atop the glue, and set the wings aside to dry. Add crayon details and construction paper antennae to the body. To assemble the showstopper, shake excess confetti from the wings and then glue the wing cutouts together so one slightly overlaps the other. Glue the butterfly body in place, and the flamboyant flyer is ready to soar.

Cheryl Mitchell
Our Lady of Mount Carmel School
Amherstview, Ontario, Canada

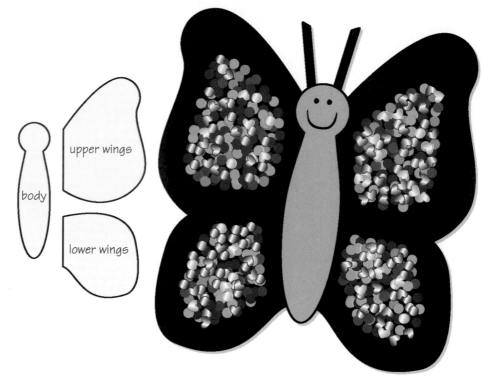

Flowers by Design

No one will guess that these gorgeous blossoms are fashioned from foil! To make a bloom, brush diluted glue over a 6" x 9" sheet of foil. Cover the foil with overlapping tissue paper squares and then apply another coat of diluted glue. The following day, cut the colorful foil into slender six-inch-long strips. Pinch together the ends of two foil strips, keeping the paper covering to the inside. Then, one by one, add in the remaining strips as you slowly turn the project. If desired, add two or three strips of green tissue paper for leaves. Next, securely wrap the base of the project with one end of a green 12-inch pipe cleaner. To open the blossom, begin at the outer edge and work inward as you gently bend each foil strip away from the flower center.

Use the blooms in colorful flower arrangements for the classroom. Or have each child make additional blooms and help him prepare his blooms for delivery. To do this, twist together the stems, wrap a paper doily around them, and secure the doily with a length of fabric ribbon. Beauteous!

Heather Miller, Auburn, IN

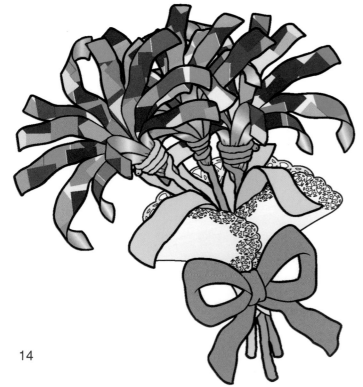

May Day Bouquets

A tisket, a tasket, it's a May Day basket! To make this cheerful arrangement, daub ink on the back side of a paper plate half using a cotton ball and a colorful stamp pad. Repeat the process with a second cotton ball and color of ink. Add a greeting to the painted plate half and then align the rim of the plate with a whole (uncut) paper plate and staple the two rims together as shown. Partially fill the resulting pocket with Easter grass or crumbled tissue paper. Also punch two holes at the top of the project, thread a one-foot length of ribbon through the holes, and securely tie the ends. Next, cut an assortment of blooms, stems, and leaves from colorful construction paper. Glue the stems to the inside front of the pocket, and glue the leaves and flowers to the stems. If the flowers fall forward, dab the back of each one with glue and secure it to the paper filling. Knock, knock! Who's there? A May Day. A May Day, who? A May Day basket for you!

Lydia Hess, Chambersburg, PA

Mother's Day Greetings

Any loved one is sure to be tickled to receive this handmade greeting! To make a card, fold in half a 9" x 12" sheet of construction paper. Keeping the fold at the top, decorate the front of the card as desired and add the phrase "[Recipient], I think you are." Then unfold the card and punch a hole at each end of the fold line. Thread a two-foot length of jute through the holes, refold the card, and tie the ends of the jute as shown. Next, cut out the shape of a T-shirt from construction paper. Decorate the cutout. Then open the card and use paper clips to suspend the cutout from the jute. Above the T-shirt write "'T-rific'!" and below it add a desired message and your signature. Very sweet!

adapted from an idea by Cheryl Rightmyer
Albion Elementary, Albion, NY

Arts & Crafts

Sparkly Suncatchers

Bring the sunshine indoors! These shiny suncatchers will brighten up your classroom windows!

Darcy Brown, Ward Elementary, Winston-Salem, NC

Materials for one suncatcher:
two 7" yellow construction paper circles
10 yellow construction paper triangles
6" circle template
8" waxed paper square
gold glitter
glue
paintbrush
scissors

Steps:
1. Brush a thin layer of glue onto the waxed paper and sprinkle with gold glitter. Shake off excess glitter.
2. Trace the six-inch circle template onto both yellow construction paper circles. Fold each circle in half; then cut along the tracing.
3. Glue one resulting yellow ring atop the waxed paper. Then trim the excess waxed paper around the circle.
4. Flip the circle and glue the construction paper triangles evenly around it. Then glue on the second yellow ring, sandwiching the triangles inside.

Magnetic Insect Clips

Buzz into summer with this three-dimensional project! Gather a class supply of wooden clothespins and two-inch magnetic strips with adhesive backs. Also make a class supply of the dragonfly patterns on page 18. To make the clip, a child colors and cuts out the patterns. She adds antennae, and then she glues the insect's body to the top of the clothespin and the wings to the back. After allowing time for the glue to dry, the youngster attaches the magnetic strip to the back of the wings along the clothespin. Clip students' papers to the insects; then post them on a file cabinet or send each child home with her clip to proudly display it on the family refrigerator.

Rita Skavinsky, Minersville Elementary Center, Minersville, PA

Star-Spangled Windsocks

This patriotic project is a breeze to complete! Have each child brainstorm six things that remind him of Independence Day. Instruct him to use a marker to write each item in the middle of a 1½" x 12" blue construction paper strip. Then have him follow the directions below to complete his windsock.

adapted from an idea by Jill Putnam, Wheelock Primary School, Fredonia, NY

Materials for one windsock:
9" x 12" sheet of red construction paper
two 4½" x 12" pieces of white construction paper
six 1½" x 12" blue construction paper strips (from above)
18" length of yarn
star template
glue
scissors
hole puncher
stapler

Steps:
1. Cut out four strips from one piece of white paper. Glue the strips onto the red construction paper.
2. Trace six stars on the remaining sheet of white construction paper and cut them out. Glue one star to the bottom of each blue strip.
3. Glue the blue strips to the back of the red paper. Then staple the 9-inch sides of the red paper together, forming a tube.
4. Punch two holes in the top of the windsock. Thread the yarn through each hole and knot it.

Dragonfly Body and Wings Patterns
Use with "Magnetic Insect Clips" on page 17.

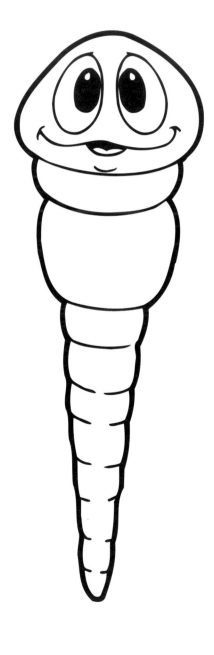

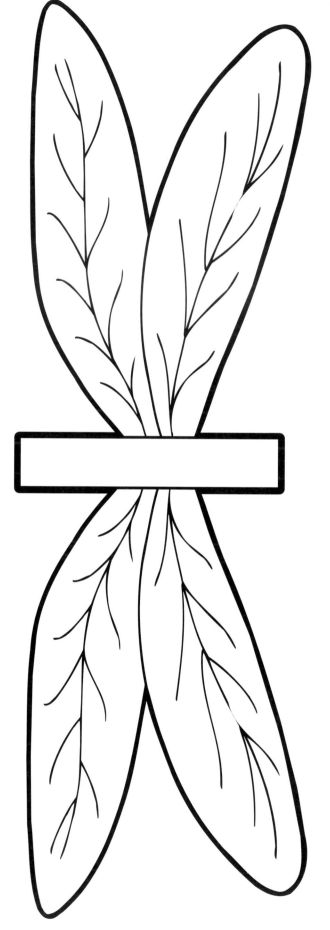

Classroom Displays

What a Great Catch!

Reel in your students' help to create this back-to-school display. Mount a fisher on a titled bulletin board as shown. Tack a length of heavy string in place for the fishing line. Have each student decorate and personalize a fish cutout (page 30). Arrange students' fish on the prepared display to show off your catch of the school year!

Laura Hess—Grs. 2–3, Providence School, Waynesboro, PA

Dish up ongoing problem-solving practice with this "scoop-er" display! Laminate two ice-cream cone cutouts and several ice-cream scoops. Use a wipe-off marker to program each cone with a problem-solving strategy and each scoop with a corresponding problem. Letter the scoops for easy reference. Mount the cutouts and a title as shown. Staple a clean, empty ice-cream container to the board for collecting student work. Change the display as you introduce new strategies. Refreshing!

adapted from an idea by Lisa Kelly
Orchard Lake, MI

F.
Each ice-cream cone has 2 vanilla scoops and 1 strawberry scoop. There are 9 scoops in all. How many vanilla scoops are there?

We Had a "Tee-rific" Summer!

Evan

Kayleigh

Lauren

Justin

Ethan

Stephen

Connor

Alina

Matthew

Megan

Reminiscing about cool summer experiences is a breeze with this student-created display! Securely attach two lengths of heavy string or plastic clothesline to a titled bulletin board. On a provided T-shirt cutout, each child writes her name and illustrates her favorite summer memory. She uses her completed T-shirt to share her experience with the class. Then she uses clothespins to suspend her T-shirt from a line. "Tee-rific"!

Carla Choy—Gr. 2, DeWitt D. Barlow School, Plainfield, NJ

This reading incentive display leads the pack! Mount the title and a class set of personalized library card pockets (colored by students to resemble crayon boxes) as shown. For each book a child reads, she completes a crayon cutout (page 30) and colors it. Then she tucks the crayon inside her box. She exchanges a predetermined number of crayons for a prize or special activity. What colorful reading motivation!

Lisa Strieker—Gr. 3
St. Paul Elementary School
Highland, IL

Whoooo's Watching the Moon?

New Moon	Waxing Crescent	First Quarter	Waxing Gibbous	Full Moon	Waning Gibbous	Third Quarter	Waning Crescent
Oct. 13	Oct. 14 Oct. 19	Oct. 20	Oct. 21 Oct. 26	Oct. 27	Oct. 1	Oct. 6	Oct. 7 Oct. 12
	Oct. 15		Oct. 22		Oct. 2		Oct. 8
	Oct. 16		Oct. 23		Oct. 3		Oct. 9
	Oct. 17		Oct. 24		Oct. 4		Oct. 10
	Oct. 18		Oct. 25		Oct. 5		Oct. 11

Turn students into sky watchers with this ongoing display! Label each of eight sections of your bulletin board with a different phase of the moon as shown. Divide students into eight groups and have each group illustrate a different phase on a paper circle. Mount the illustrations on the board. Challenge students to look at the moon each night and determine its phase. The next morning, discuss the moon phase from the previous night and write that night's date on a sticky note. Then add the note to the correct section on the board. Guide students to understand that it takes approximately one month for the moon to orbit the earth.

adapted from an idea by Stacie Stone Davis, Lima, NY

No doubt "a-bat" it—students will zero in on new books to read with this display! After a student finishes a book she enjoyed, she writes on an index card the book's title and author and a short summary and then signs her name. Next, she traces and cuts out a bat pattern like the one shown. She glues the card to the bat cutout and then decorates the bat. Mount students' work on a titled board to provide some high-flying book recommendations!

Brooke Shaw
Columbia, SC

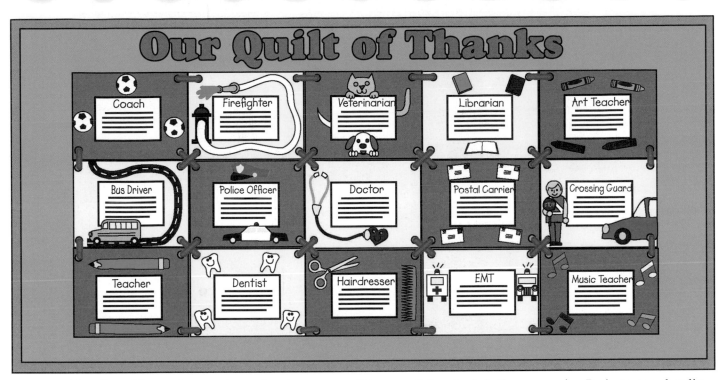

Our Quilt of Thanks

Use this quilt-making project to raise students' awareness of the many folks who help them every day. Brainstorm a class list of community helpers. Each student chooses a different helper and writes this job on an index card. Next, he writes two or more sentences that tell how this person helps others. He glues his writing on a sheet of fall-colored construction paper and decorates the sheet as desired. Hole-punch the corners and bind them with brown yarn as shown. Then display the resulting quilt.

Michelle W. Heissler—Gr. 2, Upper Freehold Regional Elementary School, Allentown, NJ

Students count the many things they are thankful for with this math-related display! Have each child write her name at the top of a large colorful paper feather. Under her name, have her list four things for which she is grateful and that can be counted (such as two sisters, three cats, two grandmothers, and 12 fish). Next, have her add up her blessings and write the sum on the feather, leaving several inches blank at the bottom. Mount the feathers, a turkey body, and a title as shown. Those blessings really do add up!

Julia Ring Alarie
Brewster Pierce Memorial School
Huntington, VT

23

CLASSROOM DISPLAYS

Bright Blends

Welcome the holiday season with a bright review of blends! Have each child brainstorm words for a chosen blend. Then have him create holiday artwork that includes one shape labeled with the blend and five or more bulb cutouts programmed with different words that include the blend. Post the projects as shown. The resulting display is sure to sparkle!

Vicki O'Neal, Lincoln School, Baxter Springs, KS

Holiday Helper
Lever's To-Do List

My name is Lever. I use levers all day long.

- Use a <u>broom</u> to sweep the floor.

- Use a <u>shovel</u> to clear a path in the snow.

- Use a <u>wheelbarrow</u> to deliver supplies in the workshop.

Show students that Santa's helpers can get a little help for themselves—from simple machines! Post an elf cutout along with a speech bubble and to-do list (without tasks) similar to the one shown. Ask students to brainstorm tasks the elf could do using his namesake, and write their suggestions on the to-do list. A few days later introduce another simple machine by replacing the speech bubble and to-do list with ones that are appropriately programmed. Ho-ho-ho, Santa sure has some good helpers!

Nell Mattingly
Walker Elementary
Savannah, TN

Season's Reading Hits

The Lorax · Jumanji · Nate the Great · Math Curse · Riptide · The Mysterious Tadpole · Gloria Rising · How Big Is a Foot? · Charlotte's Web · Arthur's Tooth

This holiday season, student-selected reading tops the charts! Ask each child to list five words that describe a book he recently read and enjoyed. Have him include the five words in a brief written review of the book, underlining each one. Then, using a permanent marker, have him copy each underlined word onto the shiny side of a promotional CD (or foil-covered circle). Display the students' projects as shown. Fa la la!

Sandi Jarvis, Riverview School, Wautoma, WI

Need a student-created display in a hurry? "Snow" problem! Have each student choose a sample of her best math work. Also invite her to cut out a snowflake for the display. Showcase the students' work samples and artwork as shown. Then add a title and other desired decorations. Encourage students to update their work samples each week. Let it snow!

adapted from an idea by Judy Lesnansky
New Hope Academy
Youngstown, OH

In honor of George Washington, it's tricorn hats off to American presidents! Have each child research a different president and complete a copy of page 31 about him. Then have the student cut out the hat shape, glue it onto dark blue construction paper, and trim the blue paper to make a border. Color details can also be added. Now there's a display that's brimming with facts!

Paula Tyszka, Peck Elementary School, Ansonia, CT

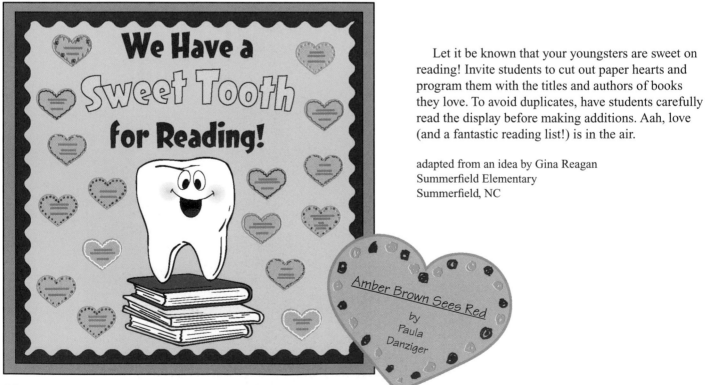

Let it be known that your youngsters are sweet on reading! Invite students to cut out paper hearts and program them with the titles and authors of books they love. To avoid duplicates, have students carefully read the display before making additions. Aah, love (and a fantastic reading list!) is in the air.

adapted from an idea by Gina Reagan
Summerfield Elementary
Summerfield, NC

Good Work Is Always in Reach!

This delightful display reminds students that exceptional work is always in reach. Have each child select a sample of her finest work for exhibit. Then, every few days, have her replace her paper with a more current example. Hey, top-notch work isn't such a tall order after all!

Laura Hess, Providence School, Greencastle, PA

Promote healthful choices with a "grape" bunch of student suggestions! Have each child write and illustrate a suggestion for good health. Then have her glue her work onto a large purple construction paper circle and add her name in black marker. Showcase the projects, a title, and desired embellishments so they look just "ripe"!

Tricia Dougherty
McNichols Plaza School
Scranton, PA

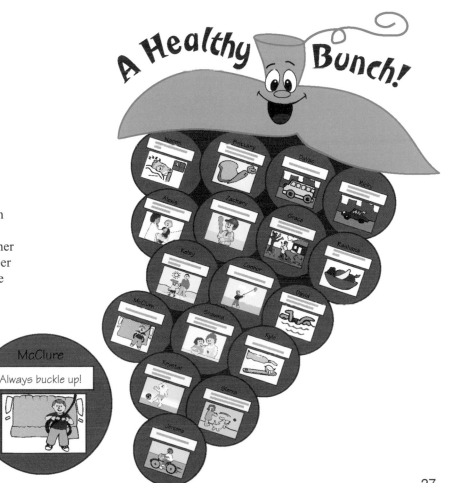

CLASSROOM DISPLAYS

April showers bring May flowers, but did you know they can bring an eye-catching and easy-to-maintain display too? Mount a title and a raindrop cutout in the center of a display area. Throughout the month, post rain-related samples of student work around the cutout. With a minimal investment of time, the display keeps growing and changing! Display a flower cutout in May and a bee cutout in June!

Vicki O'Neal, Lincoln Elementary, Baxter Springs, KS

WHAT'S THE SCOOP?

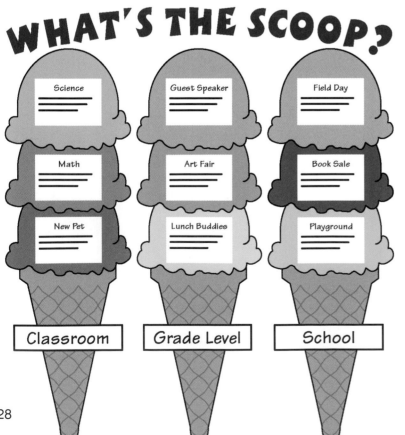

This hallway display keeps students, staff, and visitors in the know! Make an ice-cream cone cutout with multiple scoops and a label for each desired news category. Laminate the pieces for durability, cut them out, and display the cutouts with a title. Each week or two, enlist your students' help in brainstorming newsworthy writing topics and publishing paragraphs for all to read. Now that's the up-to-date scoop!

Aubrey Robertson
St. Mary School
Elyria, OH

Abloom With Great Writing!

What better way to showcase the writing of budding authors than with a display in full bloom! If possible, mount students' writing near the eye level of your youngsters. And be sure to position the paper-shaped petals for easy reading.

Laura Hess, Providence School, Greencastle, PA

Let it be known that readers reign! Have each child complete a copy of page 32 for a recently read book. Then have her fashion a crown from a half sheet of yellow construction paper and glue its lower edge to the back of a 9" x 12" sheet of purple construction paper. Use two brads to attach the child's written work to the purple paper. Display the projects and place extra copies of page 32 nearby. Plan to reward each royal reader who adds four more reviews to her literary dossier!

adapted from an idea by
F. R. Newhouse
Tiferes Bais Yaakov
Lakewood, NJ

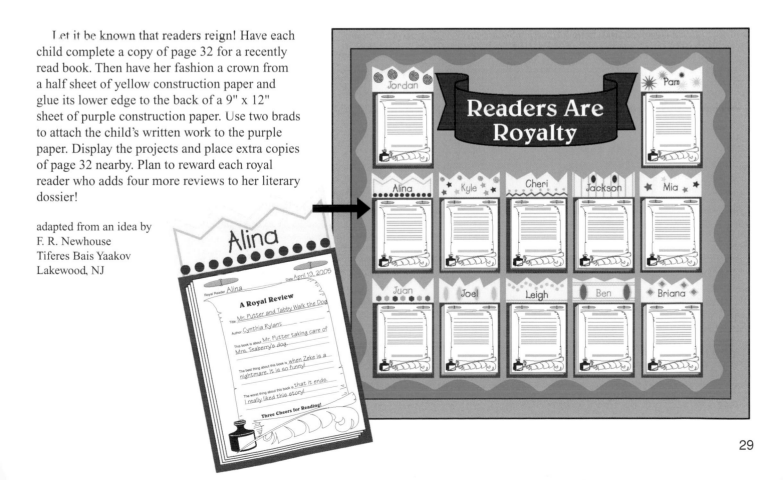

Fish Pattern
Use with "What a Great Catch!" on page 20.

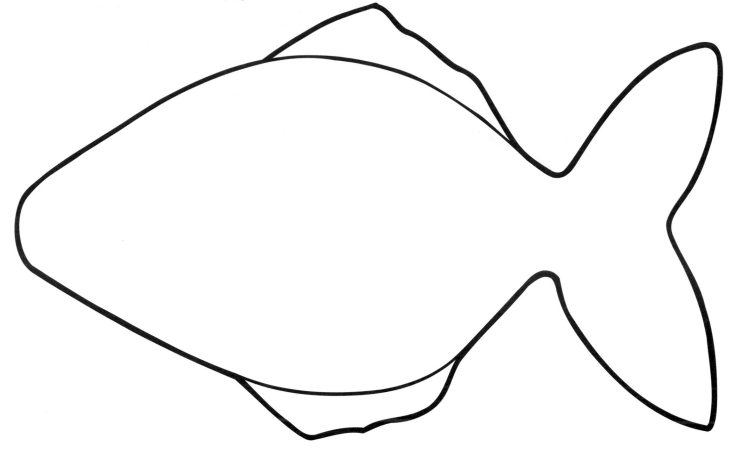

Crayon Patterns
Use with "Sharp Readers" on page 21.

_____

student name

_____

book title

Do you recommend this book? ☐ Yes ☐ No

_____

student name

_____

book title

Do you recommend this book? ☐ Yes ☐ No

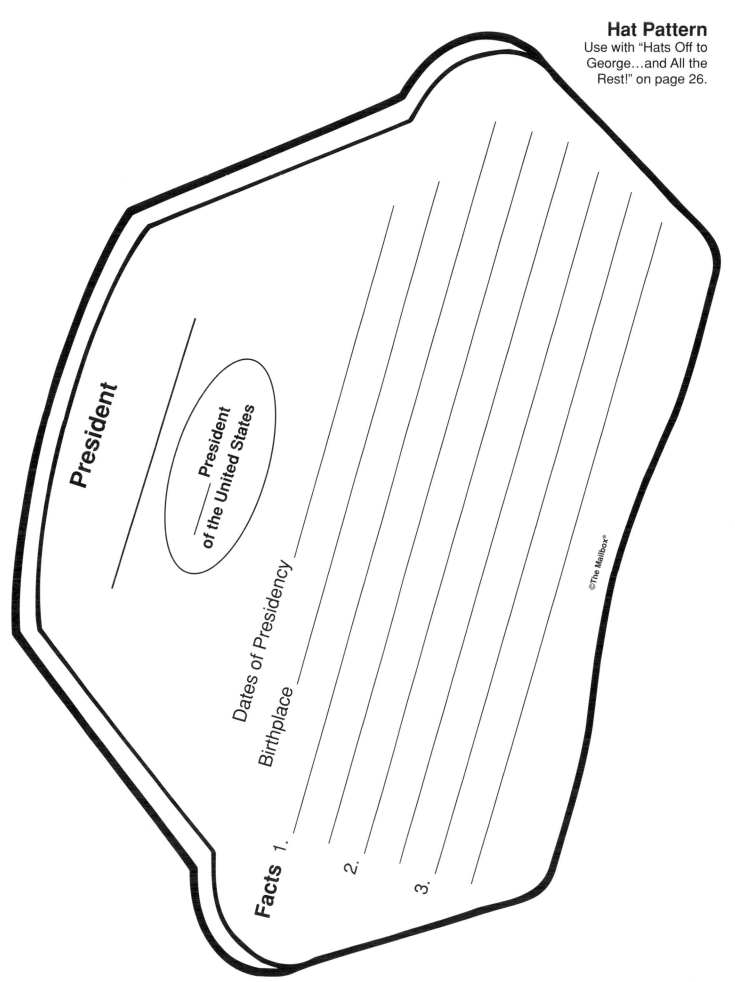

President

President
of the United States

Dates of Presidency

Birthplace

Facts 1.

2.

3.

©The Mailbox®

Royal Reader ____________________ Date ______________

A Royal Review

Title: ________________________________

Author: ________________________________

This book is about ________________________________

____

____

The best thing about this book is ________________________________

____

____

The worst thing about this book is ________________________________

____

____

Three Cheers for Reading!

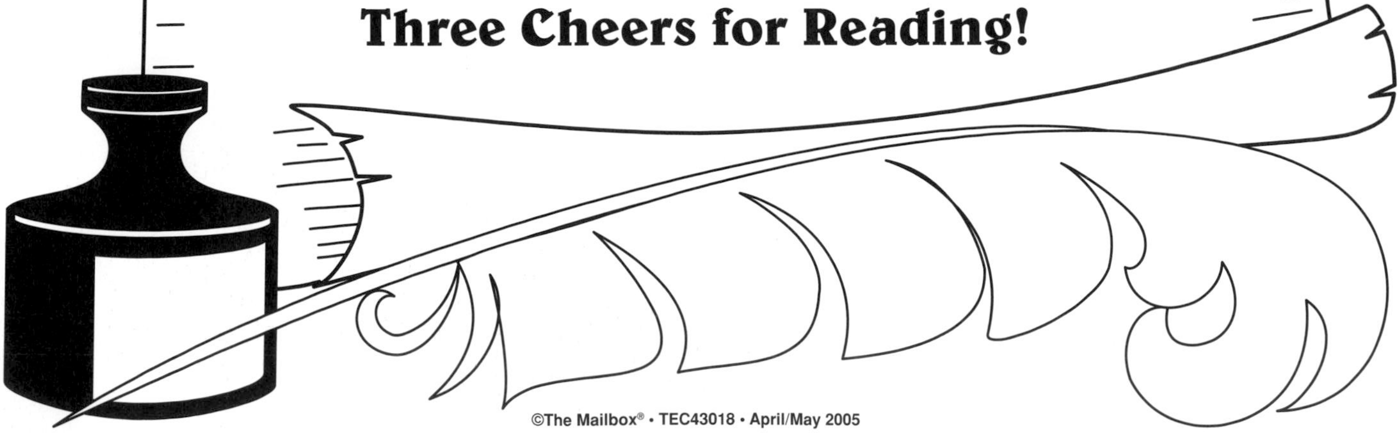

 Note to the teacher: Use with “Readers Are Royalty” on page 29.

INVESTIGATING WORDS

Investigating Words

Spin a Word

Onsets and rimes

This partner game puts a new spin on making words! Give each twosome a copy of the gameboard on page 38, two sets of game markers, two sheets of paper, and a small paper clip. To take a turn, a player uses a paper clip and pencil to spin the spinner. She combines the onset with a chosen rime and writes the resulting word on her paper. She covers the grid space with her game marker. If she cannot make a word, her turn is over. The game continues until all the grid spaces are covered. The player who covers more grid spaces wins!

"Vowel-oes!"

Long and short vowel sounds

Build vowel skills one domino at a time! Give each twosome a construction paper copy of the domino patterns on page 38. Have the partners cut the dominoes apart. Then have them follow the directions to play.

Directions:
1. Each player takes three dominoes at random and then places them faceup in front of her. Player 1 takes an additional domino and lays it faceup in the middle of the playing surface. They arrange the remaining dominoes facedown in a draw pile.
2. Player 1 checks her dominoes for a word with a vowel sound that matches one on the displayed domino. If she doesn't have one, she takes a domino from the draw pile. If she has or gets a match, she places her domino. If she has no match, her turn is over.
3. The next player takes a turn in a similar manner.
4. Alternate play continues. The winner is the first player to place all her dominoes or the player with fewer dominoes left when no more matches can be made.

adapted from an idea by Susan T. Brown, Central Elementary, Palmyra, VA

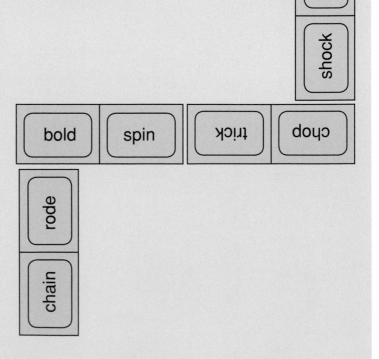

Investigating Words

Stylish Sight Words

Word recognition

With these skill-boosting necklaces, word recognition is always in style! To make a word necklace for each child, hole-punch the top of a 3" x 5" index card as shown. Thread a length of yarn through the holes. Tie the yarn at the ends and secure a paper clip at the top of the card. Have each child attach a provided sight word card to his necklace. Ask students to wear their necklaces throughout the week. During transition times, signal students to introduce themselves by their sight word names. Then, at the end of the week, have students flip their cards. Reward as desired each child who can successfully identify two classmates by their sight word names. Then collect the cards, add them to a word wall, and distribute new words.

Lydia Hess
Chambersburg, PA

spider

breakfast

school

Word Wall Lotto

Review

This group game provides some "off-the-wall" practice with words! Give each student 16 game markers and a copy of the lotto board on page 39. Direct her to choose any 16 words from the class word wall and write them on her card in random order. As students are programming their boards, write each word on a slip of paper and place the slips in a container. To begin a round, draw a slip and read the word aloud. If a student has the word on her card, she covers it. Then set the word aside and continue play. The first player to cover four numbers in a horizontal, vertical, or diagonal row wins! If desired, invite the winner to be the caller for the next round of play.

Rhonda Chiles—Gr. 2, South Park Elementary
Shawnee Mission, KS

antenna

president

tornado

insect

amazed

Investigating Words

Name That Word!
Vocabulary

Build (and review!) vocabulary during this large-group game. To play, select two student contestants to stand at the front of the room with their backs to the board. Write a familiar vocabulary word on the board, making sure it cannot be seen by either contestant. The two contestants take turns requesting clues from their classmates. A clue must relate to the word's meaning. A contestant can only attempt to name the word during his turn. The first contestant to name the word remains a contestant. The other contestant is replaced by the child who gave the winning clue. Play on!

Kay King, Ibraham Elementary, Winston-Salem, NC

Won or One?
Homophones

Which homophone is which? To review homophone pairs such as *hare* and *hair,* write each word on two cards. Decorate the backs of the cards as desired. To play this two-player Concentration game, the cards are shuffled and laid facedown. Player 1 turns over two cards. If the cards do not match, he turns them back over. If they match, the player uses the matched word in a sentence. If he uses the word correctly, he keeps the two cards and takes another turn. If not, he turns the cards over and his turn ends. Then Player 2 takes a turn. The student with the most cards at the end of the game wins. For more homophone practice, have students complete a copy of page 40.

Tonya Smith, Topeka, KS

hare

hare

The hare *jumped* behind a bush.

Spontaneous Word Study
Review

A tub of transparent bingo chips is all you need for impromptu word study during guided reading groups. Have each child keep a few chips handy so that she is ready to respond to requests such as placing a chip over a contraction, a three-syllable word, or a word with a prefix in your reading text. Quickly scan the student responses for accuracy. How's that for informal assessment?

Martha Lucas, Hunt Elementary, Cuero, TX

Investigating Words

Got It? Dot It!
Contractions

A review of contractions is in the cards—index cards that is! On the board write 15 or more contractions. Instruct each player to draw a 12-box grid on the blank side of a large index card and write in each box a different contraction from the list. Next, announce a game such as Red Dot Four in a Row. To begin play, name the two words that make a contraction shown on the board. If a player has the contraction on her card, she draws a red dot in its box. Continue play in this manner. The first student who verifies four red dots in a row wins. To play additional games, simply stipulate a different dot color for each game and, if desired, a different winning pattern. For more practice with contractions, have students complete a copy of page 41.

Twilla Lamm
Jenks, OK

I'm •	can't	he's	isn't
you're	she'll •	don't •	aren't
hasn't •	I'll	we've	that's •

Spellers' Theater
Adding -ed and -ing to base words

Audience participation is the key to this spelling production. You need a set of individual letter cards for spelling base words, another set for spelling the inflectional endings -ed and -ing, and a third set for doubling final consonants. Use a different color of marker to make each set. For the first act, announce a base word and an inflectional ending. Have volunteers from the audience hold letter cards to spell each one. Next, ask the remaining audience members to say the spelling rule for joining the base word and inflectional ending. If they say, "No change," the two groups join together to form one word. If the audience says, "Drop the final e," the child holding the e card dramatically drops to the floor before the two groups become one. If the rule is to double the final consonant, an audience member volunteers to hold the needed card so the two groups can merge. To conclude the act, ask one or more students to use the newly formed word in a sentence. Then collect the cards and begin the next act by announcing a new base word and an inflectional ending. Bravo for spelling!

Shelly Tamburro
Putnam Elementary School of Science
Fort Collins, CO

Gameboard
Use with "Spin a Word" on page 34.

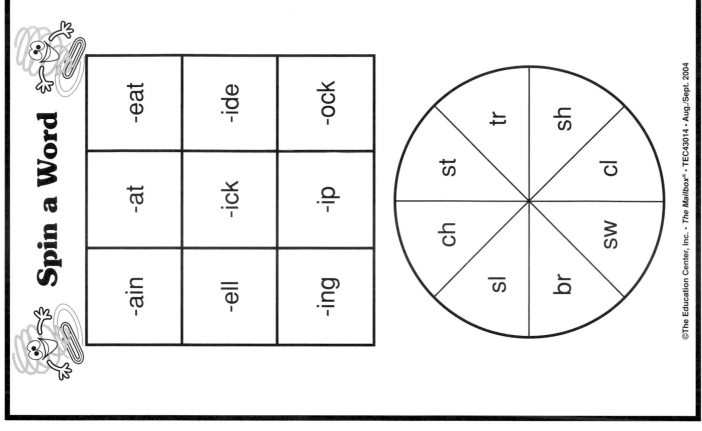

Domino Patterns
Use with "'Vowel-oes'!" on page 34.

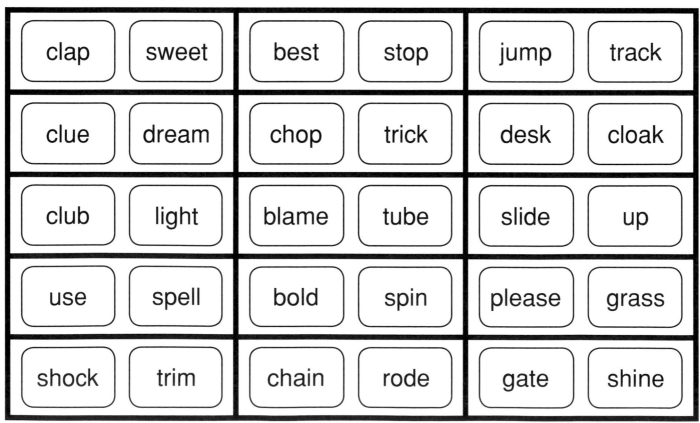

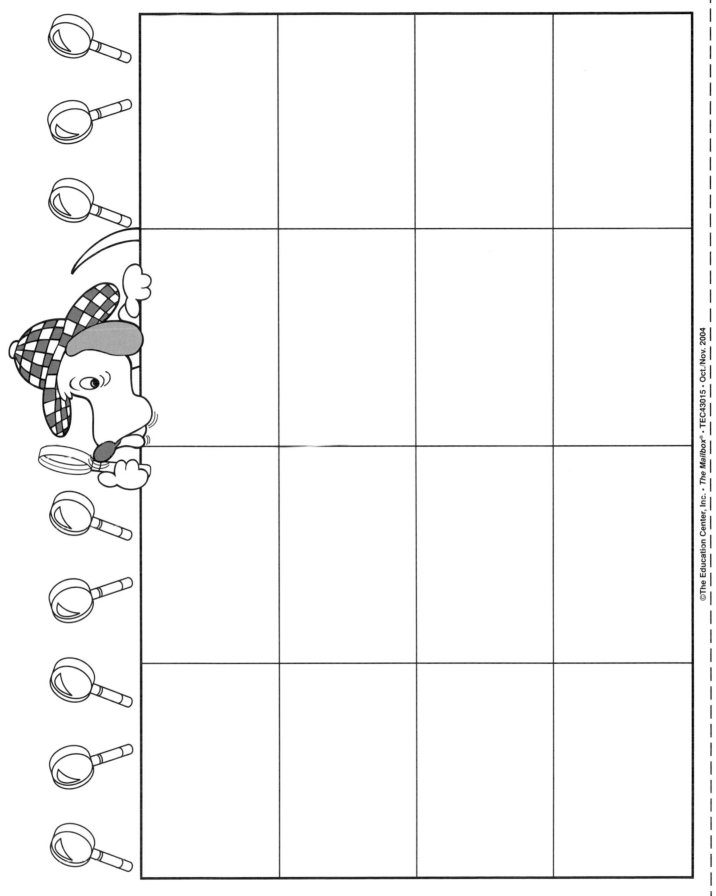

Note to the teacher: Use with "Word Wall Lotto" on page 35.

Name____

In the Mail?

Buck E. Beaver needs help.
Finish the letter he is writing.
Use the word bank.

_____________ Postal Carrier,
1

How are you? My _____________ and I moved into the _____________.
2 3

We love _____________ new home. The big _____________ bushes are
4 5

_____________ pretty. And there is more than enough _____________
6 7

for us to chew! I have only _______________ worry. My son is waiting
8

_____________ a package from his _____________. His _____________
9 10 11

is out of control. His aunt had _______________ about a _____________
12 13

kind of fur gel. She mailed him a tube of the gel _______________ days
14

ago. The package has _________________ come. Do you know what I
15

should ____________?
16

Sincerely,

Buck E. Beaver

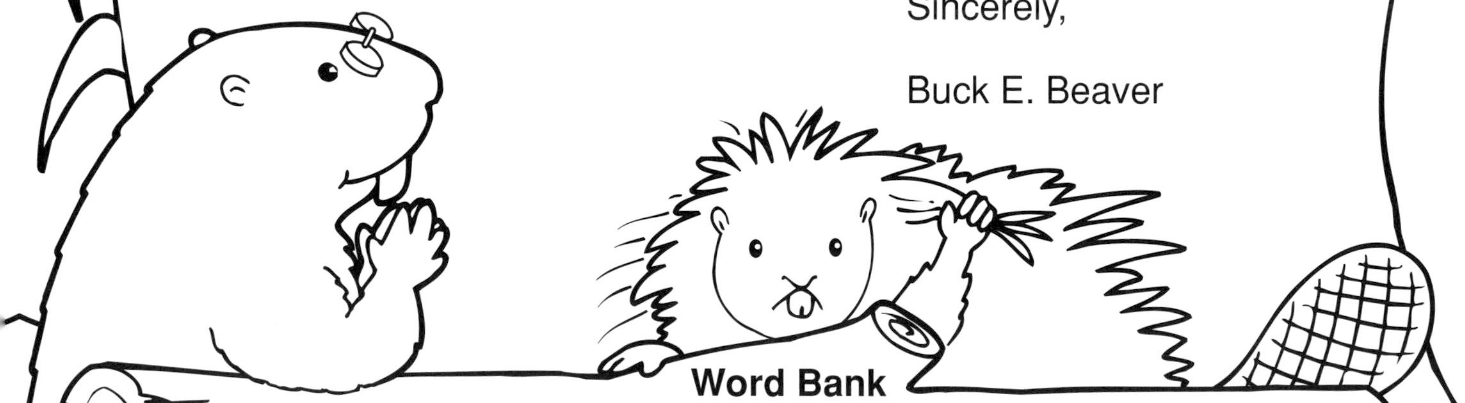

Word Bank

1. Deer/Dear	5. berry/bury	9. for/four	13. knew/new
2. son/sun	6. sew/so	10. ant/aunt	14. ate/eight
3. creak/creek	7. would/wood	11. fur/fir	15. knot/not
4. hour/our	8. won/one	12. read/red	16. due/do

Bonus Box: On the back of this paper, draw and color a picture of the gel product. Describe the gel and what it does. Use a homophone from each of the following pairs: blue/blew, no/know, to/two.

 Note to the teacher: Use alone or as a follow-up to "Won or One?" on page 36.

Pluck and Cluck

Choose a crate for each cherry.
Use the words on the cherry and the crate to make
   a contraction.
Write the contraction on the crate.

Wings of Wonder

Look across. Look down.
Circle 20 compound words.

```
c  a  m  p  g  r  o  u  n  d  a  c  p  t  a  n  x
o  p  a  j  d  t  q  s  t  a  r  f  i  s  h  o  h
o  r  y  v  o  a  k  s  n  c  t  p  t  o  d  a  y
k  u  b  a  s  e  b  a  l  l  m  b  o  o  n  g  d
b  u  e  o  c  n  q  m  l  i  c  b  u  e  p  n  c
o  s  s  k  r  d  b  n  d  f  a  k  c  o  f  i  s
o  t  a  h  u  m  e  p  e  w  r  h  z  m  b  n  b
k  e  y  b  o  a  r  d  t  b  q  x  d  a  c  y  o
j  r  e  h  m  j  f  i  h  o  d  l  o  b  z  j  w
s  q  v  p  e  v  m  u  j  a  k  a  w  y  x  f  b
u  h  f  g  m  e  i  d  w  t  o  e  n  a  i  l  a
n  g  k  c  a  l  m  t  x  u  h  y  a  w  n  z  l
r  w  i  d  u  g  o  u  t  v  g  z  y  t  x  l  l
i  s  h  t  e  r  n  l  v  m  a  i  n  b  o  x  l
s  h  f  m  g  x  a  i  r  p  l  a  n  e  s  d  a
e  i  b  i  r  t  h  d  a  y  e  i  n  d  o  o  r
o  u  t  s  i  d  e  m  l  w  k  f  e  e  p  y  o
```

Use the puzzle.
Finish each compound word.

1. to _____
2. star _____
3. snow _____
4. may _____
5. sun _____
6. cook _____
7. out _____
8. birth _____
9. touch _____
10. base _____
11. _____ boat
12. _____ box
13. _____ to
14. _____ nail
15. _____ board
16. _____ ground
17. _____ door
18. _____ out
19. _____ made
20. _____ plane

LEARNING CENTERS

Learning Centers

On the Double

When it comes to practicing **doubles facts,** this partner game is a real winner! Make a continuous trail game with 21 spaces, similar to the one shown. Mark a starting space with a thematic sticker or star. Randomly program the remaining spaces with even numbers from 2 to 20 so that there are two spaces with each number. Number a set of index card halves from 1 to 10. Store the cards, seven pennies, and two game markers in a resealable plastic bag. Place the bag and the gameboard at a center.

The players stack the cards facedown and set their game markers on Start. To take a turn, a player draws a card and announces the number. Then he states the corresponding doubles fact and moves to the next space with that sum on the gameboard. He places his card in a discard pile and his turn ends. Every time he crosses start, he takes a penny. The game continues with the next player taking a turn in a similar manner. Players reshuffle the cards as needed. The first player to collect four pennies wins!

adapted from an idea by Susan Eith—Special Education
J. W. Lilley Elementary School
Gloucester Township, NJ

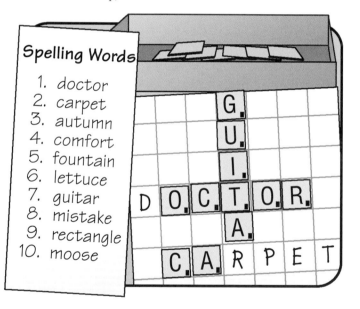

Spelling Words
1. doctor
2. carpet
3. autumn
4. comfort
5. fountain
6. lettuce
7. guitar
8. mistake
9. rectangle
10. moose

Tile It!

Here's a letter-perfect way for students to practice **spelling.** Make a class supply of grid paper (¾-inch squares). Place a collection of Scrabble letter tiles in a shoebox lid. Place the lid at a center along with the week's spelling list, copies of the grid, and pencils. A student uses the tiles to arrange a desired number of spelling words in a crossword puzzle on her grid. When she is satisfied with her puzzle, she writes each letter on the corresponding grid space.

Sherry Olfert
School District 34
Abbotsford, British Columbia, Canada

Story Savvy

Improved **reading comprehension** is the result of this partner center. Program several blank cards with statements related to a recently completed story. Be sure to include both true and false statements. For self-checking, write "true" or "false" on the back of each card. Stack the cards faceup at a center. In turn, each student selects a card, reads the statement, and declares whether it is true or false. Then he flips the card to check his answer. If he is correct, he keeps the card. If he is incorrect, he places the card in a discard pile. The player with more cards at the end of the game wins!

Betty Silkunas
Lower Gwynedd Elementary
Ambler, PA

The children in Miss Nelson's class do not misbehave.

True

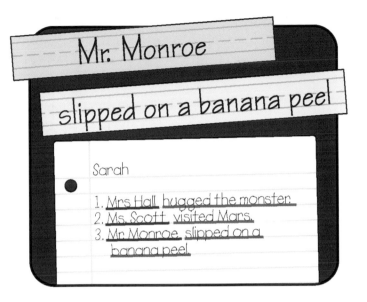

That's a Laugh!

This grin-inducing center boosts **sentence-writing skills** and helps students get acquainted with school personnel! Program one set of sentence strips with the names of faculty and staff members (subjects). Program a different-colored set with predicates. Place the strips at a center along with paper, pencils, and crayons. A student randomly pairs a subject strip with a predicate strip to form a silly sentence. She copies the sentence onto her paper, using correct capitalization and punctuation. She continues in this manner with the remaining strips. Then, for each sentence, she underlines the subject with a red crayon and the predicate with a blue crayon. Encourage students to illustrate their sentences if desired.

Tracy Kohler—Gr. 2
Chattahoochee Elementary School
Duluth, GA

Right on the Money

Coin-counting skills are sure to profit at this partner center! To make game mats, draw a piggy bank on each of two sheets of construction paper. Program eight blank cards with different monetary values that are less than 50¢. Place the game mats, cards, and imitation coins at a center.

Each player places ten desired coins atop a mat. To take a turn, a player selects a card and removes from her mat the equivalent cash amount. Player 2 takes a turn in a similar manner. If a player doesn't have the correct coins to match the amount, and the value of her coins exceeds the value of the amount she drew, she skips a turn. The first player to remove all of her coins (by drawing the exact monetary amount or an amount more than the coin value on her mat) wins!

Lisa Buccholz
Abraham Lincoln School
Glen Ellyn, IL

A Basket of Apples

ABC order is at the core of this "a-peel-ing" center. Program apple cutouts with the week's spelling words and store the cutouts in a basket. To create an answer key, list the words in alphabetical order. Place the basket and folded answer key at a center stocked with paper and pencils. A student removes the apples from the basket and arranges the words in alphabetical order. She lists the sequenced words on her paper. Then she uses the key to check her work.

Jennifer Robertson—Grs. 1 and 2
Durand Elementary School
Durand, IL

Learning Centers

Zoo Math

Give students some wild practice with **addition or subtraction facts** at this adventurous math center! Gather five disposable plates shaped like an animal's face (for example, Dixie Krazy Kritters plates or Hefty Zoo Pals plates). Stick a magnet to the back of each plate, and then attach the plates to the side of a file cabinet or other magnetic surface. Next, choose five addition or subtraction facts. Laminate five speech bubbles and program them with the answers to the chosen problems. Tape one speech bubble beside each animal. Then write math clues on index cards for four of the chosen problems, along with a sentence explaining that the zoo's most popular animal has escaped. A student reads a clue and removes the animal with the matching answer until only the featured animal remains. Call the zoo, we've found our missing elephant!

adapted from an idea by Laura Hess—Gr. 2–3
Providence School, Waynesboro, PA

Help! The zoo's most popular animal has escaped! Can you help find it?

The animal you're looking for is not 14 + 4.

Science That Sticks!

Attract plenty of student interest in **magnetism** with this seasonal center! Gather a plastic jack-o'-lantern, a magnet, and an assortment of small magnetic and nonmagnetic items. Put the items in the jack-o'-lantern. Then create a recording sheet similar to the one shown that lists the items. Place the recording sheet, magnet, and the jack-o'-lantern at a center. A student uses the recording sheet to predict which items are magnetic. Then she tests her predictions and records the results. No doubt students will be attracted to this center again and again!

Kim Field—Gr. 2–3 Multiage, Riverside School, Danvers, MA

	Prediction Is it magnetic?		After Testing Is it magnetic?	
	Yes	No	Yes	No
pencil				
paper clip				
eraser				
brass fastener				
rubber band				
hole puncher				
pom-pom				

Rhyme Time

Emphasize **word analysis** with this poetry center! Copy a short, public-domain poem or a student-written poem for each child. Then write a list of word-analysis challenges, such as circling rhyming words with a red crayon, contractions with a green crayon, and so forth. Place the list and the copies of the poem at a center. A student examines the poem and completes the challenges. Then he mounts the poem on construction paper, illustrates it, and adds it to his poetry notebook. What a fun time for rhyme!

adapted from an idea by Laurie Tracey—Gr. 2
Temple Elementary
Kennedy, NY

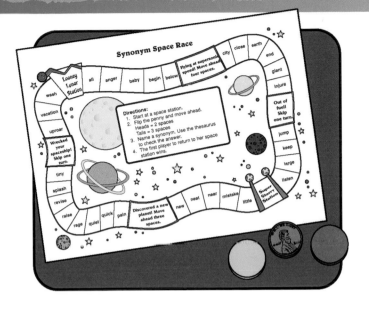

Synonym Space Race

This partner game gets students exploring **synonyms** all over the galaxy! Copy and color the gameboard on page 54. Place the gameboard, a penny, two game markers (spaceships), and a thesaurus at a center. Each student places her marker on a different space station on the flight path. In turn, a child flips a penny. If it lands on heads, she jets forward two spaces. If it lands on tails, she zooms ahead three spaces. To complete her turn, she names a synonym for the word in the space on which she lands. Then her partner uses the thesaurus to check her answer. If she is incorrect, she moves her marker back to its previous location. The first student to circle the galaxy and return to her station wins!

Debbie Patrick—Gr. 2, Park Forest Elementary, State College, PA

Story Puzzles

Piece together favorite events from a story by making **literature response** puzzles. Create a reproducible similar to the one shown. Each student chooses a favorite scene from a recent read-aloud and completes a copy of the reproducible, adding an illustration. He then cuts the sheet into puzzle pieces and stores it in a resealable plastic bag at the center. On a second center visit, a student pieces together a predetermined number of puzzles. There's nothing puzzling about these tales!

Angela Hamilton
Prentiss, MS

You have $40.00 to shop for food for Thanksgiving dinner. Six people are coming to dinner.

Turkey Time!

If you're looking for a real deal to reinforce the **guess-and-check problem-solving strategy,** this center makes "cents"! Create a sign similar to the one shown. Place the sign, several grocery store ads, and paper at a center. A student chooses items from the ads. He determines the quantity needed of each item and estimates the total cost. Next, he determines the actual sum and compares it with his guess. If he is over his budget, he adjusts his choices and recalculates. He continues in this manner, revising and rechecking his guesses until his shopping is complete and he is within his budget. Bon appétit!

Jodie Reed—Gr. 3, Marion C. Seltzer School, Cleveland, OH

47

Learning Centers

Seasonal Symmetry

Symmetry is in season at this math center! Prepare four or more symmetrical tagboard tracers of seasonal shapes, such as a candle, an evergreen tree, a snowflake, and a peppermint candy. Each shape should fit onto a quarter-sheet of drawing paper. Place the tracers with drawing paper, pencils, rulers, and crayons at a center. A student traces a different shape in each quadrant of his paper. He draws a line of symmetry through each shape and then he decorates it, maintaining its symmetry. This center is sure to shape up as a favorite!

Kerry Robertshaw
Mason Heights Elementary
Mason, OH

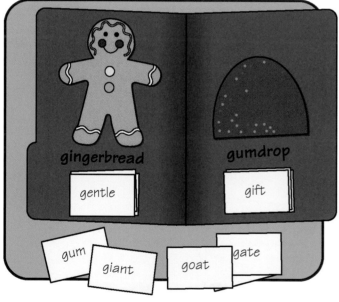

Gingerbread or Gumdrop?

Take a sweet approach to sorting the sounds of g! Use a gingerbread cookie cutout and a gumdrop cutout to prepare a file folder like the one shown. Also program a desired number of word cards with words having either the soft g sound or the hard g sound. Code the backs of the cards for self-checking and then laminate the cards and folder for durability. Place the materials at a center. A student sorts the cards by the sounds of g and then she flips the cards to check her work. Yummy!

adapted from an idea by Madeline M. Spurck
Neil A. Armstrong School
Richton Park, IL

Picture This!

Students are inspired to write and solve word problems at this picture-perfect center! Provide pencils, paper, glue, and an assortment of pictures cut from magazines. A student chooses a picture and glues it onto a sheet of paper. On the front of the paper, he writes a word problem related to the picture. Then he solves the problem on the back of his paper.

For a second center, number the students' papers (after any needed corrections are made). Slip each paper in a plastic sleeve and store the sleeves in a binder. Place the binder at the center. Solving word problems will be no problem!

Karen Fouts
Honey Creek Elementary, Conyers, GA

Kitty was petted 35 times. Then she was petted 42 times. How many times was Kitty petted in all?

Spark a Story

Give used calendars a new purpose at this writing center! Collect four or five different calendars from the past year. Cut out the pictures and laminate them. Each month stock your writing center with writing paper and the pictures for that month. What a quick and inexpensive way to spark students' creativity!

Mindy Gardzinski
Edgemont Primary
Covington, GA

Frosty Friends

These frosty pals are eager to give students a hand with contractions! Copy the patterns from page 55 onto construction paper to make several snowpals and a colorful assortment of hats and mittens. Program each hat with a contraction and program different colors of mittens with the words that make each contraction. Laminate the patterns for durability and cut them out. If desired, attach the loop side of a small Velcro dot to the back of each hat and mitten. Then attach the hook side of three small Velcro dots to each snowpal where its hat and mittens belong. A student dresses each snowpal in a hat and mittens that show a matching contraction and word pair. Very cool!

Mary Beth Godbout
Gilford, NH

"Dino-Mite"!

At this science center, students face the facts about dinosaurs. Draw a six-column grid on poster board. Title the columns as follows: "Dinosaur," "Meaning of Name," "Size," "Diet," "Protection," "Interesting Fact." In the "Dinosaur" column, list the names of dinosaurs your students have studied and, if possible, attach a sticker that shows each dino. Have a group of students research each dinosaur to locate the information needed to complete the grid. Copy the information (when verified) onto individual cards. Write the first two letters of a dinosaur's name on the back of each card in its set. Then laminate the cards and the grid before placing them at the center. A student carefully positions the dinosaur cards on the grid. Now that's some powerful learning!

Sheila Criqui-Kelley, Lebo Elementary, Lebo, KS

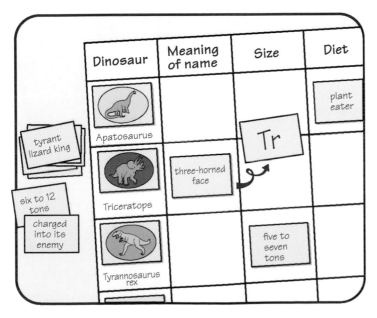

Learning Centers

Singular or Plural?

It's time to brush up on singular and plural nouns. After all, February is National Children's Dental Health Month! Program several tooth patterns with singular and plural nouns ending in *s*. Laminate the patterns, cut them out, and program the back of each one with "S" or "P" for self-checking. Place the cutouts and paper at a center. A student sorts the plural nouns from the singular nouns and then flips the cutouts to check his work. Next, he lists each plural noun on his paper and writes its singular form beside it. Students will be all smiles!

Heather Volkman
Messiah Lutheran School
St. Louis, MO

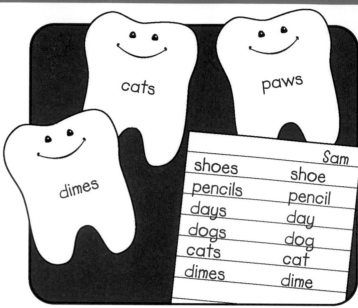

Be Mine!

Students get to the heart of organizing and interpreting data at this center! Place a colorful assortment of candy conversation hearts in a valentine tin. Next, create a graph that accommodates your candy supply and is similar to the one shown. Laminate the graph for durability. Also copy the recording sheet on page 56 to make a class supply. Place the tin of candies, the laminated grid, and the recording sheets at a center. A student organizes the candy on the graph and then completes a copy of the recording sheet. After she returns the candy hearts to the tin, she trades her recording sheet for a snack-size portion of candy hearts that she can eat!

Kelli Higgins
P. L. Bolin Elementary School
East Peoria, IL

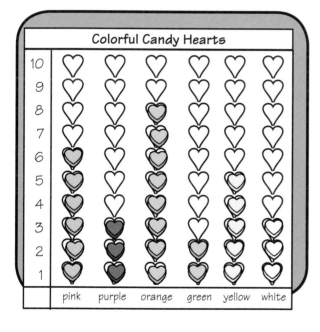

Garden Varieties

Use this idea to cultivate alphabetizing skills! Choose a variety of seed packets to be alphabetized. If desired, circle (or otherwise highlight) the seed name on each packet. Store the seed packets in a plastic pail. Then put the pail and a paper supply at a center. A student alphabetizes the seed packets and then writes the seed names in ABC order on his paper. Plan for students to plant the seeds later this spring so their learning can keep on growing!

Patty Frano
Our Lady's Christian School
Erie, PA

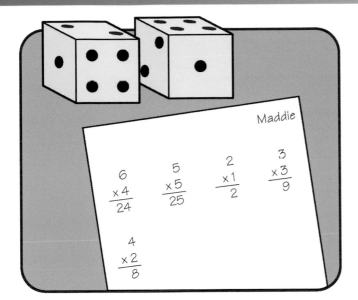

On a Roll!

Roll out reinforcement of multiplication facts with this easy-to-prepare activity. Place paper and two foam dice at a center. A student rolls both dice. On her paper she writes the rolled numbers as the factors of a multiplication problem and then solves the problem. She continues in this manner until she solves ten different facts. For a partner center, each child rolls just one die. Each partner solves the resulting multiplication fact, and then she and her partner compare answers before the next rolls are taken. Students sure will be on a roll with multiplication!

Beth Carlisle
Midland Academy
Midland, GA

Great Beginnings

No "lion," when the prefixes re- and un- are added to base words, vocabularies grow! First, program a desired number of word cards with words having the named affixes. Next, write the meaning of each word on a word meaning card (patterns on page 56). Laminate the cards for durability and cut them out. For a self-checking center, pair each word with its meaning; then flip over the pair of cards and code the backs for self-checking. Finally, use a different puzzle cut to separate each prefix and base word. A student reads a word meaning, locates the corresponding base word, and matches up the prefix. "Ewe" got it!

Kish Harris
Southampton Academy
Courtland, VA

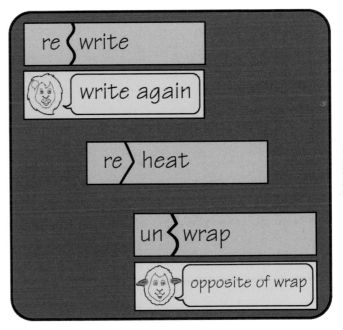

Egg Hunt!

Here's an "egg-citing" way to practice expanded form! Trace five egg shapes on each of three colors of construction paper. Program one set of eggs with hundreds, one set with tens, and one set with ones. Laminate the patterns for durability and cut them out. Store the cutouts in an Easter basket. Place the basket and a supply of paper at a center. A student removes three colors of eggs from the basket. On his paper he writes a number sentence that includes both the standard and the expanded forms of his number. Then he returns the cutouts to the basket. He repeats the process until he has written ten different number sentences. Now that's an "eggs-panded" hunt!

adapted from an idea by Anne Sheehan
General William Floyd Elementary School
Stittville, NY

Handy Rimes

Word family practice fits like a glove at this partner center! For each of four word families, label a tagboard rectangle with a rime and five tagboard circles with onsets. (See the provided list.) Laminate the cutouts and then affix a Velcro strip (loop side) to the back of each one. Use hot glue to attach a Velcro strip (hook side) to the palm and fingertips of each glove. Then place the gloves, cards, and circles at a center. A partner attaches a rime to the palm of a glove and an onset to each fingertip. Then he reads his word family aloud to his partner. Each partner repeats the activity with a different rime and onsets. What a fun way to cultivate reading skills!

Amy Barsanti
Pines Elementary
Plymouth, NC

-ain	r, p, tr, g, m
-ing	k, r, str, th, sw
-ight	br, l, f, t, m
-oat	fl, g, b, c, thr

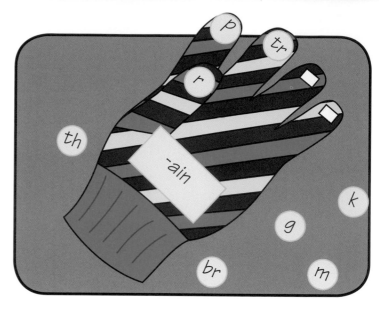

Aflutter Over Facts

At this center, students get in a flutter over multiplication facts! Make a construction paper supply of the butterfly pattern on page 285. Program each wing with a math fact and its answer. Laminate the butterflies and cut them out. To program the butterflies for self-checking, lay the cutouts facedown and code the top and the bottom of each wing. Then cut each butterfly into three pieces as shown. A student assembles the butterflies and then turns them over to check her work. Piecing together basic facts has never been more fun!

Patty Frano
Northwest Tri-County Intermediate Unit
Edinboro, PA

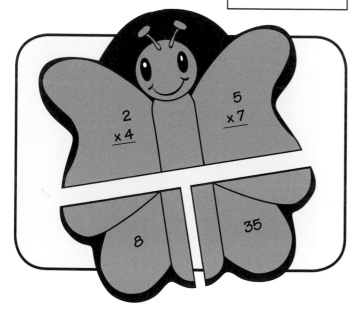

Comic Strip Rewrite

Tickle students' funny bones while providing practice with writing dialogue! Cut out student-appropriate comic strips and mount each one on construction paper. Laminate the strips for durability and then place them at a center along with writing paper and pencils. A youngster selects a strip and reads it. Then he writes the speech bubble dialogue in sentence form, providing original or known speaker names. Encourage students to use vivid verbs to convey the emotions illustrated in the comic strip.

Anna A. Walsh
M.B. Garvin Microsociety School
East Orange, NJ

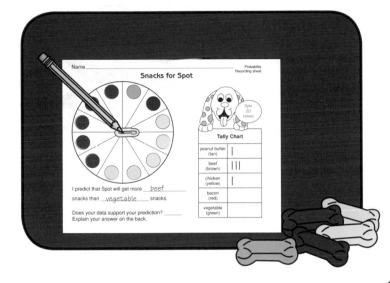

Puppy Probability

Put a pooch-related spin on probability! Place at a center a bag of flavored dog biscuits, pencils, jumbo paper clips, crayons, and student copies of the recording sheet on page 57. A child removes 12 snacks from the bag. On her recording sheet she colors the spinner wheel to match the biscuit flavors she selected. Then she records her prediction. Next, she uses a pencil and a paper clip to make a spinner. She spins 20 times and records the results in the tally box. After she interprets the data, she completes the page. No bones about it, probability is "paws-itively" fun!

Linda Masternak Justice
Kansas City, MO

Great Beginnings

Provide fine-feathered prefix practice again and again! Draw a two-tiered clothesline inside a file folder and use the patterns on page 57 to make ten construction paper birds. Program each bird with a base word. For a review of *un-* and *re-,* program the birds with the provided base words and label a small card for each prefix. Laminate the materials, cut them out, and store them at a center with paper and pencils. A youngster places a prefix card at one end of each clothesline. Next, he sets each bird on the clothesline where joining the base word and prefix make a new word. On his paper he writes each new word and its meaning. For more prefix practice, replace the prefix cards and provide corresponding base words. "Tweet"!

Judi Lesnansky
New Hope Academy
Youngstown, OH

Book Order Math

Place an order for improved computation skills! Place pencils, extra copies of book order forms, and student copies of page 58 at a center. Also provide a calculator or two for self-checking if desired. A child uses a book order form to complete the activity sheet.

Ella Duren
North Lamar ISD
Paris, TX

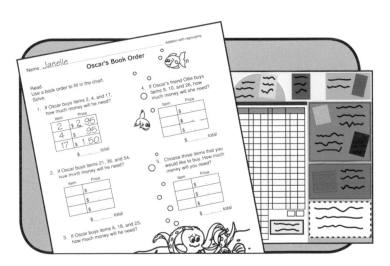

Synonym Space Race

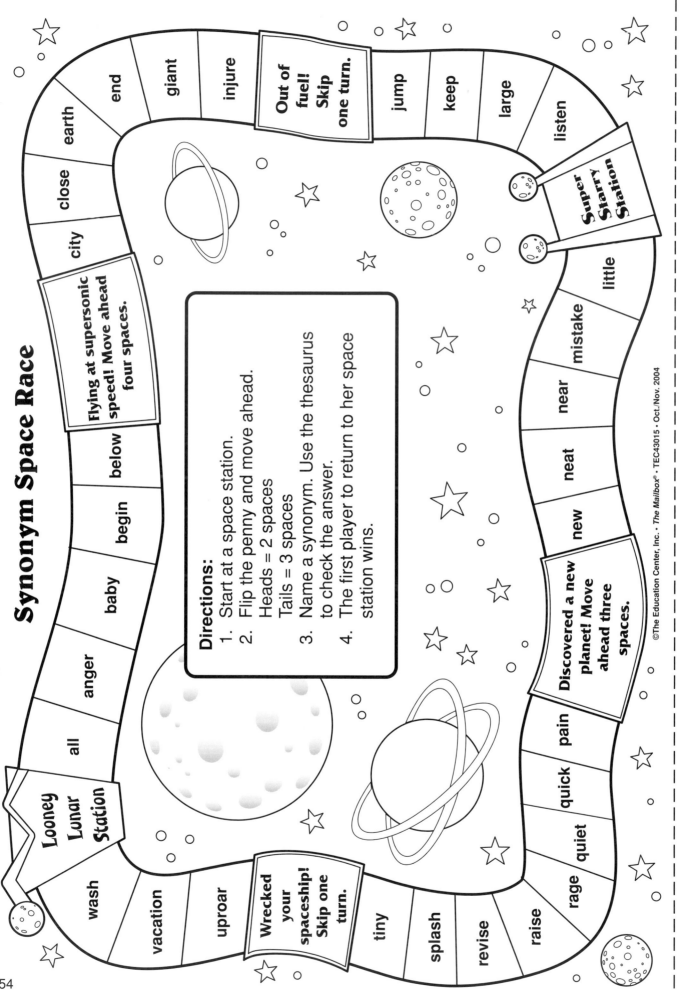

Directions:
1. Start at a space station.
2. Flip the penny and move ahead.
   Heads = 2 spaces
   Tails = 3 spaces
3. Name a synonym. Use the thesaurus to check the answer.
4. The first player to return to her space station wins.

Flying at supersonic speed! Move ahead four spaces.

Out of fuel! Skip one turn.

Super Starry Station

Discovered a new planet! Move ahead three spaces.

Looney Lunar Station

Wrecked your spaceship! Skip one turn.

earth
end
giant
injure
jump
keep
large
listen
close
city
little
mistake
near
neat
new
pain
quick
quiet
rage
raise
revise
splash
tiny
uproar
vacation
wash
all
anger
baby
begin
below

54

©The Education Center, Inc. • *The Mailbox*® • TEC43015 • Oct./Nov. 2004

Note to the teacher: Use with "Synonym Space Race" on page 47.

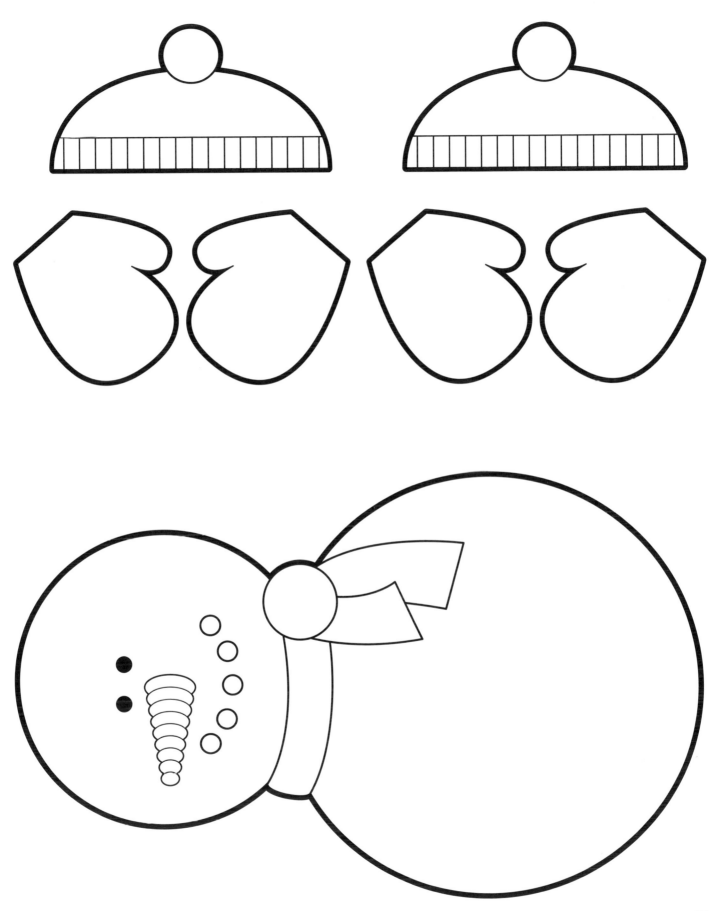

Word Meaning Cards

Use with "Great Beginnings" on page 51.

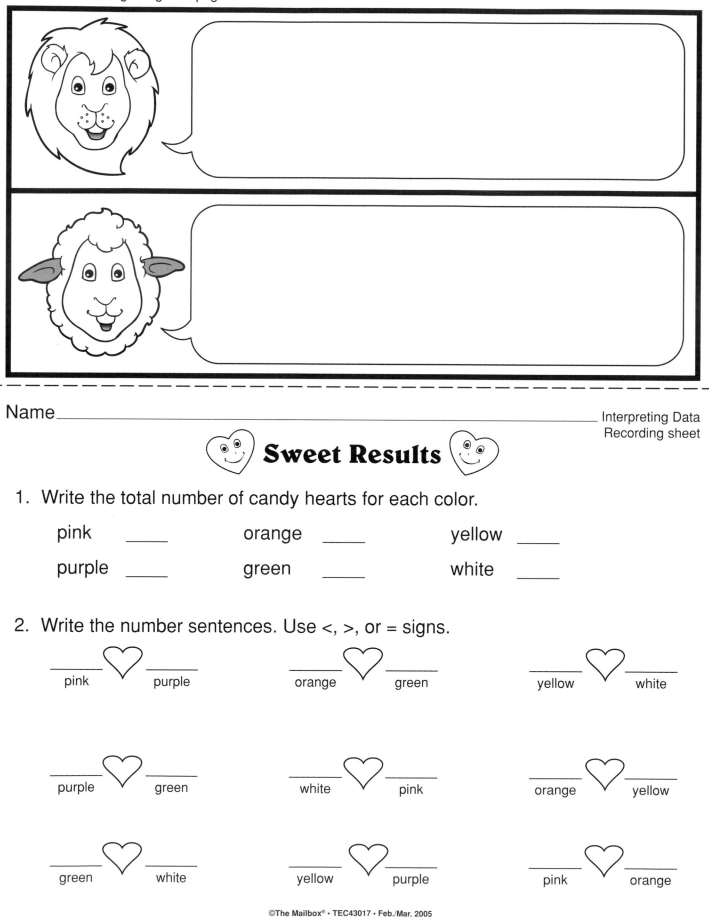

Name _____

Sweet Results

1. Write the total number of candy hearts for each color.

   pink ____   orange ____   yellow ____

   purple ____   green ____   white ____

2. Write the number sentences. Use <, >, or = signs.

   ____ ♡ ____   ____ ♡ ____   ____ ♡ ____
   pink   purple   orange   green   yellow   white

   ____ ♡ ____   ____ ♡ ____   ____ ♡ ____
   purple   green   white   pink   orange   yellow

   ____ ♡ ____   ____ ♡ ____   ____ ♡ ____
   green   white   yellow   purple   pink   orange

©The Mailbox® • TEC43017 • Feb./Mar. 2005

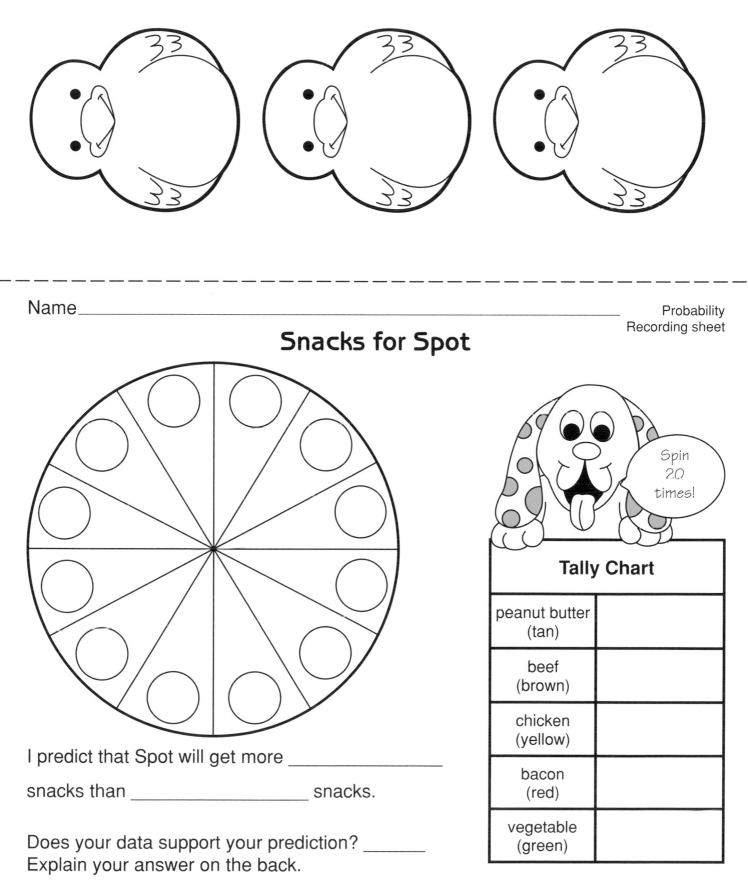

Name_____

Snacks for Spot

Spin 20 times!

Tally Chart

peanut butter (tan)	
beef (brown)	
chicken (yellow)	
bacon (red)	
vegetable (green)	

I predict that Spot will get more _____

snacks than _____ snacks.

Does your data support your prediction? _____
Explain your answer on the back.

Oscar's Book Order

Read.
Use a book order to fill in the chart.
Solve.

1. If Oscar buys items 2, 4, and 17, how much money will he need?

Item	Price
	$.
	$.
	$.

total $_____._____

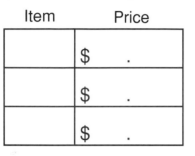

2. If Oscar buys items 21, 36, and 54, how much money will he need?

Item	Price
	$.
	$.
	$.

total $_____._____

3. If Oscar buys items 6, 18, and 23, how much money will he need?

Item	Price
	$.
	$.
	$.

total $_____._____

4. If Oscar's friend Ollie buys items 9, 10, and 26, how much money will she need?

Item	Price
	$.
	$.
	$.

total $_____._____

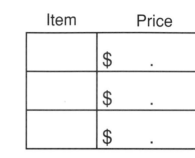

5. Choose three items that you would like to buy. How much money will you need?

Item	Price
	$.
	$.
	$.

total $_____._____

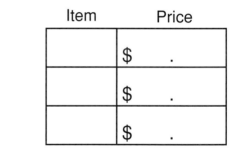

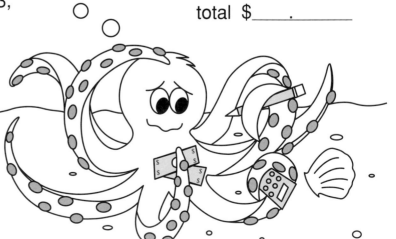

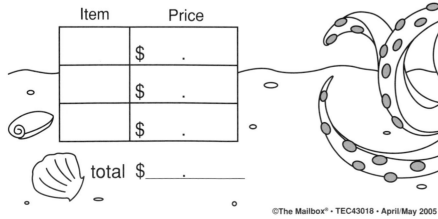

Management Tips & Timesavers

Management Tips & Timesavers

Hanging Helpers

There's no monkey business here, just a creative way to assign classroom helpers! Purchase a Barrel of Monkeys game. Use a permanent marker to initial one monkey piece for each student. Cut from green tagboard a vine and leaf cutouts (one per classroom job). Label each leaf and hole-punch the edge for a desired number of helpers. Attach the leaves to the vine; display the vine within students' view. To assign jobs, hang one or more monkeys from each leaf. Rotate the monkeys systematically to vary students' duties. What cute helpers! *Angela Nolan—Gr. 2, St. Mary's School, New Albany, IN*

By the Number

Count on this idea to keep tabs on students' belongings! Assign each child a number. Have him use a marker and self-adhesive dots to number his desktag and personal supplies. Also ask students to label any prized possessions they bring from home. The result is a surefire way for returning any misplaced belongings to their rightful owners! *Michele Daughenbaugh—Gr. 3, Park Forest Elementary, State College, PA*

Paperwork Plan

Use this organizational idea to keep track of incoming papers. Label each of several colored file folders with a desired category of paperwork (such as "Copies Needed" and "Do Today"). Place the folders in a desktop file organizer. Sort papers into the appropriate folders as they come in. Then, as time allows, address the paperwork in order of importance. No more piles of paperwork! *Michelle Mehrtens—Gr. 3, Camas Prairie Elementary, Spanaway, WA*

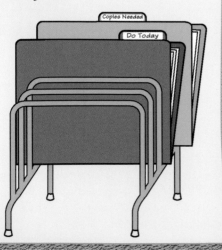

Punching Up Positive Discipline

A handheld hole puncher puts positive discipline at your fingertips. Here's how! Use yarn to suspend a laminated, personalized cutout from each child's desk. When a youngster displays exceptional behavior, hole-punch her cutout. Reward each child who earns a predetermined number of hole punches as desired. What's the added benefit? The clicking sound reminds students to monitor their behavior! *Karen Marzuk—Gr. 2, Edith Slocum Elementary School, Ronkonkoma, NY*

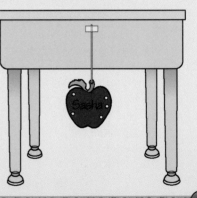

Nifty Name Badges

Here's a thrifty alternative to purchasing disposable nametags year after year. Obtain a supply of name badge holders from an office supply store. Insert a computer-generated nametag inside each holder. Have students wear their name badges during the first few days of school, during field trips, or any time they need to be easily identified. At the start of each school year, replace the existing paper nametags with new ones. *Laura Nederostek—Gr. 3, Shafer Elementary School, Nazareth, PA*

Good-Behavior Motivator

Reinforce positive behavior with an idea that's the pick of the patch! Draw a large pumpkin outline on a bulletin board. Then cut a stem and jack-o'-lantern features, such as eyes, a nose, and a mouth, from construction paper and store them in a large envelope. Add a sealed note promising extra free time, a special snack, or another class treat if students meet a series of daily behavior goals, such as keeping the classroom clean or not interrupting. Each day that the class meets the goal, add a cutout to the display. When the jack-o'-lantern is complete, reveal the reward and celebrate students' success! *Rebecca Brudwick, Hoover Elementary, Mankato, MN*

Letters Home

Provide parents with an all-in-one weekly update! Obtain a two-pocket folder with fasteners for each student. Every Friday, brainstorm a list of the week's events; then have students write letters to their parents about the highlights. As each child completes her letter, clip it to the top of the stack of letters and tuck the student's work for the week in the left-hand pocket. Remind students that parents should review the folder over the weekend and initial the student's letter, adding comments or questions and the date. Parents will appreciate these weekly updates! *Jennifer Wright—Gr. 3–4, Dry Ridge Elementary, Dry Ridge, KY*

What Are You Reading?

Aleria	Alexis	Lily	Joseph
Cassie	Owen	Ethan	Nate
Marcus	Zack	Amanda	Jon
Mary Ellen	Christine	Lloyd	Brett

Speedy Library System

Here's a quick tip for tracking books from your class library. Glue a library pocket for each student to a sheet of poster board, and then laminate. Carefully slice each pocket open and place a personalized index card inside. Each time a student takes a book from the class library, he writes the title on his index card and tucks it in his library pocket. When he returns the book, he checks it off on the card and adds his new book's title. Not only can you keep track of who has a particular book, but you'll also have a record of what students are reading! *Kathy Sherman—Gr. 3, St. Paul Catholic School, Highland, IL*

Containing Clutter

Keep students organized with this versatile tip! Collect a clean, empty icing container (no lid) for each student. Invite students to decorate their containers with construction paper or permanent markers. Then adhere one side of a Velcro fastener to the container's base and the corresponding side to the student's desk. The containers are perfect for storing pencils, bookmarks, and other easy-to-misplace items. Plus, if a student changes desks, she can take her storage container with her! *Linda Macho—Gr. 2, Delores Moye Elementary, O'Fallon, IL*

Management Tips & Timesavers

Winter Helpers

When winter weather blows in, so do numerous boots, coats, and mittens! This year appoint daily wintertime closet keepers to keep things neat. For a cute display, hang a mini clothesline near your class calendar. Then use two wooden spring-type clothespins, each labeled "closet keeper," to attach a pair of mittens to the line. Each morning, clip a second clothespin labeled with a different student's name to each mitten. Students are sure to warm up to this new responsibility! *adapted from an idea by Beth Romie, New Albany Elementary, New Albany, OH*

Magazine Routine

Make a New Year's resolution to make good use of the children's magazines to which you subscribe. Label a notebook (or computer file) with teaching topics. Each time a magazine arrives, scan it and then in your notebook list the title, page number, and issue of each article that relates to a teaching topic. In no time you'll have a ready-to-go list of kid-pleasing articles to supplement your teaching! *Sheila Kelley, Lebo Elementary, Lebo, KS*

Tic-Tac-Toe Tasks

Make the most of your early finishers' free time. Program a tic-tac-toe grid with nine independent activities and then copy the grid for each student. Make sure all the materials needed for the tasks are readily available. When a child has free time, he chooses an activity from his grid to work on. When he completes an activity, he colors the space on his grid. (Or, for a seasonal twist, have him color a seasonal shape on his grid, such as a gift for December or a mitten for January.) To keep early finishers challenged, provide a new grid each month. *Amanda Loar and Kari Gedville, Olive C. Martin Elementary School, Lake Villa, IL*

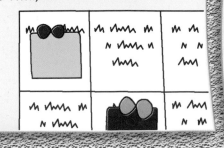

Super Goals

Tap into Super Bowl fever and help your class meet a variety of goals. Draw a football goalpost on the board. Each week program the goalpost with two or more pregame goals for the class. Then divide the class into teams of equal numbers. Designate a quarterback for each team and give her a colorful index card on which to track her team's points. Every day, each team player can score one point for successfully meeting each goal. At the end of the week, tally each team's score. Invite the winning team to choose (from a provided list) one special privilege for the class and an extra privilege for the team. Scores will soar! *Elizabeth Almy, Greensboro, NC*

Turn in homework.
Cooperate with others.

Line Up and Learn

Keep students learning even as they line up! Challenge students to line up
- in alphabetical order by first or last names
- according to their birthday months
- counting sequentially by twos, threes, fours, and so on
- naming synonyms, antonyms, or rhyming words

Brooke Shaw, Columbia, SC

Management Tips & Timesavers

Making the Grade

Save time and maintain accuracy as you write grades in your record book. Remove a name strip from an unused page and program both sides of it to match your record book. Laminate the strip and tuck it inside your grade book. As you record grades, place the laminated strip next to the column in which you're writing. No more losing your place as you move across a long line of grades! *Jo Bressan, Jefferson Park School, El Paso, IL*

Adams, Chloe
Braxton, Abby
Byrd, Arthur
Collins, Nathan
Curtis, Sarah
Daniels, Natalie
Dodge, Henry
Ferguson, Emma

Mini Bulletin Boards

Here's an easy (and portable!) way to display word lists and center directions. Cut a large, heavy-duty box into squares and then cover each square with bulletin board paper. Your mini bulletin boards are ready to use! *Crystal Perry, Chatham Charter School, Siler City, NC*

Timely Follow-Up

Try this plan for timely follow-ups with students who need to revisit an assignment. As you grade papers, put the papers that need a second look in a folder titled "See Me." Then, during independent work times, casually gather two or three students for skill review. You'll be using your extra minutes efficiently and students who need the extra help won't feel singled out. *Sr. Barbara Flynn, St. Raphael School, Bridgeport, CT*

See Me

What a Good Egg!

Put a seasonal twist on encouraging and rewarding positive student behavior. Write several class rewards on slips of paper; then place each slip inside a plastic egg. Put the eggs in a basket. Set a class behavior goal and award points for good behavior. When the group reaches the goal, invite one child to crack open an egg and announce the reward. *Danielle DeMatteo, N. Springfield Center, Springfield, VA*

15 minutes   No homework night

Surprise art p...

Ten minutes of extra rece...   Afternoon snack

This Book Belongs To...

Keeping track of personal teaching resources just got easier! Bring to school extra address labels. Place a label on each book, magazine, game, puzzle, or other item that was a personal purchase. When a colleague borrows an item she'll know whom to return it to. You'll also be able to quickly identify your materials the next time you move classrooms. *Ann Marie Stephens, G. C. Round Elementary, Manassas, VA*

Management Tips & Timesavers

Listening and Lovin' It

As spring fever sets in, challenge students to put PARROT into action! Explain that PARROT stands for **P**aying **A**ttention **R**eally **R**ewards **O**ur **T**hinking. Whenever you observe students practicing PARROT, drop a pom-pom or other marker into a clear plastic jar. When the jar is filled, reward the class with a special privilege. With this kind of incentive, students will be encouraging each other to stay focused. *adapted from an idea by Kasi Johnson, Mascoutah Elementary School, Mascoutah, IL*

Paying
Attention
Really
Rewards
Our
Thinking

Bound for Organization

Make this organizational tip a part of your spring cleaning efforts. Label a supply of tabbed section dividers to correspond with the units, skills, literature, and themes in your curriculum. Store the dividers in a large three-ring binder. As you begin to file and refile ideas from the past year, hole-punch the ones you're sure to use again next year and place them in the corresponding binder sections. Finding favorite ideas has never been easier! *Bobbie Denmark, Charleston Elementary School, Charleston, MS*

If you finish early,...

write a poem about rain

or

read and make notes about bird beaks

Early Finishers

How can you encourage students who finish their work early to engage in worthwhile tasks? Program colorful sentence strips for a pocket chart or a board display. Label the first strip "If you finish early,..." Then label several others with tasks and one with "or." Each morning, display the first strip, the "or" strip, and two task strips. The colorful strips are inviting, plus children love getting to choose between two options. *Colleen Hoover, Juniper Elementary, Hesperia, CA*

A Perfect Match

Subscribers, here's a tip for organizing *The Mailbox®* magazine's online extenders. When printing extenders from www.themailboxcompanion.com, label the bottom of each printed page with the issue and page number of the corresponding idea. Now the resources are ready to save you time—every time. *Josie Schrader, St. Bernadette School, Westlake, OH*

The Editor Is In!

This simple system helps everyone know which student editors are available to assist with editing and revising. For a pocket chart display, personalize a colorful card for each student editor. When an editor is available to help (her work is completed), she displays her card in the pocket chart. A classmate who needs assistance removes a card from the chart and asks the corresponding editor for help. When the pair is finished, the editor returns her card to the chart to signal that she is once again available. *Julie Lewis, J. O. Davis Elementary, Irving, TX*

WRITING HELPERS

José		Shane	Mark
Carlos	Vicky	Tawana	Tazmen
Nicole			

MATH MAILBAG

Math Mailbag

Rewarding Computation
Skill: computation

This idea for daily computation practice has its own rewards! Write several computation problems on the board, numbering them for identification. A student folds a sheet of paper in half and unfolds it. He copies and solves the problems on one half of the paper. Then he numbers the other half of his paper, writes each answer, and signs his name. He cuts off his resulting answer sheet, folds it in half, and deposits it into a designated basket.

Next, ask a student volunteer to solve the problems on the board, providing help as needed. Have youngsters correct any mistakes on their papers. Then randomly remove an answer sheet from the basket. If all the answers are correct, reward its owner with a sticker or small treat. (If there are incorrect answers, set the paper aside without revealing the student's name.) Repeat this with additional answer sheets as desired. Then empty the basket to prepare it for the next school day.

adapted from an idea by Ann Repsold
Gresham, OR

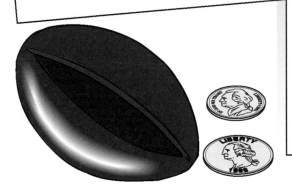

Pass the Purse
Skill: counting coins

Engage students in this modified version of hot potato to boost coin-counting skills! Place a few coins in a change purse. Seat students in a circle and hand the purse to a child. Play some lively music, signaling the child to start passing the purse around the circle. When you stop the music, tell the child who is left holding the purse to count the coins inside and announce the total amount. (Provide assistance as needed.) Then change the coins for a new round of the activity!

adapted from an idea by Cynthia Holcomb
Mertzon, TX

Measurement Mats
Skill: linear measurement

Size up linear measurement skills with these colorful mats! To make a mat, a child cuts construction paper strips of different lengths and colors. She glues the strips onto a 9" x 12" sheet of black construction paper. She lists the colors on a half sheet of paper. Then she measures each strip to the nearest half inch (or to the nearest centimeter) and writes the length beside the corresponding color word. She glues her resulting answer key to the back of her mat and submits her project for your review. For more practice, place the teacher-approved, laminated mats at a center stocked with wipe-off markers and rulers.

Tricia Walker—Gr. 2
Mellette Elementary School
Watertown, SD

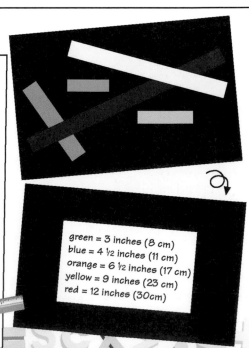

green = 3 inches (8 cm)
blue = 4 ½ inches (11 cm)
orange = 6 ½ inches (17 cm)
yellow = 9 inches (23 cm)
red = 12 inches (30cm)

Math Mailbag

Crack That Case!
Skill: addition with regrouping

For this partner game, the key to cracking the case is accurate addition! In advance, program seasonally decorated cards (cards with pumpkins, turkey footprints, and so forth) with directions likely to result in addition with regrouping, such as "+ 298." While students are out of the classroom, hide the cards around the room. To begin, ask students to pretend to be detectives who have been assigned to track down turkeys (or other seasonal critters). Instruct each child to write "200" on a sheet of paper. Then direct pairs of students to search for the cards. Once a pair locates a card, the partners follow the direction on the card, completing the problem independently. Then they compare answers and recompute if necessary. They return the card to its hiding place and continue searching for different cards until they reach a predetermined sum, at which point the case has been solved.

Danielle Conforti, Manasquan, NJ

Bank on It!
Skill: counting and comparing coin sets

Here's a small-group game that's sure to add up to improved money skills! In advance, program a spinner with coin amounts from 1¢ to 25¢. Also gather a supply of imitation coins and dollars for the bank. To play, each student, in turn, spins and withdraws the corresponding money amount from the bank. As a player withdraws her coins, she determines her total money amount and when possible, trades for coins or dollar bills of larger value to get the smallest number of coins and bills possible. The first student to reach or exceed $2.00 or another predetermined amount wins!

Mary Lanoue—Gr. 2, McGaheysville Elementary School, McGaheysville, VA

Yummy Tummy Math
Skill: place value

Students munch up place-value practice with this tasty activity! Provide each student with a napkin and a sandwich bag containing three marshmallows, three toothpicks, and 15 pieces of Froot Loops cereal. Have each student create three bases by pushing each toothpick into a marshmallow so that it stands up. Direct students to place the bases side by side on the napkin as you explain that from right to left, they represent the ones, tens, and hundreds places. Then challenge students to slide cereal pieces onto the toothpicks to make numbers as directed. For example:

- Use some or all of the pieces to make a number that is less than 300 and greater than 275.
- Use eight cereal pieces to make the largest number possible.
- Eat five cereal pieces. Then use all of the remaining pieces to make the smallest number possible.

Once students have had plenty of practice, invite them to add the goodies to a new place—their tummies!

Karen Alexander—Gr. 2, Hamilton Elementary School, Coon Rapids, MN

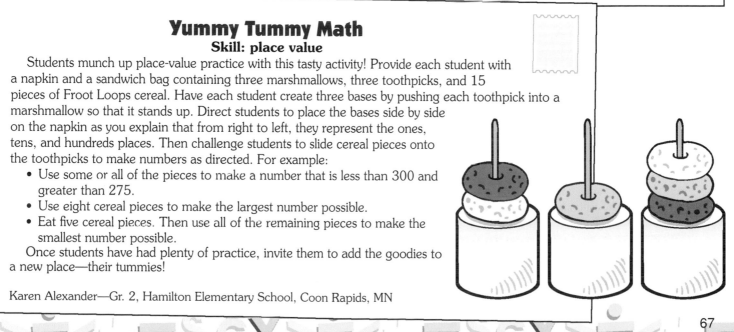

Math Mailbag

Now Boarding!
Skill: reading and comparing whole numbers

Polish your youngsters' number skills during this high-flying activity. In advance, program a class set of cards with random numbers within a desired range (such as 200–900). Store the cards in a small basket. To begin the activity, have students arrange their chairs to resemble the seats on an airplane. Then have each child take a ticket from the basket and go stand beside his desk. Call out boarding instructions such as, "Attention, passengers. Numbers between 800 and 900 may now board," or, "Good morning, flyers. Numbers less then 231 may board." As each student boards, he reads the number on his ticket aloud and hands it to you. When everyone is aboard, take students on a quick imaginary trip. Happy travels!

adapted from an idea by Michelle Bassham
St. Matthew's Episcopal School
Houma, LA

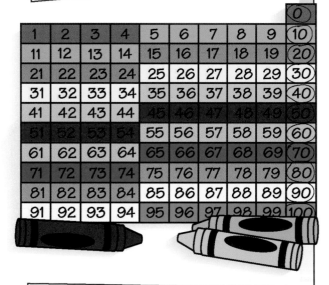

Rainbow Rounding
Skill: rounding to the nearest ten

Try this colorful approach to rounding! Give each child a hundred chart. Direct her to write a zero above the tens column and then to circle each number in that column, including the zero. Next, choose a circled number such as 10, and have students identify which numbers round to it. Then instruct each child to color those numbers and the circled number the same color. Repeat the procedure for each circled number, reminding students to use a different color each time. When each child's chart is colored, call out random numbers. Challenge each student to mentally round each number before she checks her chart. Last, have the student glue her rounding chart in her math notebook for easy reference. Remind her to use the chart when she completes "Gotta Have Gum!" on page 73. What a colorful visual cue!

Teresa Savage
Swans Creek Elementary School
Dumfries, VA

Multiplication Manipulatives
Skill: connecting addition and multiplication

Here's a hands-on way to introduce a fact table and relate it to addition. Divide students into groups, matching the number of group members to the fact table you're introducing (for example, four students per group when introducing the fours). Give each child ten manipulatives. Write a fact on the board (such as 4 x 2). Challenge each child in a group to count out the correct number of manipulatives (2), and then ask each group to add to find the corresponding product (8). Repeat the activity for each fact in the fact table.

Laura Wagner
Raleigh, NC

Eight!

Math Mailbag

Right on Time!

Skill: showing time on an analog clock

Time-related skills just keep on ticking during this large-group activity! Label 12 large cards with the times 1:00 to 12:00 to make hour cards. Also label a set of smaller cards with chosen minute amounts from :00 to :59. Then sort the cards into an hour container and a minute container. To begin, give each student a copy of page 74. Have a volunteer draw one card from each container, state the resulting time, and set the cards aside. Instruct each child to program one clock with the time and then write the time below the clock. Continue in this manner until ten times are recorded. Plan to repeat the activity at a later time, or place the containers of cards and copies of page 74 at a center. Ticktock!

Lisa J. Doran
The Children's School
LaJolla, CA

11:00 :45

Key Word Clues

Skill: solving word problems

When students have these keys at their fingertips, they're one step closer to unlocking word problems! Label one key-shaped pattern for each math operation your students use. Next, program each pattern with key words and phrases for the operation. Copy each pattern on a different color of construction paper to make a class supply and then laminate the copies for durability. Ask each child to cut out and hole-punch each key type, thread the keys onto a pipe cleaner, and twist the pipe cleaner ends to form a ring. Look who's in the driver's seat now!

Gittie Sternberg, Beth Rivkah School, New York City, NY

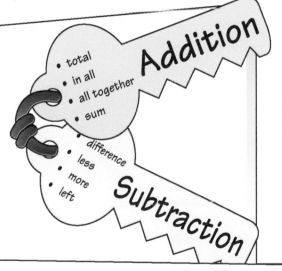

Addition
• total
• in all
• all together
• sum

Subtraction
• difference
• less
• more
• left

Signature Sums

Skill: adding larger numbers

Put addition skills into motion! For this large-group activity, cut in half one index card for every two students. Label each card with a different two-, three-, or four-digit number. Hand out the cards and instruct each student to draw a nine-box grid on a sheet of blank paper. Next, pair students. Tell each student to write and solve on his paper an addition problem that consists of his and his partner's numbers. If the partners' sums match, each student signs in the same box as his partner's problem. If their sums differ, the partners work together to find and make each needed correction. After their problems are autographed, the partners stand, and then each one pairs up with a new partner who is also standing. The activity continues until time runs out or several students have collected nine signatures.

Claire P. Chastaine, Stamford Central School, Stamford, NY

$\begin{array}{r} 1 \\ 451 \\ +\,262 \\ \hline 713 \\ \text{Mary} \end{array}$	$\begin{array}{r} 1 \\ 451 \\ +\,196 \\ \hline 647 \\ \text{Chuck} \end{array}$	$\begin{array}{r} 451 \\ +\,444 \\ \hline 895 \\ \text{Alex} \end{array}$
	$\begin{array}{r} 451 \\ +\,346 \\ \hline 797 \\ \textbf{Troy} \end{array}$	

Circus Capers
Skill: using the guess-and-check strategy

When Ringmaster Rob has a problem to solve, who's he going to call? Your students, of course! Display the information shown or hand out copies of it to students. Explain that Ringmaster Rob is organizing a one-hour circus show. He knows all the acts can't be included; however, he wants to include as many different acts as possible. Instruct students to use the guess-and-check strategy to solve Rob's dilemma. When most students are satisfied with their answers, discuss the solution as a class. (Four acts can be included in the show: Ray's Rappin' Rabbits, Elephant Parade, Lola's Laughing Lobster, Clowning Around.)

Valerie Wood Smith
Robeson Elementary Center
Morgantown, PA

Act	Length
Ray's Rappin' Rabbits	25 minutes
Monkeys on the High Wire	15 minutes
Clowning Around	5 minutes
Leo the Lion Tamer	40 minutes
Elephant Parade	20 minutes
Lola's Laughing Lobster	10 minutes

Space Race
Skill: extending a number pattern

Perfect as a center- or free-time activity, this strategic partner game strengthens number concepts and nurtures algebraic thinking. To play, one partner draws on a sheet of paper two planets that are connected by a game trail. He writes a starting number on the first planet. Next, the partners agree on a number pattern such as "add 10" or "add 3, add 2, add 5." To take a turn, a partner writes on the game trail the next number or numbers (up to three) in the number pattern. Partners alternate taking turns until the number pattern extends to the second planet. The partner who writes the last number (on the second planet) wins. Far out! Let's play again!

Laura Mihalenko
Holmdel, NJ

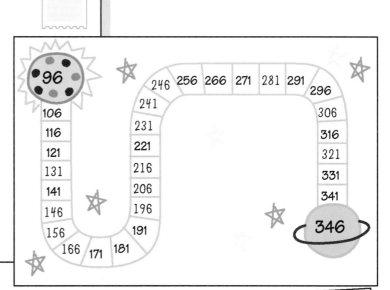

Multiplication Face-Off
Skill: reviewing multiplication facts

What does it take to win this partner game? A knowledge of facts and a bit of luck! To face off, each partner takes a turn rolling two dice. She writes the numbers she rolls on her paper as a multiplication fact and then she solves the fact. The players compare products. The greater product is circled. The lesser product is crossed out. Equal products are both circled. Players continue facing off in this manner. The player with more circled products at the end of game time wins. For a more challenging game, provide ten-sided dice. Or use masking tape to cover the dots on one die and then reprogram the tape with numerals such as 0, 4, 6, 7, 8, and 9. Roll 'em!

adapted from an idea by Jaime Saucier, Falls School
Attleboro Falls, MA

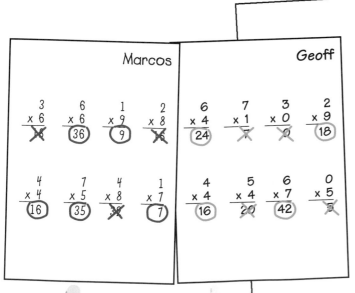

Math Mailbag

Call to Order
Skill: ordering sets of numbers

Mathematicians are on the move during this large-group activity! Label a class supply of blank cards with different three-digit numbers. Give each child a card and divide the class into three groups. Challenge each group to order its numbers from least to greatest. Verify each group's number order. Next, ask each child to trade cards with a member of his group; then provide guidelines for forming new groups, such as students who are the oldest (youngest, only) child in their families. Repeat the activity several times. Wrap up the fun by collecting the cards—in number order—for use on another day!

Joan Whitsell
East Elementary
Sheldon, IA

417   372   485

Got It!
Skill: basic facts

For spontaneous fact review, keep two flyswatters handy (for math use only). On the board write an assortment of fact answers. Divide students into two teams and ask each team to send one member to the board. With flyswatters in hand, the two players listen for a fact from you. The child who is first to swat the correct answer on the board earns one point for her team. Continue play in this manner until every child has participated one or more times. The team with more points at the end of game time wins.

Karen Marklein, St. John the Evangelist School
Spring Green, WI

What Place?
Skill: value of a digit

This nifty prop helps students make sense of place value. To make one, stack three 2" x 12" strips of colorful paper. Slide the top two strips to the left and then fold all three strips to the right to form six graduated sections. Staple near the fold and label the sections for the place values shown. Direct students to lay their props at the top of their papers and suggest that they fold back each place value with which they are not currently working. Finding the value of a digit just got easier!

Kelly Wolf
Emma Roberson Elementary
Granbury, TX

100,000   10,000   1,000   100   10   1

Pick a Card
Skill: multiplication facts

An array of fact practice is in the cards! For a partner game that reinforces facts through 10 x 10, remove the jacks and queens from a deck of playing cards and explain that aces equal 1 and kings equal 0. Also provide a times table for checking products. Partners take turns dealing the cards; the dealer plays second. For each round, the dealer shuffles the deck before he deals 20 cards facedown in a 2 x 10 array. Player 1 flips over one card in each row of ten and states the product of the numbers. If he is correct, he collects the cards. If he is not, he turns the cards over. Then the dealer takes his turn. Play continues until no cards remain. The child with more cards wins the round. Deal 'em!

Amy Barsanti
Pines Elementary School
Plymouth, NC

$\frac{1}{4}$ Litia

I have 4 pencils in my desk. Only 1 pencil still has an eraser.

Fraction Hunt
Skill: naming parts of a group

Quickly assess your youngsters' knowledge of fractions by asking each child to name, describe, and illustrate a fraction that is represented in the classroom. For example, show students that two-thirds of the class computers are turned off. Or point out that three-tenths of your fingers bear rings. Invite students to share their discoveries with the class. Then publish the papers in a class notebook titled "Fractions Are All Around!" Encourage students to add more pages to the publication.

Stacie Stone Davis, Lima, NY

Calendar Capers
Skill: using the working backward strategy

Before you make a date for this problem-solving activity, have each child complete a copy of page 76. Then guide students in working backward on their calendars to solve the following problems.
- Freddy's science fair project takes 12 days to make. The fair is May 20. What is the last day on which Freddy can start his project? *(May 8)*
- Lily practices for Croak Chorus on the second and fourth Tuesday of every month. Her cousin is coming to visit four days before her second practice in April. On what date is her cousin coming to visit? *(April 22)*
- Today is May 21, the day of the leapfrog contest! Willy spent the last five days training in the pond. Before that Willy trained for six days at Hopping Camp. The day before camp he saw his granny. On what date did Willy see his granny? *(May 9)*

Cynthia Holcomb, Mertzon, TX

Name _Alex_

Hop to It!   Making and using a calendar

Finish each calendar.

April

Sun.	Mon.	Tues.	Wed.	Thurs.	Fri.	Sat.
					1	2
3	(4)	5	6	7	8	9
10	11	12	13	14	(15)	16
17	18	(19)	20	21	22	23
24	25	26	27	28	29	(30)

May

Sun.	Mon.	Tues.	Wed.	Thurs.	Fri.	Sat.
(1)	X	3	4	5	6	7
8	X	10	11	(12)	13	14
15	X	17	18	19	20	(21)
22	X	24	(25)	26	27	28
29	X (31)					

Follow the directions.
1. Draw a green line under the name of each month.
2. Draw a blue circle on the first and last day of each month.
3. Draw a red X on each Monday in May.
4. Draw an orange ▲ on each Thursday in April.
5. Draw a yellow box around each day of the week.
6. Use green to circle the following dates on the calendars. On each line write the day on which each event takes place.

Saturday	May 21	Leapfrog Contest
Friday	April 15	Pond Taxes Due
Thursday	May 12	Bug-Eating Picnic
Wednesday	May 25	Croak Chorus Concert
Monday	April 4	Tadpole Tour
Tuesday	April 19	Save the Pond Day

Gotta Have Gum!

Name _____

Round each number to the nearest ten.
Write your answer.
Color by the code.

Color Code
number rounded up = yellow
number rounded down = green

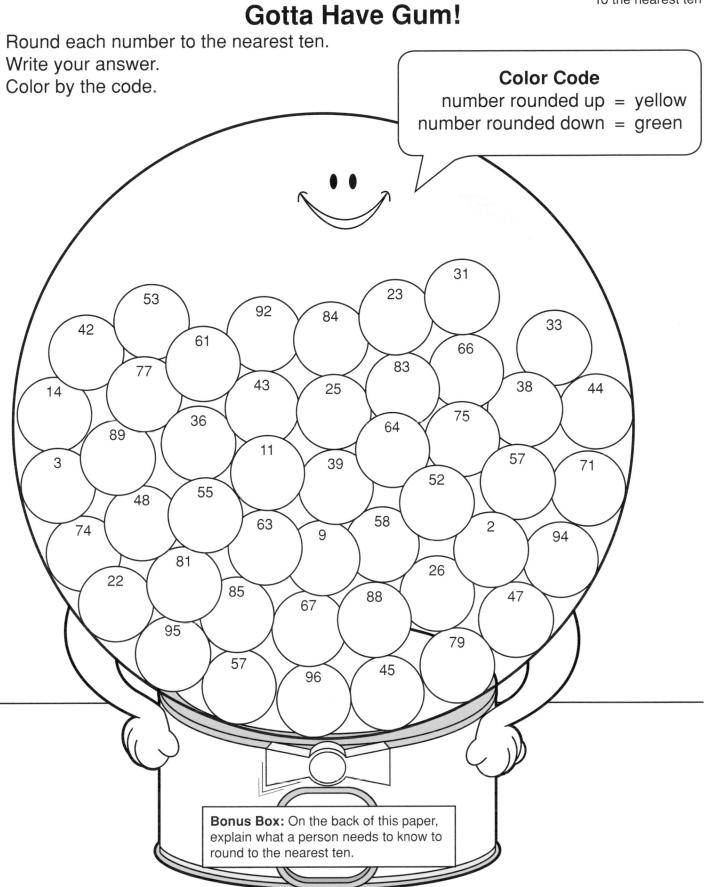

Bonus Box: On the back of this paper, explain what a person needs to know to round to the nearest ten.

Note to the teacher: Use alone or as a follow-up to "Rainbow Rounding" on page 68.

Right on Time!

____ : ____   ____ : ____   ____ : ____   ____ : ____

____ : ____   ____ : ____   ____ : ____   ____ : ____

____ : ____   ____ : ____

COCK-A-DOODLE-DOO!

Sold!

Name the place value of each
  underlined digit.
Color by the code.

Shelby's
Auction House
17

Color Code
thousands = yellow
hundreds = red
tens = green
ones = blue

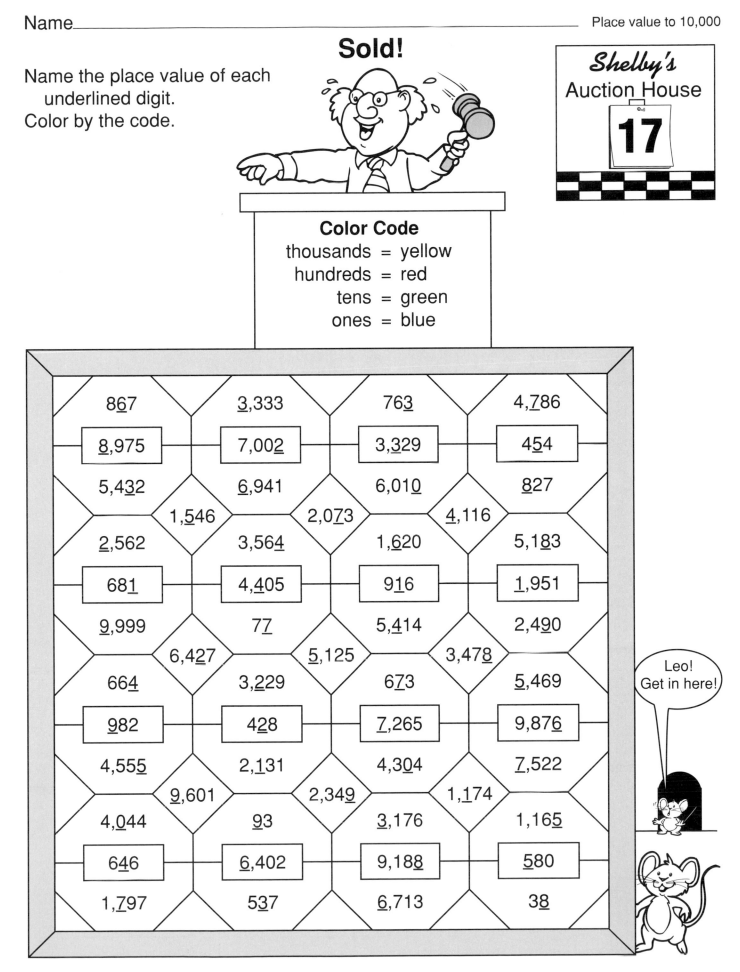

Leo!
Get in here!

Hop to It!

Finish each calendar.

April						
Sun.			Wed.		Fri.	Sat.
					1	
			6			
10	11					
					22	
						30

		Mon.	Tues.		Thurs.	
			3			
	8					
					20	21
			31			

Follow the directions.

1. Draw a green line under the name of each month.
2. Draw a blue circle on the first and last day of each month.
3. Draw a red X on each Monday in May.
4. Draw an orange ▲ on each Thursday in April.
5. Draw a yellow box around each day of the week.
6. Use green to circle the following dates on the calendars. On each line write the day on which each event takes place.

_____	May 21	Leapfrog Contest
_____	April 15	Pond Taxes Due
_____	May 12	Bug-Eating Picnic
_____	May 25	Croak Chorus Concert
_____	April 4	Tadpole Tour
_____	April 19	Save the Pond Day

Freddy's Flies

Read the sentences.
Cut and paste to complete the picture graph.
Use the graph to answer the questions.

Freddy ate 6 flies on Sunday,
    Wednesday, and Thursday.
Freddy ate 18 flies on Saturday.
Freddy ate 9 flies on Monday.
Freddy ate 12 flies on Tuesday.
Freddy ate 3 flies on Friday.

Number of Flies Eaten by Freddy Frog

Sunday	
Monday	
Tuesday	
Wednesday	
Thursday	
Friday	
Saturday	

Each 🪰 = 3 flies

1. On which day did Freddy eat the fewest flies? _____

2. On which day did Freddy eat the most flies? _____

3. How many flies do you think Freddy usually eats? _____

    Why? _____

4. How many flies did Freddy eat during the whole week? _____

5. Last week Freddy ate 42 flies. Did he eat more or less flies this week?

_____ How many? _____

Daring Dolphins

Each dolphin does a different trick for the show.
Find out which trick each dolphin is doing.

Read each clue and record what you know on the chart.
If a dolphin cannot do the trick, color the box.
If a dolphin can do the trick, draw a star in the box.

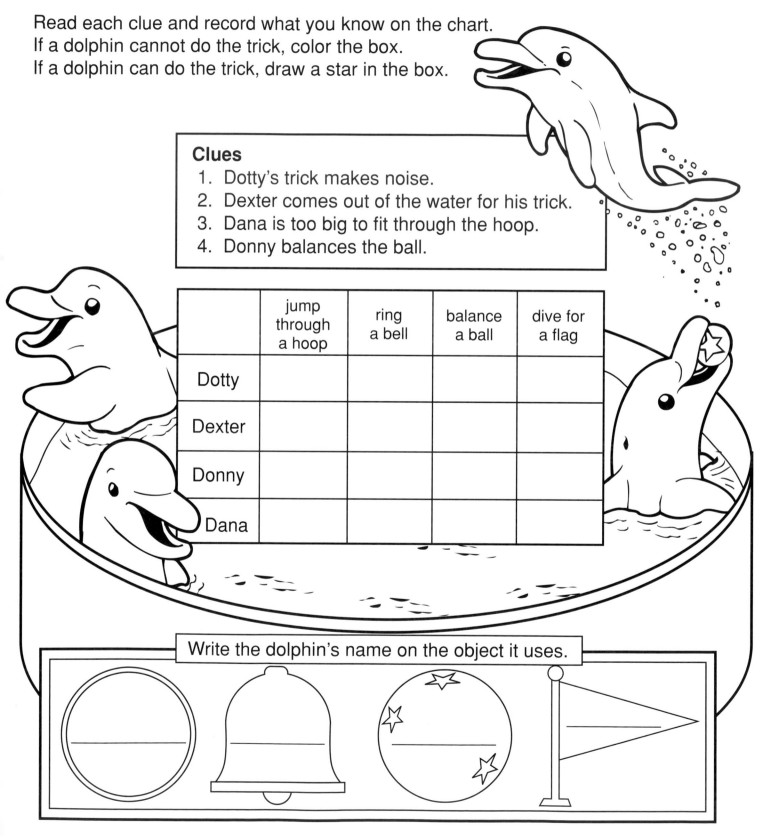

Clues

1. Dotty's trick makes noise.
2. Dexter comes out of the water for his trick.
3. Dana is too big to fit through the hoop.
4. Donny balances the ball.

	jump through a hoop	ring a bell	balance a ball	dive for a flag
Dotty				
Dexter				
Donny				
Dana				

Write the dolphin's name on the object it uses.

©The Mailbox® · TEC43019 · June/July 2005 · Key p. 311

OUR READERS WRITE

Our Readers Write

Meet and Greet

This activity puts a spin on first-day introductions! Divide students into two equal groups. (Plan to participate if there is an odd number of students.) One group stands in an inner circle, facing outward. The other group stands in an outer circle with each member facing a partner from the inner circle. Each student in a twosome shares her name and a fact about herself, such as an interest or something she did during the summer. At your signal, members of the inner circle take one step to the right, and the new pairs share information. Continue for a desired number of rotations.

Jamie Zidle—Gr. 2, Washington Avenue Elementary School, Chatham, NJ

Mr. Brody,

Please visit our class on Tuesday. We want to learn about what a school bus driver does.

Thank you,
Ms. Lewis

Back to School With the Black Lagoon

Introduce school staff with this kid-pleasing literature series. In each installment of Mike Thaler's Black Lagoon series, a child confronts his outlandish fears about meeting a staff member. Read aloud one or more selected titles. Then arrange for your class to visit each selected staff member for a personal introduction and a quick job description. Cool!

Julie Lewis—Gr. 2, J. O. Davis Elementary, Irving, TX

Memorable Writing Motivation

This idea for providing writing motivation results in a class scrapbook at the end of the year. Throughout the year, use a decorative container to store photographs of students engaged in various school activities. When a child needs writing inspiration, she selects a photograph and mounts it to the top of her writing paper. Then she writes about what is happening in the picture. She places her edited work in a three-ring binder. Share the resulting scrapbook with students in May or June for a year-end reflection. How memorable!

Jessica Hines—Clarksville Elementary, Clarksville, TX

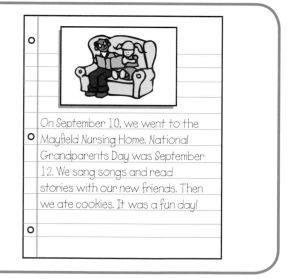

On September 10, we went to the Mayfield Nursing Home. National Grandparents Day was September 12. We sang songs and read stories with our new friends. Then we ate cookies. It was a fun day!

Compare and Contrast

Here's a picture-perfect way for students to get acquainted! Pair students. (Plan to participate if there is an odd number of students.) Have the students in each pair draw a Venn diagram on a large sheet of paper, label it with their names, and draw their self-portraits. Then have each pair jot similarities and differences in the corresponding sections of the diagram. Provide time for sharing.

Ruthie Jamieson Titus—Gr. 3, Union Elementary, Poland, OH

80

Sentence ABCs

This unique activity reinforces the ABCs of writing sentences. Challenge students to write humorous sentences using words that begin with a selected alphabetical sequence of letters. Have each child copy his favorite sentence on a blank sentence strip, using a different color for the first letter of each word. Invite students to read their sentences aloud, applauding students with the longest sentences.

Bears come down every Friday.

Heather Colbert—Grs. K–6, West Lee Center of Creative Learning, Wytheville, VA

Problem Solving
Remarkable Police Save Lives.
e	l	o	o
a		l	o
d	a	v	k
	n	e	
			b
			a
			c
			k

Instant Recall

Help students remember the problem-solving process with a mnemonic device. List the problem-solving steps used in your classroom. Then enlist students' help in using the first letter of each step to brainstorm sentences that will help them remember the process. Display the sentences and corresponding steps on a decorated poster, as shown, for a student reference.

Dawn Maucieri—Gr. 3, Signal Hill Elementary, Dix Hills, NY

A Gift of Reading

Celebrate students' birthdays with birthday books! Collect one book for each child. (If desired, use bonus points from a classroom book club, or ask parents to donate new or gently used books.) Attach a personalized bookplate to each special book. On a child's birthday, read his story to the class; then present the book to the birthday student. Have him keep it in the classroom library and then take it home at the end of the school year.

Jan Schoenherr—Gr. 3, Hughes Elementary, Marshall, MI

It's in the Cards

These cards put countless opportunities for math review at your students' fingertips! Each child will need ten index cards. He cuts each card in half and numbers both halves of each card with a number from 0 through 9 to make two sets. If desired, he decorates the back of the cards. He uses his cards to play math games, review facts with a partner, or display an answer to a math problem. When they're not in use, he stores the cards in a resealable plastic bag and places the bag in his desk for safekeeping.

Margaret Wanat—Gr. 3, St. Eugene School, Chicago, IL

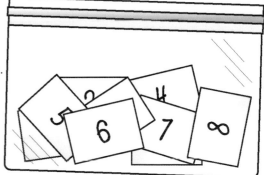

Silent Reading Share Time

Stick with this idea for making the most out of independent reading! Place a stack of sticky notes near your classroom library. When a child selects a book, he also takes a note. After reading, he locates a part of his reading that caught his attention and flags the page. Then he shares his observation with a partner during a designated "Sticky Note Talk Time!"

Dawn Maucieri

Grandma's
Famous
Chocolate
Chip Cookies

1 c. butter
1 c. sugar
1 c. brown sugar
1 tsp. vanilla
2 c. flour
1 tsp. baking powder
1 tsp. salt

Cooking Up Good Handwriting

Here's a clever idea for handwriting practice that culminates with a keepsake cookbook. Ask parents to contribute simple recipes on a particular theme, such as Thanksgiving favorites, yummy desserts, or ethnic recipes. Each day, write one recipe on the board or overhead. Direct students to copy it using their best handwriting and to add an illustration if desired. Once students have copied all of the recipes, have each child staple the recipes behind a decorated cover. Encourage students to present their cookbooks to their parents. Now that's some tasty handwriting practice!

Tina Alvarado—Gr. 3, Houston Elementary, Mineral Wells, TX

Highlight of the Day

Do your students forget to put their names on homework papers? Give each student a highlighter and explain that before turning in homework, he should highlight his name at the top of the page. No more anonymous papers!

Jen DeWaard, Armour, SD

It Matters!

The idea that gases take up space but don't weigh much can be confusing to youngsters. Here's how to make the concept clear! Purchase a helium-inflated, holiday-themed mylar balloon, such as a turkey or pumpkin. Tape two index cards to the balloon's ribbon. On the first card write "Does all matter take up space? Yes!" and add an arrow pointing to the balloon. On the second card write "Is all matter heavy? No!" and draw another arrow to the balloon. The concept will be much clearer!

Judi Lesnansky, New Hope Academy, Youngstown, OH

Does all matter take up space? Yes!

Is all matter heavy? No!

Open a New Chapter

Celebrate National Children's Book Week (November 15–21, 2004) by creating these inspiring bookmarks. Request outdated book catalogs from your school or public librarian. Have each student cut out pictures of interesting books and glue them to a bookmark-size piece of tagboard. Then laminate the bookmarks if desired. Not only are these bookmarks great for marking current books, but they also provide inspiration for future reading!

Ann Marie Stephens, G. C. Round Elementary, Manassas, VA

Eerie Cue for You

Add a touch of suspense to silent reading time! Play spooky music to signal the start of silent reading. If desired, darken the classroom and provide students with flashlights to read by. And finally, encourage youngsters to read mystery stories to add an air of suspense. Boo! What are you reading?

Glenda Muccitelli—Gr. 3, Wright Elementary, Altoona, PA

Conferences With Confidence

Put parents at ease prior to parent-teacher conferences with this idea. Several days prior to conferences, send home a letter that lists the topics you'll cover and provides a place for parents to write down any questions they have. When each letter is returned, make a note of comments and concerns to discuss at the conference. Parents will know the agenda ahead of time and won't have to worry about forgetting their questions. Everyone will be more at ease!

Deb Martin—Gr. 3, Starside Elementary, De Soto, KS

Classy Art

Wondering what to do with the precious artwork that students make just for you? Create a classroom artists' book! Bind 12" x 18" sheets of construction paper behind a laminated cover with a title such as "Our Classroom Artists." Display students' drawings at your desk for several days, and then staple or tape them into your book. Students love looking at their own artwork!

Laura Frederick—Gr. 3, Cannon Falls Area Elementary School Cannon Falls, MN

Neat and Tidy Stamps

Clean old ink from your rubber stamps in seconds with this tip. Fold a baby wipe in quarters, then press the stamp onto it several times. Your stamps will be like new!

Alesia Richards—Gr. 2, Redbud Run Elementary, Winchester, VA

Book Order Express

Add a dose of geography to your next class book order! Explore your book club Web site to see if it offers order tracking. If so, show students how to track the class order. Then have one student check the order status each day and mark the location with a sticky note on the class wall map. Students can predict when the order will arrive, calculate how far it traveled in a day, and so forth. This activity makes the waiting a little easier—and more exciting!

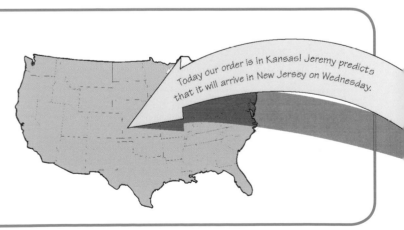

Laura Nardi—Gr. 3, Marlton Elementary School, Marlton, NJ

You've Got Mail!

Holiday mail provides a perfect opportunity for learning about the U.S.A.! Post a large black and white U.S. map, and send home five index cards with each child. After a child gets a parent's permission, he reads envelopes that come through the mail for postmarks (or address labels) from different states. He attaches one postmark to each index card. Next, he finds a fact about the state. He writes it on the card and draws a small illustration. When a student returns a card, have him name the state, read the corresponding fact, and then display the card near the map. If he is the first to name a state, he colors that state on the map.

Julie Rezash, Whitman Elementary School, Milwaukee, WI

This mail came from Iowa. A lot of corn grows in Iowa.

This mail came from Florida. Florida is called the Sunshine State.

Cool Custom

After you read aloud a favorite story for Hanukkah, give students a chance to experience a Jewish custom—playing the dreidel game. Small, inexpensive dreidels are available at department stores. Pennies, counters, or candies can be used for tokens. After several rounds of play, invite students to modify the playing rules by changing the amount of tokens that are put into or taken out of the kitty. Math plus social studies equals holiday fun!

Mia Valentine, Albany School of Humanities, Albany, NY

The More, the Merrier!

Turn plural practice into a volume of holiday cheer! To make a class book, have students brainstorm nouns that relate to a specific holiday. List the words in singular form on the board. Each child chooses a different word from the list and writes it in the top right-hand corner of a sheet of drawing paper. Then she writes the plural form of the word, writes a sentence that includes the plural form, illustrates her sentence, and decorates the page. Hole-punch the papers and organize them alphabetically in a three-ring binder. Invite students to make additions to the book throughout the holiday season.

Danielle Conforti, Old Mill School, Sea Girt, NJ

candy cane
candy canes

We have lots of candy canes on our Christmas tree.

All Clear!

Checking word searches just got easier! To make a key for student use, place a sheet of clear plastic over a puzzle and use a permanent marker to complete the puzzle. A student simply places the transparency over his paper to check his work. Easy!

Tina Ceratti, College Square Elementary School, Beaver, PA

Quick Spin

Make a spinner in a jiffy! Prepare and laminate a desired spinner card, and super-glue a large safety pin shut. Poke a brad through the small opening at the bottom of the pin and then poke the brad through the center of the spinner. Fasten the brad and then the spinner is ready!

Jill Shock, Syracuse Elementary, Syracuse, IN

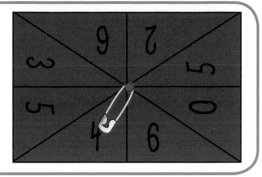

Keeping in Touch

Here's a New Year's resolution for communicating with parents that's easy to keep. Each day write a brief note to one student's parent(s). Share a good deed, an accomplishment, or an amusing anecdote about the child. Call it your one-a-day plan. It's certainly a healthy way to promote positive relationships with parents!

Julia Ring Alarie, Williston, VT

No Recess? No Problem!

Indoor recess goes smoothly when students build snowpals! Give each of several small groups a length of white bulletin board paper. Challenge each group to cut a snowpal's body from the paper and then creatively decorate it using construction paper scraps and markers. If your classroom has windows, suggest that groups make their snowpals two-sided. You'll have just what you need for a wintery window display. Let it snow!

Marlene Gaffner, Possum Elementary, Springfield, OH

Pleasing Practice

Reinforce that penmanship practice really is just practice. Laminate a sentence strip for each child and provide a class supply of dry-erase markers and cloth rags. Students are more likely to enjoy practicing forming cursive letters when they know they can quickly erase the letters that don't come out just right!

Ilah Breen, Clay Hill Elementary, Jacksonville, FL

100th Day Shopping Spree

Mark the 100th day of school by sending students on an imaginary shopping spree! Provide catalogs, sale flyers, calculators, scissors, glue, and construction paper. Tell each child she has $100 to spend. Instruct her to design a shopping cart and then, inside the cart, glue cutouts (and the prices) of her purchases. Require each shopper to keep a running total of money spent. Students shop until their pockets are empty!

Kim Barton, Blanding Elementary, Blanding, UT

In Honor of Abe

Abraham Lincoln is top of mind during this timeline project. Program a penny pattern for each year of your students' lives and then copy the patterns on construction paper to make a class supply. A student cuts out a penny for every year of his life, beginning with the year in which he was born. He glues the pennies in order along one side of a piece of paper, and then he draws and programs a timeline of personalized events (with the help of a parent). You can count on students being eager to share their timelines. Who knows, there could be a future presidential candidate in the bunch!

Lisa Strieker, St. Paul Elementary, Highland, IL

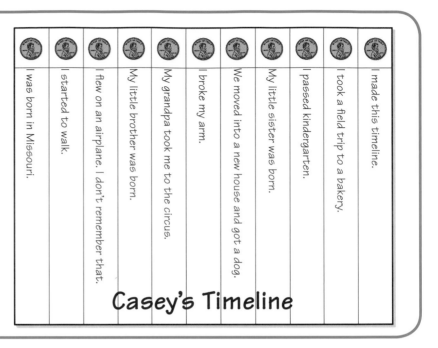

Casey's Timeline

- I was born in Missouri.
- I started to walk.
- I flew on an airplane. I don't remember that.
- My little brother was born.
- My grandpa took me to the circus.
- I broke my arm.
- We moved into a new house and got a dog.
- My little sister was born.
- I passed kindergarten.
- I took a field trip to a bakery.
- I made this timeline.

Sedimentary Snack

Here's a party snack that feeds tummies and rocks brains! For a valentine party, use a heart-shaped cookie cutter to cut semi-frozen bread, making at least two heart shapes per student. Also gather an assortment of kid-pleasing sandwich fixings. As students add layers to their heart-shaped sandwiches, remind them that sedimentary rocks form when assorted materials settle into layers and become pressed together. There you have it—a party snack that reinforces a science standard!

Barbara Marks, St. John LaLande School, Blue Springs, MO

Party Game

If there's time for a valentine party game, try this one! Conceal all but three prizes from a class supply of heart-shaped candies or mini erasers. Also cut an equal number of heart shapes from pink and red craft foam. Show students the cutouts before dropping them in a gift bag. To play, each student, in turn, guesses the color of heart she'll pull from the gift bag. If she's correct, she earns a prize. The cutout goes back in the bag at the end of each turn. When the three prizes have been awarded, explain that the next player with a correct guess must snatch her prize from another classmate by saying, "[Student's name], please give me your heart!" A quick game tempo means prizes change hands quickly and it keeps students paying close attention. When it's time to conclude the game, surprise students by handing out the remaining prizes. Everyone wins!

Isobel Livingstone, Rahway, NJ

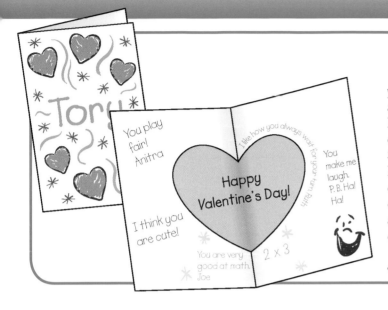

Valentine Card Exchange

Valentine's Day is a perfect time to get to the heart of your students' special qualities! Have each student make and personalize a large construction paper card. Then have him trade cards with a classmate and, inside the card, describe a special quality of the child who made it. Students may sign their notes or leave them anonymous. Have students repeat the exercise several more times, each time confirming that they have received neither their own cards nor cards they have already signed. If time allows, collect the cards and add a personalized note to each one. Happy Valentine's Day!

Julie Lewis, J. O. Davis Elementary, Irving, TX

Flash Card Totes

If you routinely send home flash cards with your students, keep reading! To protect the cards and reinforce their return, provide each child with a personalized flash card tote. The vinyl folders in which some photo centers (such as in Wal-Mart stores) return photographs work perfectly. Each morning, put a sticker on each returned tote. Now that's a flash of inspiration!

Mederise Burke, Courthouse Road Elementary, Spotsylvania, VA

Spill-Proof Paint

Try this idea for eliminating messy paint spills and for storing leftover paint. Pour paint into empty 35mm film canisters and then set each canister inside the lid of a spray can that has an inner lid (such as those from spray paint). When students are finished painting, snap on the film canister lids. Spilled paint easily rinses off the canisters and holders. Cleanup is a snap, and so is storage!

Jill Shock, Syracuse Elementary, Syracuse, IN

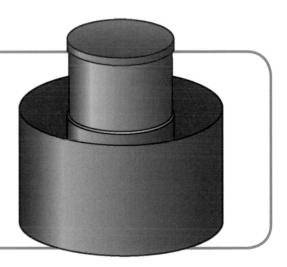

Million Dollar Words

$$$ Million Dollar Words $$$

atrocious—very bad

astonishment—surprise

miserable—unhappy

Take a million dollar approach to building your students' writing and speaking vocabularies. Display a poster titled "Million Dollar Words." Join students in pointing out highly descriptive words found in the students' reading. List these words on the chart using one color for the word and a second color for the definition. In no time at all, students will be using a wealth of new vocabulary!

Pat Hart, W. S. Freeman, Troy, IL

Poetry for Breakfast

During April, National Poetry Month, invite parents and guests to your classroom for an early morning poetry breakfast. Prior to the big day, have each child create a small anthology that includes poetry he wrote and other poetry he enjoys. On the morning of the poetry breakfast, have student volunteers share with your guests their favorite original poems. Then have students and parents gather in small groups throughout the classroom to discuss the anthologies while they nibble on light refreshments.

Peggy Bruno, Squadron Line School, Simsbury, CT

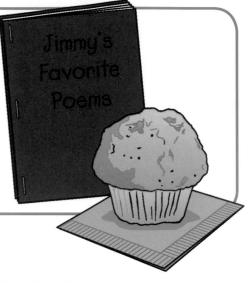

Suffix Jingle

Teach your students this song, sung to the tune of "I'm a Little Teapot," so they can easily remember the placement and role of suffixes.

I'm a little suffix, short and stout.
The end of a word is where I hang out.
When I join a root word,
Better watch out!
'Cause I'll change its meaning;
There's no doubt.

Amber Leigh Barbee, Deaf Smith Elementary, Wharton, TX

Our Wonderful World

This crowd-pleasing Earth Day show is inspired by "What a Wonderful World," a song made famous by Louis Armstrong. To prepare, begin by taping 20 blank poster board cards to a wall, forming a 4 x 5 grid. Project a simple smiling earth design onto the cards and trace it.

Give each card to a child and have him initial it before coloring his portion of the earth according to your directions. (If you have more than 20 students, give the remaining students other tasks related to the show.) Reassemble the earth design on the floor and then flip the entire design over as a unit. Attach a sticky note to each card. Then, in the sequence of the song, label each note with a phrase to illustrate or a word to copy. After the cards are programmed by students (and the notes removed), play a recording of "What a Wonderful World." Guide children in revealing their cards as the corresponding song parts are sung. On performance day, have children sing along and display their cards as practiced. At the song's end have them flip their cards in unison and showcase the large earth design. Oh, yeah!

Mary Mattivi, Holy Rosary School, Johnsonburg, PA

Dear Teacher

Slip a little more letter writing into your students' week with this suggestion. Every now and then, ask that children write a letter to you in their journals instead of making their usual journal entries. Each time, respond to the letters by writing responses in letter form. If you're unable to respond in writing to each one, respond to half of them in writing one time and half the next. This creates opportunities for students to practice writing friendly letters, while opening up a new channel for helpful dialogue.

Bonnie Kinniff, St. Agatha School, Columbus, OH

Find It in a Flash

Here's a habit that will help you find your favorite ideas from issues of *The Mailbox*® magazine in a flash. When you thumb through your current issue of *The Mailbox*® magazine, flag and label the ideas you want to eventually use. Then, when you need one of the ideas that caught your eye earlier, you can refer to your flags to find it—pronto!

Stephanie Raymoure, Patterson Elementary, Holly, MI

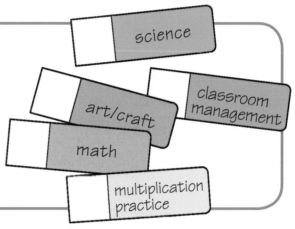

Pasta Aplenty

Do you use pasta a lot in your classroom for counting, sorting, or art projects? Here's a simple tip to keep your supply plentiful and varied. When buying pasta to prepare for your family, purchase different pasta shapes rather than always buying the same kind. Whenever you prepare pasta at home, put some of the unused uncooked pasta in a plastic bag to take to school. Not only will your students enjoy their ever-changing pasta supply, but your family will enjoy the variety too.

Pat Piechowski, Annunciation Regional School, Bellmawr, NJ

Cute-As-a-Button Gifts

These soon-to-be-treasured keepsakes are as much fun to make as they are to give for Mother's Day gifts or end-of-the-year mementos. In advance, collect candid photos or group photos for the project. Then prepare or purchase frames made from cardboard, craft foam, or other suitable material. Have students use craft glue to glue buttons all around the frames. When the glue has dried, have children attach their pictures and, if necessary, poster board backing. Moms, staff, or volunteers will be delightfully surprised to receive this one-of-a-kind gift of appreciation.

Susan Stires, Sam Houston Elementary, Wichita Falls, TX

Quotation Queen

If your students are perplexed about where to place quotation marks, send the queen to the rescue. Create a poster similar to the one shown and laminate it. Use it to explain that quotes are placed around words that are spoken. As you give an example, use a wipe-off marker to write the spoken words above the mouth so that children see the quotation marks around what was said. Wipe off the example and have children propose some other examples. Thanks, Queen! You make it easier to remember!

Jamie Zidle, Washington Avenue Elementary School, Chatham, NJ

Math Workout

This spring engage students in exercise and data analysis. Ask some higher-grade students to measure the distance around the school playground and calculate how many laps equal one mile. Invite children to join you in walking laps during recess. After each day's walk, have students tally the total distance for the day. Encourage them to determine how close you are to one mile, estimate when you'll reach the five-mile mark, and so forth. Now that's great exercise!

Katy Hoh, WCK Walls Elementary, Pitman, NJ

A Minute for Spelling

When you have a minute or two to spare between lessons, use the time to help children with spelling. If several of your children commonly misspell *because,* for example, suggest this mnemonic sentence: **B**ig **e**lephants **c**an **a**lways **u**nderstand **s**mall **e**lephants. On another day, when you have a couple of minutes to spare, ask your class to invent a mnemonic sentence for another troublesome spelling word. What a great way to get a lot of mileage from a minute or two!

Kathleen Doherty, Christa McAuliffe School, Tinley Park, IL

big elephants can always
Understand small elephants

b-e-c-a-u-s-e

Chip Clips

When children are writing reports using computers, this little tip makes it easier for them to refer back to their notes or drafts. Simply place a clean, empty Pringles can near the computer and clip a clothespin to the top. When a student comes to the computer to write a report, he just clips his paper to the can and goes right to work. It's so much easier to view an entire page when you don't have to crane your neck to get a good look at it.

Susan Russell, Durham Elementary, Durham, NY

WRITE ON!

Write On!

Ideas and Tips for Teaching Students to Write!

Hats Off to Labor Day!

Jordan

Code
Mirror = Tell something about yourself.
Book = Write about the last book you read.
Empty wallet = Describe what you would do with a million dollars.
Sports hat = Tell whether or not you like sports and why.
Measuring cup = Write a recipe.
Postcard = Describe a place you have visited.

Timely Prompts

When it comes to boosting writing skills, these Labor Day **prompts** pay off! Tell students that Labor Day, the first Monday in September, honors working people. Further explain that many laborers wear hats that help them perform their jobs. Invite students to share some examples. Next, each youngster uses a hat-shaped template to make two booklet covers from construction paper and two pages from writing paper. He staples the hats together, as shown, and responds to a provided prompt inside. Then he adds a title and desired crayon details.

- Think about a job you would like to have one day. What would you wear to perform that job? Tell why.
- Imagine that you are the boss and need to hire a new worker. List five questions you would ask.
- Write a thank-you note to someone (such as a parent or a teacher) whose hard work makes your life better.

Unpacking Ideas

Writing **ideas** are in the bag with this suggestion! Prepare a code similar to the one shown. Laminate the code and place it inside a backpack along with each of the items. When a youngster has trouble thinking of a writing topic, encourage her to randomly select an item from the backpack. Have her refer to the code and write about the topic. Then tell her to return the item for another student to use. To maintain interest, periodically restock the backpack with different items and change the code.

Johna Berg—Gr. 3, Blaine Elementary School, Blaine, WA

Knock, Knock!

Students won't knock this kid-pleasing **creative-writing** activity! Share a selected knock-knock joke book with students for inspiration. Then have each child try his hand at writing an original joke. He writes his teacher-approved joke on a vertically positioned 4" x 6" unlined index card. He staples another card on top and embellishes the resulting door with crayon details as desired. To make a door knocker, he threads a short pipe cleaner length through a bead and staples the pipe cleaner ends to the door as shown. Then he shares his joke with his classmates. What rib-tickling writing motivation!

Ann Zisser—Gr. 3, The Solomon Schechter School of Westchester, White Plains, NY

Write On!

Ideas and Tips for Teaching Students to Write!

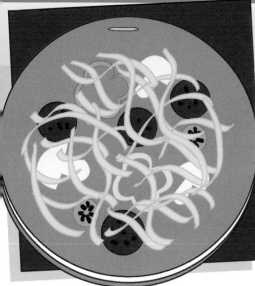

Timely Prompts

Any way you slice it, these tasty **prompts** are perfect for celebrating National Pizza Month (October)! Have each student create a pizza-shaped journal by stapling circles of lined paper between two slightly larger circles of brown construction paper. The student then adds toppings by using construction paper, yellow yarn (cheese), markers, and glue. Then he writes pizza-inspired paragraphs in response to the prompts below.

- If you could have only one topping on your pizza, what would it be? Write a persuasive paragraph about why this topping is best.
- Your pizza has just been delivered. It is burnt and hard as a rock. What else could you do with the pizza besides eat it?
- A new student has just moved to your town. Write directions for how to drive to your favorite pizza place.

"Spook-tacular" Stories

Here's a hauntingly fun way to encourage students to **revise their writing by adding descriptive details.** Brainstorm nouns related to a haunted house; then challenge each student to write a story about a haunted house using a set number of the nouns. Next, have each student use colored pencils to underline all of the nouns in his story (not just those on the original list) and then revise it by adding an adjective before each noun. If a noun already has an adjective, have him add a second one. Each student writes a final copy of his story on lined paper. Then he uses construction paper scraps to create a picture of the haunted house on the left side of a 12" x 18" sheet of construction paper. He then attaches his paragraph to the right side of the construction paper. Descriptive writing isn't scary at all!

Dawn Maucieri—Gr. 3, Signal Hill Elementary School, Dix Hills, NY

> Creak! That's the sound that the big wooden door made when brave Eva pulled it open. She peered inside the dark hallway and saw big gray pieces of dust floating around on the dirty floor. She took a deep breath and stepped inside. The spooky house was quiet except for a low whooshing sound. What was it? she wondered.

"Fall-ing" Into Writing Practice

"Be-leaf" it or not, students will fall right into **descriptive writing** with this seasonal activity. Gather a variety of colorful fall leaves or purchase silk leaves at a craft store. Have each student choose one and study it. Then challenge her to write a paragraph that's so descriptive that a reader could picture the leaf without actually seeing it. Staple each finished paragraph to a sheet of fall-colored construction paper, attaching it at the top only to create a flap. Number it under the flap. Then glue each leaf to construction paper and give it the corresponding number. Post leaves and paragraphs separately. Challenge each student to read each description, choose the leaf that inspired the paragraph, and check her conclusion by lifting the flap. Fall leaves may crumble, but students' descriptive writing lives on!

Melinda Blackwill, Hays, KS

> My leaf is bright red with yellow in the middle. It has five pointy tips. There is a brown spot on the middle one, maybe where an animal or insect chewed a little hole. The stem is broken off. I think the leaf is from a maple tree because it looks like the ones in my front yard.
> by Claudia

Write On!

Ideas and Tips for Teaching Students to Write!

Candy canes, snowy lanes,
Candles on my windowpanes.
Candle flames spreading light.
Sure wish you were here tonight.
One more thing I want to say:
Have a happy holiday!

Timely Prompts

Candle-related writing **prompts** keep students' writing bright! Prompt a class discussion about the important roles candles play in a variety of holiday celebrations, including Hanukkah, Christmas, and Kwanzaa. Then have each child respond to a selected prompt. To publish her writing she staples her final draft to a piece of slightly larger construction paper and then attaches a candle flame fashioned from yellow paper. The result is a glowing example of writing!

• Think about the most spectacular candle you've ever seen. Describe the candle, where it was, why it was there, and how it made you feel.

• Many holiday greeting cards feature a poem. Write a poem about candles for a holiday card.

• The phrase "burn the candle at both ends" describes someone who is trying to do too much. Write about a time when you or someone you know was burning the candle at both ends.

Rudolph, the Purple-Nosed Reindeer
by Caroline

One afternoon Rudolph took a long walk. He was very hungry, and he walked past a huge blueberry patch. "Yummy," he thought. He stuck his red nose into a blueberry bush and ate a berry. Then he ate more berries and more berries. When he was full he had blueberry juice all over his nose. Now his red nose was purple! "Oh no," Rudolph thought. "What will the other reindeer say?"

A Purple-Nosed Reindeer?

When Rudolph's nose changes color, **writing an explanation** is in order! Have on hand a colorful supply of pom-poms (excluding red) and a class supply of paper toppers like the one shown. Ask students to ponder what could cause Rudolph's nose to change color. As each child does this, have him color a paper topper, cut it out, and glue a colorful pom-pom nose on it. Then have him write an explanation for how Rudolph's nose became this color. Display each child's explanation and paper topper together. Who "nose" what creative tales your writers will create?

Lori Geelen, Woodland Elementary School, Emporium, PA

Seasonal Cinquains

Thoughts of winter provide inspiration for **writing cinquain poetry.** Engage students in brainstorming activities, foods, and clothing associated with winter. Then ask each child to choose a topic and compose a cinquain about it. When his writing is complete, have him cut it out, glue it onto drawing paper, and illustrate it. The poem may be just five lines, but it sure does say a lot!

Rebecca Brudwick
Hoover Elementary
North Mankato, MN

Cocoa
Creamy, sweet
Sipping, slurping, smacking
Yummy to my tummy
Winter drink

The five lines of a cinquain:
one-word title
two adjectives
three action words
four feeling words
synonym for title

Write On!

Ideas and Tips for Teaching Students to Write!

Timely Prompts

These chocolate-themed **prompts** make the writing experience oh so sweet! Have each student respond to a favorite prompt and then work with a partner to edit and revise her writing. To publish her work, have her make a candy-shaped booklet from brown construction paper and writing paper, write her final draft inside the booklet, and decorate its front cover. Showcase the projects on a large heart cutout. Now that's a big box of chocolates!

- The school principal is coming to dinner. You know the principal loves chocolate. Describe the dinner you will serve. Be creative!
- The store where your family shops for groceries will no longer carry chocolate products. Write a plan for persuading your family to shop elsewhere.
- There are chocolate-covered raisins, cherries, and strawberries. It's time for a chocolate-covered vegetable! Which vegetable should it be? Why?

March 17, 2005

Dear Leprechaun,
How are you? I hope you feel like sharing some good luck with me! I have been wishing for a dog and a big backyard. I also wish I had a pot of gold to give my mom. Thank you very much!

Sincerely,
Derrick

I wish I had a dog.
I wish I had a backyard.
I wish I had a pot of gold.

Dear Leprechaun

Who better to **write a letter** to on St. Patrick's Day than a little green leprechaun? First, have each child cut matching heart shapes from three squares of green paper and write on each heart cutout one wish he'd like a leprechaun to grant. Then instruct each child to write a letter for the purpose of sharing his three wishes. When his letter is written, have him glue the heart cutouts and a stem cut from green paper in the shape of a shamrock on his correspondence. How nice!

Theresa Waltner, Our Lady of Visitation School, Cincinnati, OH

Main Idea

Having a baby brother is fun.

High-Flying Details

Here's an idea that makes **planning a paragraph** a breeze! To make a reusable planner, prepare and laminate one kite and four kite bow cutouts similar to those shown. Then use a hole puncher and a length of yarn to make a kite string. Place the cutouts and a wipe-off pen in a zipper bag. To plan a paragraph, a student uses the provided pen to program the cutouts with her main idea and supporting details. After she arranges the details in a desired order along the kite string, she's ready to write. When her paragraph is complete, she uses a paper tissue or towel to wipe the planner clean. Students' success at writing paragraphs is sure to soar!

adapted from an idea by Cindy Barber, Fredonia, WI

Detail
He giggles at me.

Detail
He makes funny faces.

Detail
He has fun toys.

Detail
We look at books together.

Write On!

I think it would be more fun to be a tree frog because I could live in a tree. It would be like staying in my tree house all the time! I could look down and see all the things that are going

Popcorn
Yellow, lumpy
Sweet, salty
Rough, bumpy
Crunchy, crackling
Buttery, delicious
Kernels

by Hannah

Step 1
Step 2
Step 3
Step 4
Step 5

How to Give a Dog a Bath
First, fill the tub with warm water. Put your dog inside the water and get it wet all over. Then pour shampoo into your hand and rub your hands together. Next, rub your hands over the dog's fur. Make sure you don't get

Timely Prompts

Leap into spring with these "ribbit-ing" **prompts**! Invite each child to respond to a favorite writing suggestion. To publish his work, he copies his edited writing onto quarter sheets of writing paper. Next, he cuts out a green construction paper frog (pattern on page 99). The youngster adds details to his frog, including eyes and a long tongue. Then he stacks his writing pages in sequential order and staples the stack to the frog. If desired, lay a large lily pad cutout on the floor and invite each author to stand on it as he reads his writing to the class.

- How would your day change if you woke up one morning and discovered that you now leapt like a frog?
- Pretend you are a frog. Describe your ideal lily pad.
- Would you rather be a tiny tree frog or a large bullfrog? Why?

"Sense-sational" Poems

This **poetry** idea will have your students popping with excitement! Give each child a small serving of popcorn. As students munch, ask them to describe how the popcorn feels, tastes, looks, sounds, and smells. Write students' thoughts on the board, categorizing them by sense for easy reference. Next, have each child write a six-line poem titled "Popcorn." For each of the first five lines, she uses a different sense to describe popcorn in two words. The last line is another word for popcorn. For a satisfying conclusion, have each youngster write her poem on precut writing paper and then glue it to a popcorn bag.

Linda Masternak Justice, Kansas City, MO

Squeaky Clean!

Every student can shampoo his way to **writing clear directions**! As a prewriting activity, show students how to bathe a pet by acting out the process with a stuffed animal. Say each step aloud, and have each youngster note the steps on an organizer. After a quick review of signal words, direct him to use the notes he made to write a clear set of directions on story paper. Then have him illustrate his work. With this activity, writing directions is good clean fun!

Natalie Tanner, Adam Elementary, Houston, TX

Write On!

I want to do "s'more" reading and math. I want to learn how to multiply bigger numbers. I want to read "s'more" chapter books. I also want to play "s'more" soccer and become a better goalie for my team. I can't wait until next year!
by Matt

We Want S'more!
Creative writing

This end-of-the-year writing project is oh so sweet! Ask each child what he learned this school year that he wants to learn more about next year. Then have him write his ideas on the center of an eight-inch white construction paper square. Next, he paints the outside edges of the square with a half-and-half mixture of glue and shaving cream, creating a puffy marshmallow. After allowing 48 hours for his creation to dry, he glues a dark brown paper strip (chocolate) to the bottom of the marshmallow. Finally, he sandwiches his chocolate-marshmallow section between two light brown paper strips (graham crackers) to complete the s'more. If desired, provide s'mores to snack on as students share their writing. Yummy!

Cindy S. Barber, Saints Cecilia and James Catholic School, Thiensville, WI

Write On!

Timely Prompts
Journal prompts

Beat the heat with these cool summertime prompts! Lead a class discussion about students' favorite ice-cream treats. Next, have each student make a sundae-shaped booklet using the pattern on page 100 and half sheets of writing paper. She staples the pages together as shown, cuts around the shape, adds crayon details, and then responds to a selected prompt inside. Mmm, good!

- If you could be any type of ice-cream topping, what would you be and why?
- Describe your favorite ice-cream flavor without naming it. Give lots of details that describe how it looks, tastes, and smells.
- Imagine that you live in a world where everything is made of ice cream. Describe what it would be like living in this world.

Ice-Cream World
If I lived in a world where everything was made of ice cream, I would always be cold. The temperature would have to be freezing so the ice cream wouldn't melt. I'd have to wear a heavy jacket and winter clothes all the time. The water in the ocean would taste sweet instead of salty, and the oceans would all be different colors. I would like it because everything would have a flavor, and I could taste whatever I wanted.

Personal Timelines
Writing a sequence of events

Celebrate student achievements with this activity! Discuss as a class what students have accomplished throughout the year, both in and outside school. Next, give each child four index cards. The student labels each card with a different season and writes a memorable event that happened during that season. Then he uses a hole puncher and lengths of yarn to attach the cards in chronological order. Finally, he uses crayons and construction paper to make a head and feet, and he adds them to his personal timeline. Post students' time-lines in the hallway under the title "Celebrating the Seasons of _____ Grade."

Anne E. South, East Oro Public School, Orillia, Ontario, Canada

Stories From the Shore
Descriptive writing

Sand, sun, and fun combine for a great descriptive-writing activity! Begin by having students close their eyes while you describe a beach scene. Next, have students imagine that they are grains of sand on the beach. Instruct them to use their senses to brainstorm adjectives and other descriptive words. List students' responses on the board. Then have each youngster use words from the list to write a story on a sheet of lined paper about her day as a grain of sand. She staples the completed story in the center of a 12" x 18" sheet of white construction paper, folding the left and right sides to the middle to make a booklet. Then she illustrates the cover of the booklet with a scene from her story. Invite students to share their stories before posting them on a bulletin board titled "Stories From the Shore."

Tracy Meabe, Crawford-Rodriguez School, Jackson, NJ

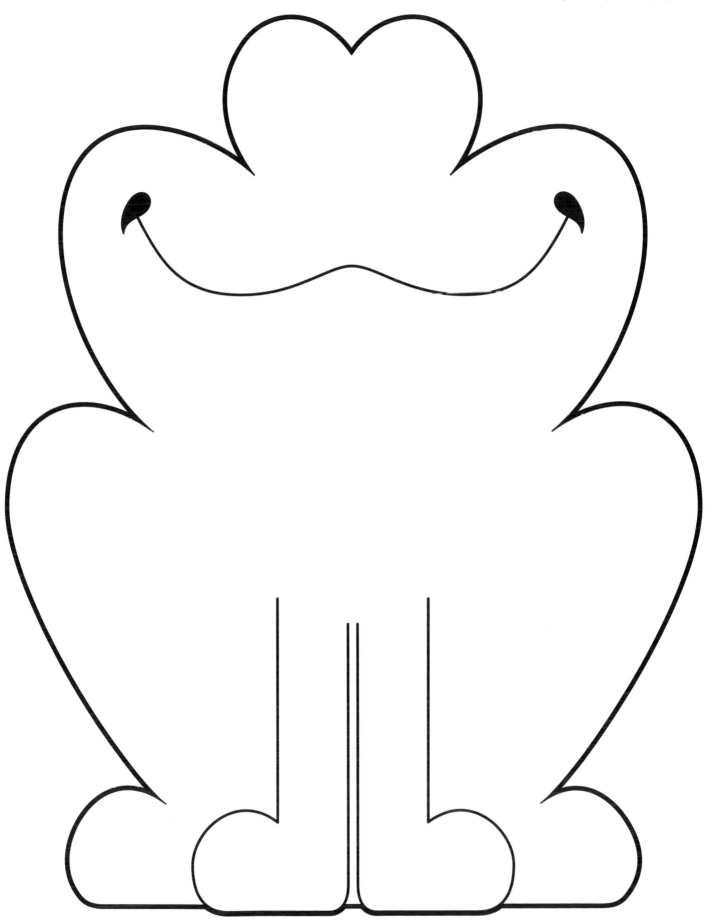

Sundae Pattern

Use with "Timely Prompts" on page 98.

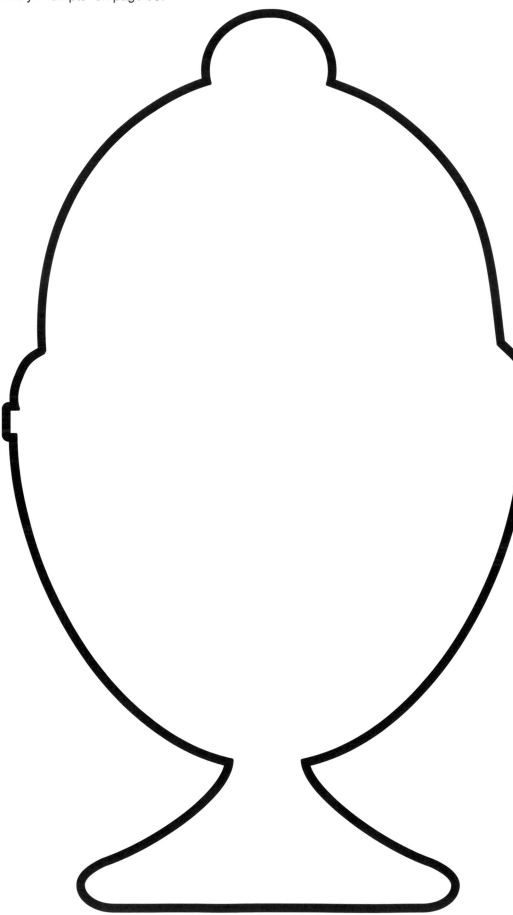

LANGUAGE ARTS UNITS

Quack for Compound Words!

Whether you're planning a review of compound words for a student or two or the entire class, you'll find activities that fill the bill right here. And that's just ducky!

ideas contributed by Kelli S. Jones, East Clayton Elementary, Clayton, NC

flower

From Two to One

"Quacking" this case requires students to decode compound words and provide evidence of their meanings. To make a flip booklet for the investigation, have each child stack two 4½" x 12" sheets of blank paper and position the stack horizontally. Next, have her slide the top sheet about a half inch to the left, fold the papers to the right to create four graduated layers, and staple near the fold. Then assign the child a compound word that can be illustrated. (See the list for suggestions.) To decode the word, a student writes and illustrates the first part of the compound on the first booklet page, adding a plus sign after the word. She writes and illustrates the second part of the compound on the second booklet page, drawing an equal sign after the word. She writes and illustrates the entire compound word on the third booklet page. Then, on the last booklet page, she writes an explanation of its meaning. After a student cracks her first case, she may be eager to crack a second case, so be sure to have plenty of paper on hand!

Ready-to-Illustrate Compound Words

sunflower	keyboard
footstool	sunburn
dragonfly	notebook
football	moonlight
eggshell	seafood
butterfly	rattlesnake
flagpole	sunglasses
flowerpot	baseball
houseboat	watermelon
ladybug	cookbook

footstool

Picture This!

Picture clues keep junior detectives engaged in this game for two teams. In advance, program individual cards with compound words that can be illustrated. (See the list for suggestions.) Stack the cards facedown and flip a coin to determine which team plays first. Teams will alternate play. To take a turn, a team selects one member to draw on the board. This student takes the top card. She has one minute to illustrate the compound word (or the two words that form it) and have her team say it. If she succeeds, her team earns one point and the card is placed in a discard pile. If she does not, no point is awarded and the card is placed on the bottom of the stack. The team with more points after an equal number of turns wins.

Teresa Pfeiffer, Payne Elementary, Payne, OH

Community Investigations

What happens when you pair a review of compound words and a review of community types? You build your students' compound word vocabularies! Title one sheet of chart paper for each of the following community types: urban, suburban, and rural. Then challenge students to name compound words that describe features of these communities. List each word on the corresponding paper. Next, have each child title a six-inch square of blank paper for one community type and draw a line across the bottom of the square, using his ruler as a guide. Have him illustrate the community in the center of the square and include four or more compound words from the class list. Ask him to write below the line each compound word pictured. Encourage students to look for pictured compound words in their classmates' illustrations.

If desired, have each child complete the activity for each community type. Then have him mount his work on a 9" x 24" paper strip and prepare his project for hanging. Very impressive!

Top Secret Collage

Here's a compound case that can be investigated during center time, independent time, or free time! Provide a stack of magazines and a stack of file folders that are no longer in use. Challenge each sleuth to find and cut out compound words and pictures of compound words from the magazines and then glue the cutouts inside a file folder. Instruct her to label each picture with its corresponding compound word. Then ask each sleuth to keep a tally of the words contained in her top secret collage. Periodically invite sleuths to share with the class the progress of their investigations.

Hot on the Trail

Flushing out high-frequency compound words keeps student pairs hot on the trail of this case. For a center activity, copy and color the gameboard on page 104. Mount the gameboard on construction paper and then laminate it for durability. Place the gameboard, a penny, and two game markers at a center. A pair of students plays the game by following the directions on the gameboard.

Or send home a copy of page 104 with each student. Suggest that he color the gameboard and then challenge a family member or friend to a round of 'Quack' the Case!

"Quack" the Case!

| Start | where . | body ? | In a hurry. Take another turn. | thing ! |
| | | | | one . |

| body ! | one ? | thing . | Hot on the trail! Move ahead two spaces. | where ? | body . | Confused! Go back one space. |

| thing ? | **Place your markers on Start.** 1. Choose a word from the briefcase. 2. Flip the penny and move according to the code: Heads = 1 space Tails = 2 spaces 3. Make a compound word. Use it in a sentence that has the end mark shown. 4. The first player to reach Finish wins! | | | one . | where ? | thing ! |

| See a friend. Miss one turn. | | | | | | |

| body ! | one ! | where . | thing ? | Hear a noise. Move ahead one space. | | Dropped briefcase. Go back one space. |

| | | | | | | body . |

| Finish | Too tired to waddle. Rest for one turn. | one ? | body ? | where ! |

©The Mailbox® • TEC43017 • Feb./Mar. 2005

Daily Specials for Journal Writing

Looking for a way to help students spice up their journal entries? These ideas are made-to-order for writing success!

ideas contributed by
Natalie Tanner, Adam Elementary, Houston, TX

Foods I Like
I love meat loaf! My mom makes the best meat loaf in town. She puts sausage in it. My brother doesn't like meat loaf. I always take his piece. I wish we could have her meat loaf in school. It's so good!

Prompts by the Letter

Generating journal topics

Serve up a month's worth of student-selected journal topics! Divide students into small groups. Assign each group a range of letters from the alphabet. Challenge the group to brainstorm a word or phrase that begins with each letter and has journal-writing potential. Ask each group to read its list to the class. Record their ideas on a copy of page 108, replacing any inappropriate topics as needed. Distribute student copies of the page and have each child glue it on a blank journal page. For each journal-writing session, a child selects a topic and colors the corresponding letter. She copies the topic on a blank journal page, using a crayon to write the first letter. Then she writes her journal entry. There you have it—journal topics from *A* to *Z*!

Hot Topics

Using a prewriting strategy

Budding writers are sure to benefit from this enlightening strategy! Write a topic on the board. Each student draws a sun with several rays on a sheet of paper. He labels the sun with the topic and writes a related word on each ray. Then he writes sentences about the topic on a blank journal page, including one of the words in each sentence. Before he knows it, he'll have a journal entry with several sentences!

Memorable Writing

Writing to record reflections

Show students that meaningful writing prompts can be found in their own memories! Write a memory-inducing topic on the board, such as "My Birthday" or "A Family Outing." Each student recalls a memorable experience related to the topic. He begins his entry with "I remember the time when…" and writes about his experience, being sure to detail the events in chronological order. If desired, he adds an illustration as if it were a photograph taken of the event. Now that's a purposeful trip down memory lane!

Describe how you would make a new classmate feel welcome.

I would slap him on the back with my flipper. I would tell him a joke. I would ask him to do cannonball splashes in the water with me. Then I would sing a very loud song for him.

Tacky the Penguin

Literature Link

Writing from a character's perspective

Add a bit of character to everyday journal writing! Write a prompt on the board. Tell each child to write a response from the perspective of a favorite story character. Encourage him to incorporate story details into his writing. Then have him sign the character's name. The result is an exercise that boosts writing skills *and* reading comprehension!

Dear Bear,

I wanted to play Cinderella in the school play, but my teacher made me be the ugly stepsister. My best friend gets to play Cinderella. What should I do?

Signed,
Grumpy in Greenwood

Words of Wisdom

Writing to record ideas

These advice-column prompts provide plenty of writing motivation! Tell students that many newspapers and magazines have columnists that give advice to readers who send in letters. For inspiration, read aloud several advice-column letters appropriate for students. Also point out that a popular way to sign letters is with a nickname that tells how the person is feeling and where he or she is from (such as "Confused in Colorado" or "Sad in San Diego.")

Next, announce to students that they are advice columnists! Write a kid-related problem on the board, signed by a fictitious child. Have each student write a solution to the problem in his journal. Then invite him to share his letter with the class.

Alleen Carletta Porter—Gr. 3, Merrywood Elementary School
Greenwood, SC

Should students be allowed to chew gum in school?

Yes. Chewing gum is harmless. We would promise to be careful and not get any on the floor. We would not blow bubbles.

Prompts for Pairs

Writing to record ideas

Take this partner approach to journal writing! On the board, write a question that requires youngsters to give their opinions, such as "Should students be allowed to chew gum in school?" In his journal, each child copies the question, states what he believes, and explains why he feels that way. Then he trades journals with a partner and reads the other child's entry. After a brief discussion, he gets his journal back and writes a summary of his partner's opinion below his own, stating whether his partner agrees and giving a brief explanation. Students are sure to agree—everyone's opinion matters!

Time to Share!

Use the following ideas to help students share their journal entries with a partner, the whole class, or you!

- Color-code the journals with self-adhesive dots so that there are four groups. Announce a color each day and have those students share a selected entry with the class. Or collect those journals for your review.
- Have each student trade journals with a classmate. The child reads the entry and writes a relevant question. When the student gets his journal back, he uses the question to add details to his entry.
- When a child would like you to read a journal entry that is especially meaningful to him, have him flag it with a self-adhesive note. Respond to the entry on the note before returning his journal.

Journal Prompts From *A* to *Z*

Choose a topic.
Color the letter.

A _____

B _____

C _____

D _____

E _____

F _____

G _____

H _____

I _____

J _____

K _____

L _____

M _____

N _____

O _____

P _____

Q _____

R _____

S _____

T _____

U _____

V _____

W _____

X _____

Y _____

Z _____

Note to the teacher: Use with "Prompts by the Letter" on page 105.

Hooray for Vowel Teams!

Use this winning lineup of ideas with a variety of vowel teams, and you'll have a perfect game plan for improving students' reading and spelling skills!

ideas by Julie Douglas
St. Louis, MO

sleep

ea	ee
beak	sheep
leaf	deep
heat	

ee

Which Team?
Recognizing words with the same vowel team

This ongoing display idea will have your students rooting for their favorite long-vowel teams! Choose a long-vowel sound and two or more corresponding vowel teams. Divide a bulletin board into columns so that there is one column for each vowel team. Head each column with a labeled pennant cutout as shown. Prepare an equal number of word cards for each column. Then scramble the cards and place them in a lidless box.

To begin, assign a vowel team to each student, and group students accordingly. Announce the number of cards for each vowel team. Explain that the goal is to be the first group to post all of its words. In turn, have one student from each group take a card from the box at random, read it aloud, and show it to her group. Ask her group members to signal with a thumbs-up or thumbs-down whether the word has their assigned vowel team. If it does, post the card in the correct column. If it doesn't, have the student return it to the box. Continue alternating turns until one group posts all of its words. Then tack up the remaining card(s). After students are familiar with the resulting vowel team rosters, encourage them to add different words over several days. The result will be a word reference that can't be beat!

Give a Cheer!
Reading words with vowel teams

What better way to get students in the spirit of reading than with a rousing cheer? Prepare six word cards that feature the same vowel team. Have volunteers stand at the front of the classroom and hold the cards. As you lead the class in the cheer shown (adapted as necessary), invite students to incorporate movements, and prompt each volunteer to hold up her card at the appropriate time. Three cheers for vowel teams!

ai

Cheer
Read each word loud and clear;
It's time for the [a, i] cheer!
[Train, wait, paid],
[Brain, paint, maid].
Yay, vowel team!

Spell to Score!
Spelling words with vowel teams

Bring knowledge of letter patterns into play with this quick and easy idea. To begin a round, secretly choose a word with a familiar vowel team. On the board, draw a blank for each letter in the word and then write the vowel team in the appropriate blanks. Nearby write "SCORE" and draw a large circle.

Next, challenge students to identify the mystery word with fewer than five incorrect guesses. To do this, have students sit in groups to facilitate collaboration and then ask the groups to take turns guessing letters. For each incorrect guess, draw a line through one letter in "SCORE" and write the letter in the circle. For each correct guess, write the letter in the appropriate blank. (If the letter appears more than once, write it in each corresponding blank.) If the students complete the mystery word before all of the letters in "SCORE" are crossed out, invite a volunteer to present the next mystery word. If they do not, fill in the remaining blank(s) and then present a different mystery word.

Vowel Team	Letters	Words
ai	a, e, i, l, m, n, p, r, t	rain, train, main, mail, pail, pain, paint, painter
ea	a, b, d, e, l, m, n, s, t	seat, seal, meal, mean, bean, bead, lead, least
oa	a, b, c, g, l, o, s, t, t	oats, boat, goat, goal, coal, coat, coast, toast

The "Write" Team
Forming and using words with vowel teams

Coach your students to complete vowel team booklets! In advance, draw lines to divide a 1" x 9" paper strip into nine equal sections. Then choose a vowel team from the chart and program each section with a corresponding letter. Copy the letter strip to make a class supply. Have each student fold a 4½" x 12" strip of construction paper in half and then staple four quarter sheets of white paper (4¼" x 5½") inside to make a booklet. Instruct him to label a T-shirt cutout with the chosen vowel team, add desired crayon details, and then glue the cutout onto his booklet cover.

Give each student a letter strip and have him cut apart the letters. Say the first word for the vowel team and ask him to form it. Confirm the spelling and have him label his first booklet page with the word. Then announce the next word and ask him to add or change one or more letters to form it. Instruct him to write the correct spelling on the back of his first page. Continue in this manner with the remaining words, asking him to use the front and back of each page. Later, have him use each word in a sentence on the appropriate page. Now that's an approach to word study sure to gain plenty of fans!

Name _____

Today Is the Day!

Read each sentence.
Write **ea** or **ee** to complete the words.

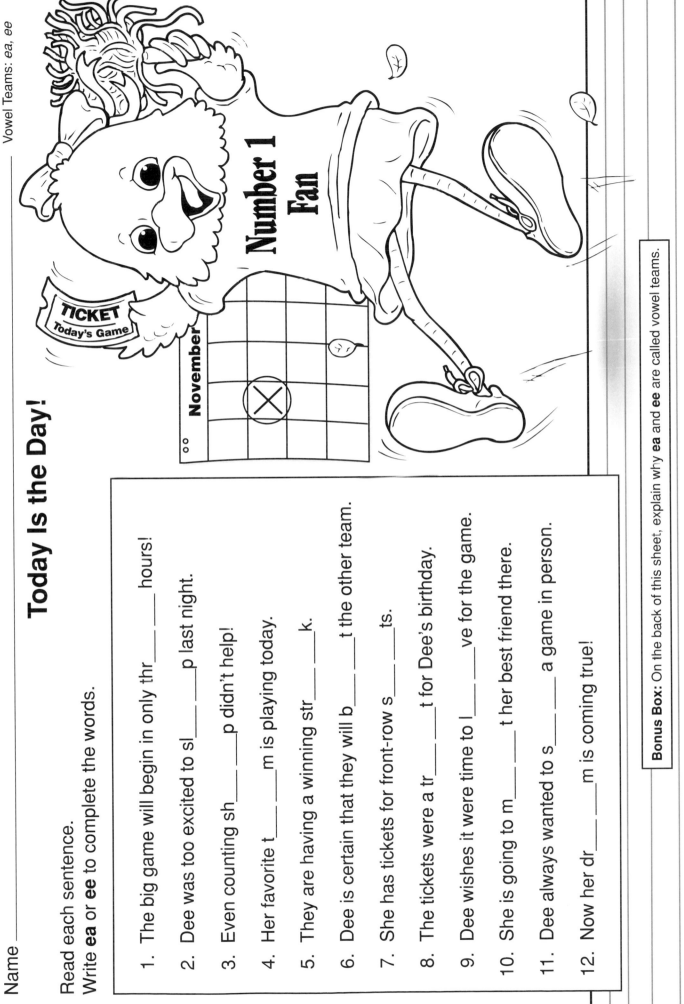

TICKET
Today's Game

Number 1
Fan

November

1. The big game will begin in only thr____ hours!

2. Dee was too excited to sl____p last night.

3. Even counting sh____p didn't help!

4. Her favorite t____m is playing today.

5. They are having a winning str____k.

6. Dee is certain that they will b____t the other team.

7. She has tickets for front-row s____ts.

8. The tickets were a tr____t for Dee's birthday.

9. Dee wishes it were time to l____ve for the game.

10. She is going to m____t her best friend there.

11. Dee always wanted to s____ a game in person.

12. Now her dr____m is coming true!

Bonus Box: On the back of this sheet, explain why **ea** and **ee** are called vowel teams.

©The Education Center, Inc. • *The Mailbox®* • TEC43015 • Oct./Nov. 2004 • Key p. 311

111

A Parts-of-Speech Safari

Add adventure to your parts-of-speech studies! Select your favorite activities from this collection and then take your students on safari—a parts-of-speech safari that is! Soon students will be spotting nouns, verbs, adjectives, and adverbs everywhere!

ideas contributed by Laura Wagner, Raleigh, NC

Person, Place, or Thing?
Classifying common nouns

Create a little hoopla with this large-group noun review! To prepare, collect three plastic hoops, and write each of the following noun categories on a colorful card: person, place, thing. Review the three categories of common nouns with the class; then ask each child to write one noun from each category on an individual index card. Collect these cards, shuffle them, and give three to each child. Position the three plastic hoops on the floor, and place each card that you labeled inside a different hoop. Next, gather students (with their cards) around the hoops. Have each child, in turn, name the noun on his top card, identify it as a person, place, or thing, and then place the card in the corresponding hoop. Continue in this manner until all the cards are sorted. Then place the cards and hoops at an independent center for additional reinforcement.

Teresa Pfeiffer, Payne Elementary School, Payne, OH

Person

Place

jungle

Thing

camera

giraffe

Vote on Land Gets Zoo a Big Addition

Common Nouns	Proper Nouns
monkeys	November
camera	Africa
teacher	Rex
airplane	Lex

Nouns in the News
Identifying nouns, distinguishing common and proper nouns

Students get the scoop on nouns—both common and proper—during this newsworthy activity! Cut out a class supply of student-appropriate newspaper articles. Give each child one and ask him to circle the nouns in it. Next, have him trade his article with a classmate and read his classmate's article to verify that every noun is circled and that every circled word is a noun. After students return the articles and discuss their findings, have each child fold a sheet of paper in half lengthwise, unfold the paper, and label the resulting columns "Common Nouns" and "Proper Nouns." Instruct each student to carefully copy each of his circled nouns into the appropriate column on his paper. Extra! Extra! There are many nouns in the news!

Spring Into Action!
Naming action verbs

Here's a unique way to leave a lasting impression with students about action verbs. Prepare a spiral pattern like the one pictured. Copy the pattern onto light-colored construction paper for each child. Instruct each youngster to write an assortment of action verbs on his pattern, making sure he stays within the lines. Next, have him cut along the solid lines. After he makes the spiral cut, have him bend back the center piece of the pattern (creating a small tab) and gently pull the spiral upward. Suspend the students' action-packed verb banks at a writing center. Or have each child glue the outer rim of his project to a slightly larger paper as shown. Either way, there'll be plenty of verbs to go around!

Dawn DuBell—Gr.3, Lake Elementary, Millbury, OH

prance   send
dare   sob   hurry
tease   drank   blow
sift   bark   curdle   eat
take   crawl   sold   sing
put   tell   sew
juggle

Pam Crane

walk
tiptoe
skip
prance
stroll
hike
march
saunter

talk
whisper
yell
exclaim
chatter
shout
holler
murmur

Getting Specific
Naming specific action verbs

To build your youngsters' action word vocabularies, challenge them to get specific with verbs! On chart paper, write and circle the verb *walk*. Have a volunteer demonstrate the action. Then challenge students to name other verbs that describe the action in greater detail, such as *tiptoe, skip, prance,* and *stroll*. Write their suggestions on the chart paper and, if desired, invite volunteers to demonstrate the different actions. Explain that more specific action verbs paint clearer pictures. Display the chart paper along with a second sheet labeled "talk." Tell students that you'll meet with them the following school day to list their verb suggestions on each of the two posted charts. Repeat the activity several times, each time adding one more verb chart to the collection. Along with growing your youngsters' verb vocabularies, you'll be building an awesome verb wall!

Picture This!
Naming appropriate adjectives

You've heard the saying "A picture is worth a thousand words." During this independent activity students brainstorm several of those words! To prepare, cut from old magazines colorful and age-appropriate pictures of nouns. Store a class supply of cutouts in a large container. Ask each child to remove a cutout from the container and glue it in the center of a blank sheet of paper. Then, around the picture, have her write adjectives that describe the noun.

To extend the activity, have each child write a descriptive paragraph about the pictured noun and use several of the adjectives in her writing.

yellow   ripe
fresh
big
smooth
delicious

backpack

big
green
black
empty
slick
clean
useful

Adjective Carousel
Naming appropriate adjectives

When students step onto this carousel, they take a ride with adjectives! In each of several classroom locations, display a different nonbreakable object and a large sheet of paper labeled with the name of the object. Divide students among the locations, appoint a recorder in each group, and give each recorder a different color of marker. Begin the carousel ride by instructing each group to name describing words for the provided object. Have each recorder write the words on the paper. After a short amount of time, direct each group to rotate clockwise. Instruct group members to read the word list in their new location and then name additional adjectives for their group recorder to add to the list. Continue in this manner until each group has listed adjectives in each location. After students return to their seats, help them evaluate each group of adjectives to be sure the words on the list accurately describe the corresponding object. Wheee! That was fun!

Stacy Shaener—Gr. 3, Bi-Cultural Day School, Stamford, CT

A Verb's Best Friend
Comparing adverbs to verbs

Recalling the role of an adverb isn't always easy. Use this little jingle to help students remember that an adverb is a verb's best friend!

(sung to the tune of "London Bridge")

Adverbs tell us about verbs,
About verbs,
About verbs.
Adverbs tell us about verbs.
They are helpful.

Adverbs tell us when, where, how;
When, where, how;
When, where, how.
Adverbs tell us when, where, how.
They are helpful.

Adverbs often end with *-ly,*
End with *-ly,*
End with *-ly.*
Adverbs often end with *-ly.*
They are helpful.

adapted from a song by Kathleen Morrison—Gr. 2
St. Thomas More Cathedral School, Arlington, VA

How? When? Where?
Naming appropriate adverbs

Three verb-related questions lead students to a variety of adverbs. For each child, precut a white 3" x 5" card and three 1" x 4" strips, each from a different color of construction paper. On the board, write a simple sentence, such as "The dog ate" or "The hat fell." Ask each child to copy the sentence on his card and underline the verb. Next, have him answer the verb-related question "How?" on a specific color of paper strip. Explain that the answer must be one word and should tell how the verb action happened. Guide students through a similar process to program the two remaining strips with answers to the adverb questions "When?" and "Where?" Then have each child glue his three strips to the bottom of his card as shown. Students will have a grand time orally incorporating their adverbs into the simple sentence.

To double the learning and the fun, have each child turn his project over. Then, on a second 3" x 5" card, have him write another simple sentence and underline its verb as before. After he programs the blank side of each colorful strip with the answer to a different adverb question, have him glue together the blank sides of his cards.

The dog <u>ate</u>.

noisily   yesterday   upstairs

115

Some Monkey Business

Who mixed up the adjectives?
Rewrite the list.
For each noun write an adjective that makes sense.

The adjectives are all here.

They are just in the wrong places!

1. tiny elephant _____

2. spotted zebra _____

3. scaly gorilla _____

4. clear giraffe _____

5. puffy lion _____

6. striped leopard _____

7. blue cheetah _____

8. fast sky _____

9. noisy clouds _____

10. hairy snake _____

11. tall water _____

12. huge flea _____

Name_____

A Risky Snapshot

Underline the verb in each sentence.
Then circle the adverb and write it on the chart below.
The first one is done for you.

1. Rex <u>walks</u> (toward) a sleeping lion.

2. He firmly holds his camera.

3. Lex hides behind Rex.

4. Yesterday, Lex scared a rhinoceros.

5. Today, Lex remembers to be quiet!

6. Rex steps over a tree trunk.

7. The lion quietly moves one eye.

8. Now Rex takes a picture.

9. The lion roars loudly.

10. Lex and Rex stand still.

11. Soon the lion falls asleep.

12. Lex and Rex sneak away.

How?	When?	Where?
		toward

A Serving of Story Elements

Build comprehension skills with these appetizing entrées!

The House of Bricks Restaurant

Please Join Us!

Identifying and describing setting

One thing leads to another when students complete this setting-related writing activity! When a story's setting has been clearly established, ask students to invite a chosen school celebrity (such as the school principal, librarian, secretary, or nurse) to pretend to join them there. Emphasize the importance of providing in their written invitations details about the time and the place the story occurs. When the celebrity drops by your classroom, ask students to share with that person what has happened thus far in the story. Students who have been absent are sure to appreciate invitations and/or story recaps too!

Julie Lewis, J. O. Davis Elementary, Irving, TX

Dear Ms. T,
  Please join us! We just traveled to the plains of Africa with Jack and Annie in their magic tree house. There are lots of zebras and giraffes. There is a very wide river. It is almost summer. Please hurry to visit our classroom! This is going to be an adventure!

  Sincerely,
  Wayan

Miss Nelson Is Missing

Book Setting
at school during the day

New Location
camping in the woods at night

New Location

Understanding the importance of setting

Today's special is the link between a story and its setting! Have each child fold a sheet of drawing paper in half, unfold the paper, and turn it horizontal. Instruct students to write at the tops of their papers the title of a picture book you'll be reading aloud. Then have each child label the left half of her paper "Book Setting" and the right half "New Location." After reading the picture book, ask each child to describe and illustrate the story's setting on the left half of her paper. Next, have students brainstorm other possible settings for the story. For each setting suggested, welcome your students' thoughts on how the location might change the story. To complete the activity, ask the child to describe and illustrate her favorite change of location for the story. Your students' understanding of the importance of setting is sure to be strengthened!

Changes in Character

Observing change in a character

Open a window to an author's underlying message with an examination of how the main character changes throughout the story. Title a length of bulletin board paper with the character's name and then divide the remainder of the paper in half. Label the two resulting columns "In the beginning" and "In the end." Ask students to describe the actions and feelings of the character for each part of the story. List their comments on the chart. Invite students to summarize how the character changes during the story. Then prompt further thought and discussion with questions such as the following: What change in the character do you think most affects the other characters in the story? Why do you think the author changed the character's actions (feelings)?

Lilly

In the beginning
She loves school.
She is happy.
She wants to be a teacher.
She wants everyone to see her purse.
She wants her way.

In the end
She knows how bad it feels to be mean.
She learns to take her turn.
She is happy.
She wants to be a teacher.

Planning a Vacation

Relating to a story character

How well do students understand a main character? Why not find out! Ask each child to choose a vacation destination for the character based on what he knows about the character's likes and dislikes. Then instruct the student to pack a vacation suitcase for the character. To do this, he folds in half a 9" x 12" sheet of construction paper. Then he unfolds the paper, cuts a handle shape from a scrap of construction paper, and glues the handle to a short end of the larger paper. Next, he cuts out magazine pictures or illustrations he's drawn and glues them on the construction paper, avoiding the fold line. When the glue is dry, he refolds the paper. He makes a suitcase tag from construction paper and personalizes it for the character. Then he attaches the tag to the vacation bag and embellishes the bag with desired details. Be sure to set aside time for students to share the vacations they envision for the character. You can quickly assess each child's understanding of the character's traits and interests.

Julie Suh, Churchill Public School, Toronto, Ontario, Canada

Handy Solutions

Introducing problem and solution

Use this handy introduction to problem and solution. Label each of a few hand cutouts with a different everyday problem such as "I forgot my lunch," "I can't find my eraser," and "My desk wobbles." Then, for each hand cutout, cut a simple tool shape from construction paper. Tape one hand cutout to the board and read aloud the problem described. Invite students to brainstorm possible ways to fix the problem, reminding them that there's usually more than one solution for every problem. Then, with your students' input, select one solution to write on a tool shape. Tape the shape near the hand cutout. Repeat the procedure for each remaining problem. Keep the cutouts on display as a reminder of problem and solution.

Take a similar approach when identifying the story elements of problem and solution. Instruct each child to trace the outline of his hand on a sheet of blank paper, label it "Problem," and describe inside the outline a problem the main character faces. Then have him draw the outline of a tool, label it "Solution," and describe inside the outline how the problem is solved. Very clever!

Julie Lewis, J. O. Davis Elementary, Irving, TX

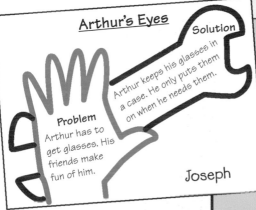

Arthur's Eyes

Solution
Arthur keeps his glasses in a case. He only puts them on when he needs them.

Problem
Arthur has to get glasses. His friends make fun of him.

Joseph

Story Element Express
Recalling story elements

Here's the ticket to keeping students on track with story elements! On a shower curtain (or length of heavy plastic) use a permanent marker to draw the outline of a train engine followed by four boxcars and a caboose. Working from front to back, label the parts of the train as follows: "Title and Author," "Characters," "Setting," "Beginning," "Middle," and "End." To assess one student's understanding of story elements, ask the child to board the train by stepping onto the engine. Then have him walk down the train, stopping on each train car to share the appropriate story information. Or ask six students to each board a different train car. Then, starting with the child on the engine and ending with the child on the caboose, have each child take a turn providing story details. When the train is not being used, fold it up for easy storage. All aboard for a story element review!

Rebecca McNeill and Angela Howell
Cameron Park Elementary
Hillsborough, NC

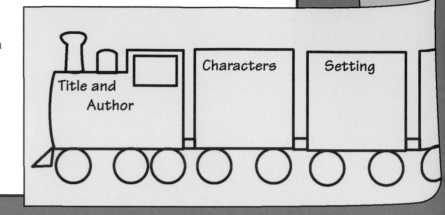

Story Box
Identifying story elements

It's not a boom box and it's not a jack-in-the-box. However, a story box does speak volumes about a chosen story! Collect a class supply of empty cube-shaped tissue boxes. To make a story box, a student covers a box with colorful paper. Next, she cuts out a white paper rectangle sized to fit the top of the box and labels it with the title and author of the story she is describing. After she glues the prepared rectangle on her box, she cuts out four more rectangles from white paper, each sized to fit on a side of the box. She labels one cutout "Character(s)." On this cutout she describes and illustrates the main character(s) of the story. She labels a second cutout "Setting." On this cutout she describes and illustrates the story setting. She labels the remaining cutouts "Problem" and "Solution." She adds a corresponding description and illustration to each. Then she glues each of the four cutouts to a different side of her story box. What a fun way for students to show what they know about a story!

Vicki Dabrowka, Carrollwood Day School, Odessa, FL

Here's the Proof!

Draw a main character in the frame.
Write the character's name and the
book title below.

_____

character name

from

_____

_____

book title

Write three traits of this character.
Give examples from the story.

Trait of	Trait of	Trait of
_____	_____	_____
when	when	when
_____	_____	_____
_____	_____	_____
_____	_____	_____
_____	_____	_____

Name _____

It Begins Like This...

Write the title of the story.
Describe what happens in each part of the story.

_____
title

Beginning

Middle

End

122

Taking the Plunge Into Paragraph Writing

Whoopee! It's the perfect time to make a big splash over paragraph writing! Use the ideas and reproducibles that follow to reinforce the "bear" essentials of writing a paragraph—a main idea and supporting details.

Search and Circle
Recognizing paragraphs

What happened when the paragraph wrecked its car? It got indented! To reinforce the fact that paragraphs are indented, give each child a newspaper page that features several paragraphs of text. Challenge each child to circle the first word in each paragraph she finds. Then have students exchange papers and critique their classmates' work. Look at this! Every paragraph starts on a new line!

One Topic, Please
Building paragraph knowledge

Student-pleasing practice for staying on topic is in the bag! Label each of four or more paper grocery bags with a topic familiar to your students and then place in each bag an assortment of related items. For example, in a bag labeled "Playground," put a Frisbee toy, jump rope, glove, knit cap, and winter scarf. In a bag labeled "Kitchen," put a measuring cup, mixing spoon, salt shaker, spatula, and dish towel. Then add to each bag one or two items that are clearly off topic, such as a toothbrush and a pepper shaker in the bag labeled "Playground."

Remind students that a paragraph is a group of sentences about one main idea. Then group students and have each group evaluate the contents of a different bag. Ask each group to report to the class which items in its bag are and are not on topic. Or have each group record its findings and then rotate the bags through the groups until each group has evaluated the contents of and recorded its findings for every bag.

For independent practice, give each child a copy of page 125 to complete.

A Plan of Action
Planning and writing a paragraph

Have students take this approach to planning and writing paragraphs, and you can expect a downpour of details! On the board, draw the outline of a large umbrella and four large raindrops. Remind students that one sentence of a paragraph tells the main idea and the other sentences tell details about the main idea. Inside the umbrella, write a main idea such as "Our school is special." Next, ask students to describe specific ways in which their school is special. Write a different student-suggested detail inside each raindrop outline. (If you wish to introduce students to a concluding sentence, write one on the umbrella handle.) Then engage students in transforming the plan they've made into a written paragraph. If desired, write the paragraph on the board, using two colors of chalk or ink: one color for the main idea and a second color for the details. Very impressive!

Natalie Tanner
Adam Elementary
Houston, TX

Spiffy Portfolios

Planning and writing a paragraph

Keeping your young authors inspired just got easier! Make a colorful supply of the paragraph planner on page 126 and then copy the paragraph starters to make a class supply. Have each child glue his copy of the paragraph starters inside a file folder and then personalize and decorate the outside of the folder. A student chooses a writing topic from his folder, plans his paragraph on a copy of the planner, and then writes the paragraph on writing paper. When his writing is complete, he dates it and staples it to his planner. Then he files his writing inside his folder, making sure to color the corresponding prompt on the inside of his folder. Every few days, meet with individual students and invite them to share with you recent paragraphs that they've written.

Dot It!
Editing for paragraph form

Students will agree that the five-dot paragraph edit is easy and fun! Display the editing guidelines provided. To complete a five-dot edit, a child awards herself one dot for each guideline she has successfully completed. Ask that she draw her dots in the bottom right-hand corner of her paper for easy reference. When a child has less than five dots, she revisits her paragraph on the dot!

adapted from an idea by
Natalie Tanner

Five-Dot Paragraph Edit
Color a dot for each of the following:
- The first line is indented.
- One sentence tells the main idea.
- Three or more sentences tell details about the main idea.
- Each sentence begins with a capital letter.
- Each sentence ends with punctuation.

Name _____

Having a Ball!

Read each main idea.
Circle one detail in each list that
does not stay on topic.

sports
pencil
baseball
soccer
golf

bedroom
bed
teddy bear
pillow
corn

pizza
olives
pepperoni
mushrooms
bat

fruit
apple
banana
cereal
pear

flowers
hot dog
tulips
rose
daisy

sandwich
bread
fog
cheese
chips

computer
keyboard
screen
cord
salt

theater
movie
popcorn
ticket
ruler

pond
frog
fish
shark
duck

tools
saw
hammer
bread
shovel

plants
grass
sky
leaves
tree

pet
puppy
island
fish
kitten

breakfast
roof
pancakes
egg
juice

car
horn
lizard
radio
tire

Bonus Box: On the back of this paper, write the main idea "recess." Below it, list three details that stay on topic.

©The Education Center, Inc. • *The Mailbox®* • TEC43016 • Dec./Jan. 2004–5 • Key p. 311

Note to the teacher: Use independently or as a follow-up to "One Topic, Please" on page 123.

Paragraph Planner and Paragraph Starters

Use with "Spiffy Portfolios" on page 124.

Name_____   Paragraph Planner

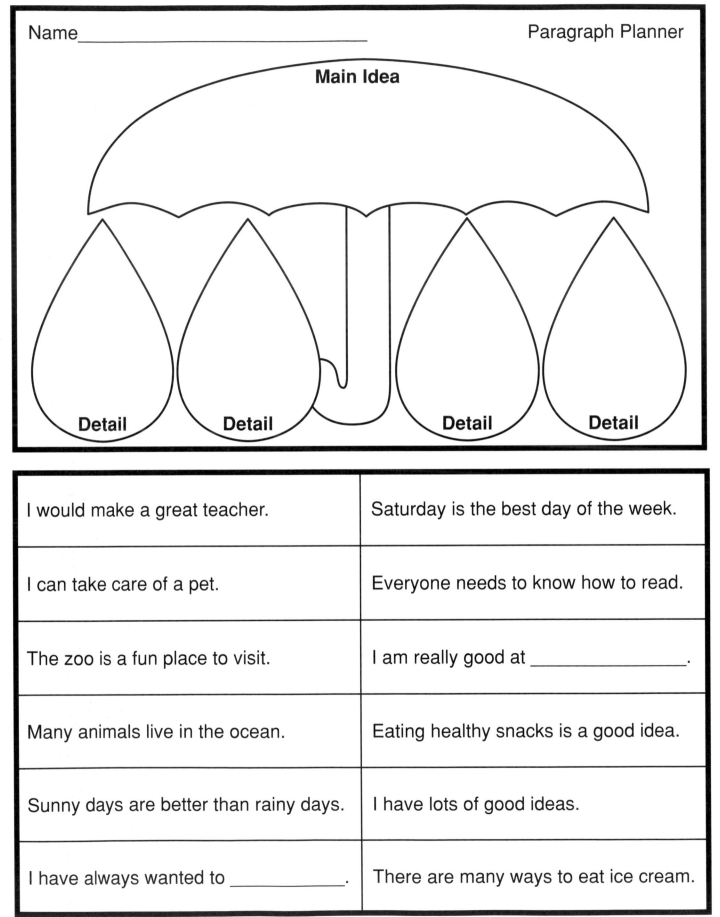

Main Idea

Detail   Detail   Detail   Detail

I would make a great teacher.	Saturday is the best day of the week.
I can take care of a pet.	Everyone needs to know how to read.
The zoo is a fun place to visit.	I am really good at _____.
Many animals live in the ocean.	Eating healthy snacks is a good idea.
Sunny days are better than rainy days.	I have lots of good ideas.
I have always wanted to _____.	There are many ways to eat ice cream.

An Oasis of Information

Comprehending Nonfiction Text

Continue to nourish your youngsters' nonfiction reading skills with this wellspring of teacher-tested ideas! You'll find thirst-quenching suggestions for replenishing comprehension before, during, and after reading.

Before Reading

Reading Warm-Up
Previewing the selection

Activate prior knowledge and introduce select vocabulary words during this prereading warm-up. Prior to reading a nonfiction passage, lead students in a few body stretches. As you do this, remind students that athletes understand the importance of stretching out their muscles before engaging in physical activity. Tell students that good readers do something similar. Ask students to be seated and lead them through previewing the reading selection. Direct the students' attention to the title and ask them to predict what the selection is about. If photos, illustrations, graphics, or headings are a part of the selection, direct their attention to these, too. Invite students to share their knowledge about the reading topic. Also ask students to name topic-related words they might encounter as they read the text. Write these words on the board and familiarize students with them. Then congratulate the students on completing a thorough reading warm-up. It's time to read!

Kelly Hanover, Vernon Elementary School, Kenoaha, WI

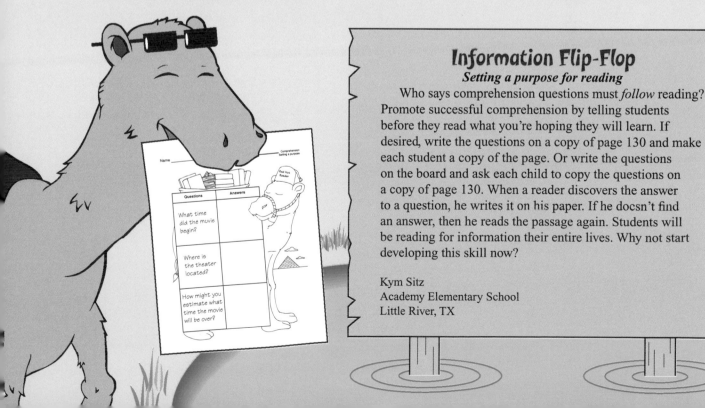

Information Flip-Flop
Setting a purpose for reading

Who says comprehension questions must *follow* reading? Promote successful comprehension by telling students before they read what you're hoping they will learn. If desired, write the questions on a copy of page 130 and make each student a copy of the page. Or write the questions on the board and ask each child to copy the questions on a copy of page 130. When a reader discovers the answer to a question, he writes it on his paper. If he doesn't find an answer, then he reads the passage again. Students will be reading for information their entire lives. Why not start developing this skill now?

Kym Sitz
Academy Elementary School
Little River, TX

Right on Target
Reading for details

A supply of colorful arrow flags is just what you need to monitor your students' comprehension during group activities. Give each child an index card with a similar collection of flags attached to each one. Before students begin to read a nonfiction passage, ask them to read for specific details and flag each detail when they find it. You can even pair a flag color with a specific detail, such as marking *where* an event happens with a green arrow and *when* it happens with a yellow arrow. Students enjoy using the colorful arrows and find comfort in knowing that if they target incorrect information, the arrows are easy to reposition. Collect the cards of arrow flags at the end of a reading session for later use, but consider making them accessible for students to use during independent reading time too.

Susan Hughes
Ty Ty, GA

Stop and Summarize
Monitoring comprehension

It's difficult to ignore a stop sign, and that's the secret behind these nifty bookmarks! Make a double octagon template like the one shown. To make his bookmark, a child traces the template onto red tagboard, cuts out the shape, and folds it in half. He glues a jumbo craft stick between the folded shape as shown. Next, he writes "STOP" on a scrap of white construction paper two times and cuts an oval shape around each word. He glues one cutout to each side of his red octagon. Last, he uses a fine-tip permanent marker to write "Summarize" on each side of the craft stick. The colorful (and demanding!) bookmark reminds a student to stop and monitor his comprehension as he reads!

Barclay Marcell
Theodore Roosevelt Elementary School
Park Ridge, IL

Something New, Something Known
Making connections

When students compare newly learned facts to prior knowledge, comprehension flourishes! To make a class notebook of fact connections, have each student draw a line to divide a sheet of blank paper in half. Instruct her to explain and illustrate on the left half of her paper a fact she learned from her reading. On the right half of her paper, ask her to compare the fact to something she already knows. Slip each child's completed project inside a plastic page protector and then assemble the protected pages in a three-ring binder labeled "Something New, Something Known." Place the book in the class library for all to enjoy. Encourage students to continue contributing pages to the publication. After all, each time a student makes a connection with a new fact, she helps her classmates connect with the fact too!

My outside ear is made of cartilage too! Ronda

A shark doesn't have a skeleton made of bones. Its skeleton is made of cartilage.

Fact Pyramids
Reading motivation

Promote reading interest by inviting students to share interesting facts from their nonfiction readings. For a super shelf display, provide copies of the pyramid pattern on page 131. (For a larger project, use a copy machine to enlarge the patterns.) When a child finishes a nonfiction selection, he completes the programming on a copy of the pyramid by writing his reading topic and three facts he learned while reading. After he illustrates his work, he cuts along the bold lines and folds along the thin lines. He glues the bottom (the side with his favorite fact) where indicated, keeping the programming to the outside and lining up the dots. Then he continues to assemble the project to make a pyramid. Display the projects on an easily accessible classroom shelf. Be sure to remind visitors to read the favorite fact that's found on the bottom of each pyramid.

Rita Skavinsky
Minersville Elementary Center
Minersville, PA

Bye Bye!

Venus Flytraps
Reading Topic

The Venus flytrap eats flies, ants, and bees.
Fact

Ask Before You Read

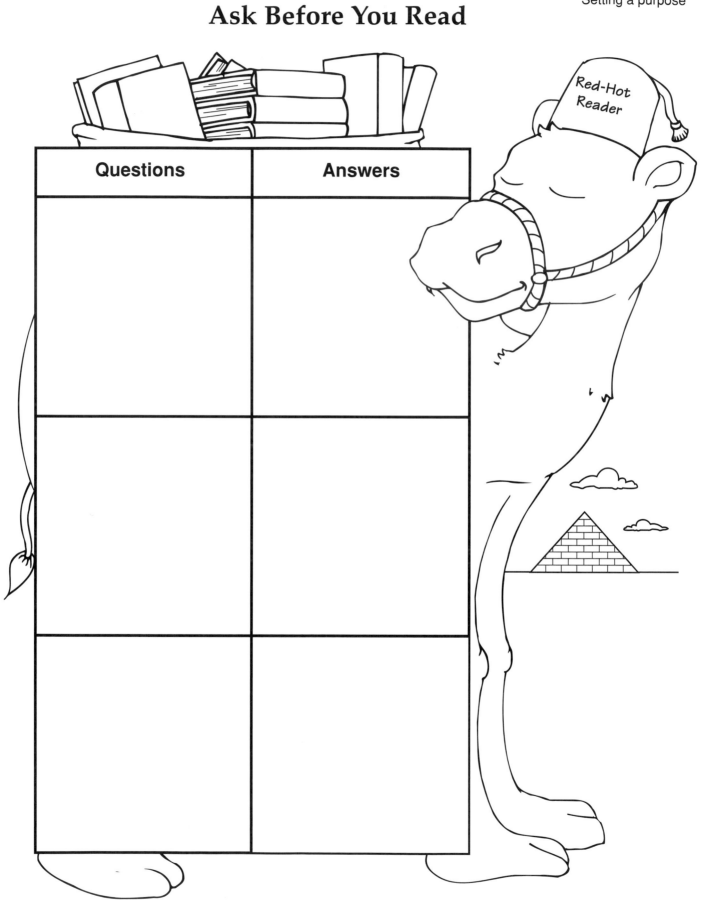

Questions	Answers

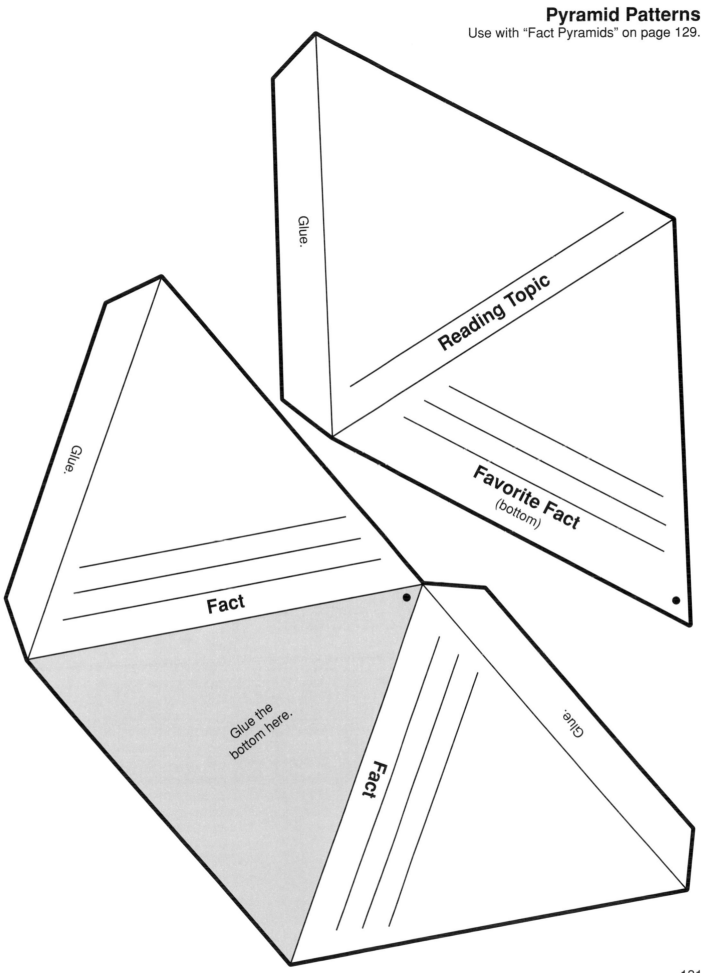

Glue.

Reading Topic

Favorite Fact
(bottom)

Glue.

Fact

Glue.

Glue the
bottom here.

Fact

Getting to the Heart of Descriptive Writing

What's at the heart of descriptive writing? A healthy dose of details! Use these ideas to coach young writers on observing details, organizing details, and using details in their writing. "Bee-dazzling" descriptions are just a heartbeat away!

See "Details, Please!" on page 305 for a fun group activity.

Book It!
Identifying descriptive language

Whet students' appetites for descriptive language by reading aloud picture books packed with descriptive details. During a second or third reading, ask students to listen carefully for words that help them "see" the story. Write the student-selected words on chart paper. Then challenge each child to use the posted language as inspiration for an original story or a retelling of the one that was read.

Kelli Jones
East Clayton Elementary
Clayton, NC

Simply Delicious!
by Margaret Mahy

double-dip
lumpy
bumpy
rainbow
cool
rare
delicious
ferocious
giant
bounded

arched
bumping
fluttered
hovering
perched
snarled
baffled
croaked
lunged
glided

It is a mailbox but it is shaped like a big fish. It sits on a post. It is gray and white. There is a flag on its side.

Picture This!
Understanding the importance of specific details

Get right to the point of specific details with a jaw-dropping description! First, cut photos from outdated catalogs and tuck one cutout in each of a class supply of envelopes. Next, describe for students your favorite kind of dog—one that is short, plump, and rather red. Ask students to quickly illustrate on scrap paper the dog they envision. Then show them a picture of a hot dog! Help students who illustrated canines understand that because you did not give specific details, your description was easy to misunderstand.

Hand each child a prepared envelope and a sheet of story paper. Challenge her to write a detailed description of the pictured item in her envelope. Next, pair students. Ask each child to read her partner's description and illustrate what she believes has been described. Then have the partners return their papers. Details will be the buzz of the conversations that follow!

Susan DeRiso
John W. Horton School
Cranston, RI

Critter Lineup
Using specific adjectives

Specific adjectives are the reason these critters get identified. Name two animals and ask each child to prepare a detailed illustration of one. Then have him write on another sheet of paper several sentences that describe the animal he drew. If he has less than four sentences, ask him to add more details to his illustration. Next, collect the drawings and tape them to the board in two groups of like animals. For easy management, number the drawings in each group. Ask several volunteers to read aloud their descriptive details and challenge their classmates to identify the animals they drew. Continue until all the animals are identified or time runs out. A few days later repeat the activity, but this time name only one animal for students to illustrate. Even more details will "bee" needed!

adapted from an idea by Carolyn Riffel
Mill Neck School for the Deaf,
Mill Neck, NY

Have you heard the buzz? Descriptive details are a writer's best friend!

A "Sense-ible" Approach
Organizing sensory details

What's at the heart of specific details? The five senses! To help students generate and organize sensory details for a descriptive writing project, have each child fold a sheet of blank paper in half two times and then unfold the paper to reveal four boxes. Have her draw a large heart in the center of the page and label it with a writing topic. Or have her glue a picture cutout in the center of the page and draw a heart shape around it. After she traces over the fold lines that extend beyond the heart, have her label the boxes with different senses and list observations about her writing topic in each one. When all five senses can be used for observation, have her label one box with two senses. A hearty amount of descriptive details is a writer's best friend!

Looks
fat yellow sun
bright blue sky
red-breasted robins
slimy brown worms

Feels
wonderful
lighthearted
warm
breezy

Springtime

Sounds
birds chirping
dogs barking
lawn mowers rumbling
balls bouncing
skateboard wheels spinning

Smells
sweet flower scents
fresh-cut grass

Designer Duds

Editing for word choice

Creativity and details bring down the house when students illustrate and describe costumes for a possible school play. First, have students brainstorm appropriate roles. Then give each child a sheet of drawing paper on which to illustrate herself in costume. Also give her an index card and ask her to list words on it that describe the costume she's designing. Conclude this portion of the activity by collecting the cards.

After privately reviewing the cards, write several words on the board that could be more specific. Explain to students that these are good words; however, you'd like to make them even better! Beside each word write your students' suggestions. Then return their word cards and challenge each child to edit her card for stronger and more engaging words. Last, have her use the words on her card to write a paragraph that describes the spectacular costume she's designed.

Kelli Higgins
P. L. Bolin Elementary School
East Peoria, IL

Salli

stretchy black tights and top
sunshine yellow leotard
fuzzy, jet black stripes
two gigantic wings
black headband
shiny silver antennae

Dear Squirrel,
I am writing to tell you about a wooded area I think you will love! Trees tower overhead. You can hear the patter of acorns dropping to the ground. There is cool shade everywhere. I think you will find this place very relaxing. I didn't see any big barking dogs that might try to catch you!

Sincerely,
Bumble

This Is the Place!

Using sensory details in writing

To set the scene for this activity, show the class a colorful scenic photo from a book or magazine that depicts a natural habitat. Ask students to imagine that they are sitting quietly in this location and then prompt them to describe things they see, sounds they hear, emotions they feel, and smells or tastes they experience. Write students' thoughts on the board, categorizing them by sense for easy reference. (Or have each child complete an organizer like the one described in "A 'Sense-ible' Approach" on page 133.) Then ask each child to write a letter to an animal he believes will find the location to be an extraordinary home. Encourage students to include plenty of sensory details in their descriptions of the location. When each child shares his letter with the class, ask a classmate to recall one or more details from the letter that he especially likes.

Kelli Higgins

swarmed

buzzed

"Bee-Loved" Words
Revising for word choice
Here's a honey of an idea for creating a buzz about well-chosen words! Divide students into small groups. Assign each group a commonly overused word—such as *big, little, pretty, good, said,* or *went*—and challenge the group to brainstorm a list of more specific alternatives. Next, ask each group to share its word list and invite the rest of the class to suggest other suitable words. When each group has updated its list, edit it for correct spelling. Then give each group a yellow construction paper copy of the bee pattern on page 136, two construction paper copies of the wing pattern on page 136, a black marker, glue, and scissors. Help the group members work together to create a bee of "bee-loved" words that is similar to the one shown. Display these student-made bees (and others like them) buzzing around a hive cutout titled "'Bee-Loved' Words." Encourage students to buzz by this word reference whenever they're revising their writing.

tiptoed
sprinted
strolled
skipped
hurried

went

crawled
rushed
flew
raced
wandered

Pig!

Descriptive Riddles
Writing for a specific purpose
Some riddles are written to baffle readers, but not these! Tell students that their task is to describe an animal so well that a classmate can identify it without being told its name. Have each child choose an animal and then think about the animal's physical characteristics, movements, habits, and habitat. Next, have him write a list of eight to ten descriptive observations about it. To write his riddle, a student uses his observations to compose four descriptive phrases. He concludes his riddle with the question "What is it?" Invite each child to gather feedback on his riddle from two different students before he takes a turn sharing it with the class.

Kelli Higgins
P. L. Bolin Elementary School,
East Peoria, IL

A wet, pink snout
A round belly
Four short, pudgy legs
A tail that curls like a

What is it?

Bee and Wing Patterns

Use with "'Bee-Loved' Words" on page 135.

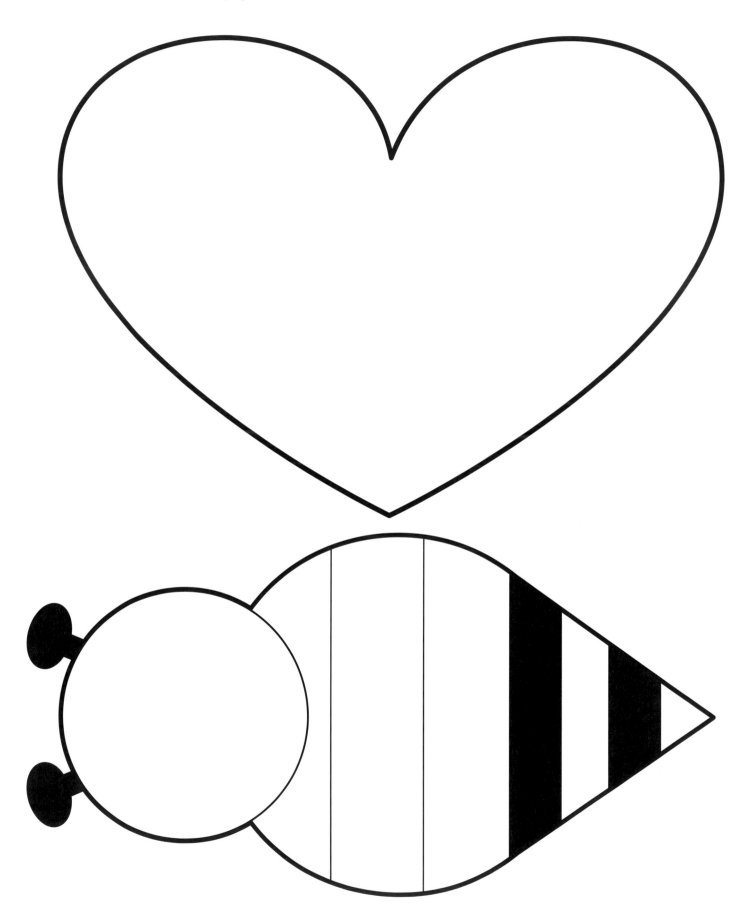

NUTTY OVER 'NYMS!
Using Synonyms and Antonyms

Get your synonyms and antonyms right here! Each activity is packaged for quick and easy review. Choose between the whole-group variety, the partner variety, and the individual variety—or sample them all! All varieties are guaranteed to nourish vocabulary skills and shell out success! Better get crackin'!

ideas contributed by Kelli Jones, East Clayton Elementary, Clayton, NC

By the Pocketful

When students need **synonyms,** have them search these pockets! To make the pocket chart shown, label each of several library pockets with commonly overused words. Then glue the pockets onto a sheet of poster board and title the sheet "Synonyms by the Pocketful." Also cut index cards (or something of similar durability) into pocket-size word strips. Over a period of several days, engage students in brainstorming synonyms for the overused words you've selected. Write their suggestions on the precut strips and tuck the strips in the corresponding pockets. When a student spots an overused word in his writing, he consults the chart for a replacement. This handy reference can be a great center activity too. Simply remove all the strips and have students return them to the correct pockets!

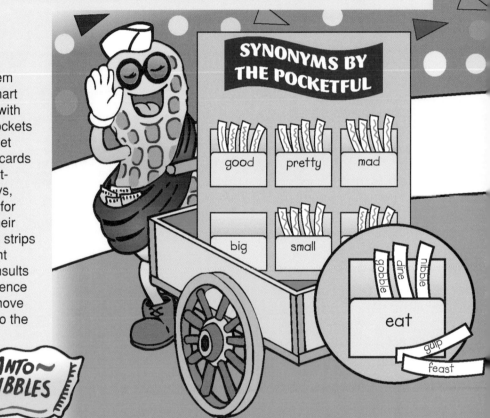

Silly Sentences

Antonyms are the focus of this large-group activity, though students' writing and listening skills definitely come into play! Begin by asking students to name words that have opposite meanings, such as *hot* and *cold*. Write several word pairs on the board. Next, write a sentence on the board that includes the wrong word of an antonym pair, such as "The campfire was so *cold* my marshmallow melted." Ask a volunteer to correct the sentence with an antonym. Repeat the activity with another sentence, such as "The box was too *tiny* to pick up." Next, challenge each child to write a sentence in which she replaces a desired word with its antonym. Have her underline the incorrect antonym and then write the correct one below it. Be sure to set aside time for students to share their silly sentences with their classmates. Listening skills are sure to be sharp!

Go Nuts!

In a nutshell, this **synonyms and antonyms** game is for two or more players. However, you can count on every child wanting her own copy! Give each student a resealable plastic bag, a paper clip, and a construction paper copy of page 139. Have her personalize the title card, cut out the card and the game pieces along the bold lines, and then store the cutouts and the paper clip inside her plastic bag. To play, a student shuffles one set of game cards and stacks the cards facedown. Players alternate drawing cards. A player reads her card aloud; then she completes the task on the card or she uses the paper clip and a pencil to spin for a task. In both cases, if she can complete the task, she keeps the card. If she cannot, she places the card facedown on the bottom of the stack. When the last card in the stack is played, the game is over. The player with the most cards wins.

Four in a Row

It takes a knowledge of **synonyms and antonyms**—and a bit of luck—to win this large-group game! Have each student draw a 4 x 4 grid on a blank sheet of paper. Then instruct him to use the numerals 1 through 6 to randomly number the boxes. Start each turn by rolling a die. Announce the number rolled and one word of a synonym or an antonym pair. If a player has an empty box on his grid labeled with the announced number, he writes the provided word inside it. Then he awaits a second direction from you as to whether to add to the box a synonym or an antonym. The game continues as described. When a player has programmed four boxes in a row, he declares, "Four in a row!" To verify his win, he reads aloud the programming from each box in his winning row and identifies each word pair as synonyms or antonyms. If time permits, continue the game by announcing a new game variation such as Four Corners or Blackout.

Go Nuts!

Name _____

grin	discover	stormy
small	quiet	hard
cold	wet	rough
many	friend	thin
end	tidy	right
happy	Give an antonym.	Give a synonym.
Go nuts! Take a card from another player.		
Go nuts! Give away one of your cards.	Give both an antonym and a synonym.	Make a sentence.
Go nuts! Take another turn.		

Word Snacks!

Draw a red box around each pair of synonyms.
Draw a blue box around each pair of antonyms.

Peanut Stadium
Where Rivals Are Roasted!

HOME	88:88		VISITOR
sad glad	enemy friend	dry wet	mistake error
messy sloppy	gift present	narrow wide	alike same
east west	relax rest	fast quick	question answer
drowsy sleepy	neat tidy	tame wild	add subtract
short tall	shout whisper	sad unhappy	buddy pal

Home of the Fighting Legumes!

I sold ten snacks!

I sold ten snacks too!

bright
sweet dull
sour
Antonyms

cold
chilly jump
leap
Synonyms

Pop! Bang! Boom!

Using Figurative Language in Writing

SHOWY SPARKLERS
Writing Similes

This festive collection of comparisons is sure to light up students' descriptive writing! Start by displaying several simile starters. (See the box for suggestions.) Ask each child to copy and complete a different starter on each of five ¾" x 9" paper strips. Remind him to leave a one-inch margin at the left end of every strip.

To make a sparkler, a student covers a paper towel tube with a 6" x 11" rectangle of red, white, or blue construction paper. Then he uses construction paper scraps and foil stars to decorate the tube to his liking. Next, he glues or tapes his paper strips inside the rim, keeping the programming to the inside. Last, he uses his finger or a pencil to loosely curl each strip outward. Hip, hip, hooray for similes!

The floor is as slippery as ice.

The sand is hot like a baked potato.

The car is as noisy as a beehive.

The shoes are as shiny as…	The water is smooth like…
The sand is hot like…	The kitten's fur is as soft as…
The tree is as tall as…	The mattress is lumpy like…
The chips are salty like…	The floor is as slippery as…
The car is as noisy as…	The table is hard like…

141

Make students' writing something to cheer about
with this investigation of figurative language!

by Stacie Stone Davis, Lima, NY
and Jennifer Kohnke, Nature Ridge Elementary, Bartlett, IL

SOUNDS OF LANGUAGE
Onomatopoeia

Energize students' writing with this sound idea! Have students think of an Independence Day celebration. Then ask them to brainstorm words that sound like the sounds they describe, such as *bang, pop,* and *boom.* Next, divide students into small groups and give each group a sheet of paper titled for a different location. Ask each group to list on its paper words that describe the sounds heard in that setting. Set aside time for the members of each group to read their clues aloud. Challenge the remaining students to use the examples of onomatopoeia to guess the group's location. Be sure to place each group's word list in a writing center. Have students use words from the list in a story.

AS RED AS AN APPLE
Similes

Enhance students' writing with these colorful comparisons! Use construction paper to make a large sun and apple. Label each with the simile starters shown. Display the apple and ask students to brainstorm other objects that are red. List their suggestions on a large sheet of paper. Next, display the sun and repeat the process with objects that are yellow. Then post each cutout along with its corresponding list. Refer students to the word lists when they are writing. If desired, create additional simile displays by using other colors.

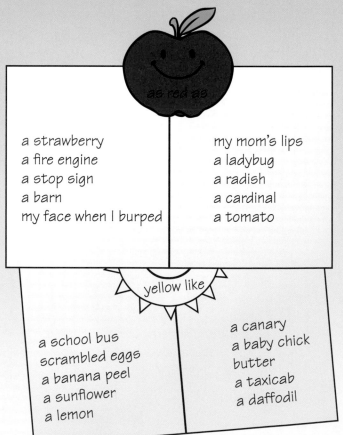

Claire was tired, so she [hit the hay / went to bed]

IN A PICKLE!
Idioms

Why does a writer use a phrase that doesn't mean what it says? Students find out during this activity! Write idioms on the board and confirm their meanings with the class. Next, ask each child to fold a 3" x 5" index card in half (to 1½" x 5"), copy an idiom onto the front of her folded card, and write its meaning inside. Then, on a sheet of blank drawing paper, have the student incorporate her idiom into a sentence and illustrate her work. Set aside time for students to share the two versions of their sentences with partners—one with the idiom and one with its meaning. Most likely students will agree that idioms add interest to writing!

PERSONALITY PLUS
Personification

Giving a teddy bear human qualities is a fine example of figurative language! Post a teddy bear cutout like the one below. Next, have students share words that describe the thoughts, feelings or actions of the bear if it were human. List students' ideas on the board. Then have each child choose a word from the list and write it on a sticky note. Invite each child to use his chosen word in a sentence and then post it on the bear cutout. As a follow-up activity, have students contribute to a class story using words posted on the cutout. No doubt student interest will demand that other everyday objects be personified.

143

Picnic Lunch

Read each sentence.
Use an idiom below to rewrite the sentence.

 1 Finding our picnic spot was easy.

_____

 2 We listened carefully while the directions were read.

_____

 3 But we had a problem because we forgot a blanket!

_____

4 Ellie was thinking ahead and found a good place for us to sit.

_____

 5 The food was great!

_____

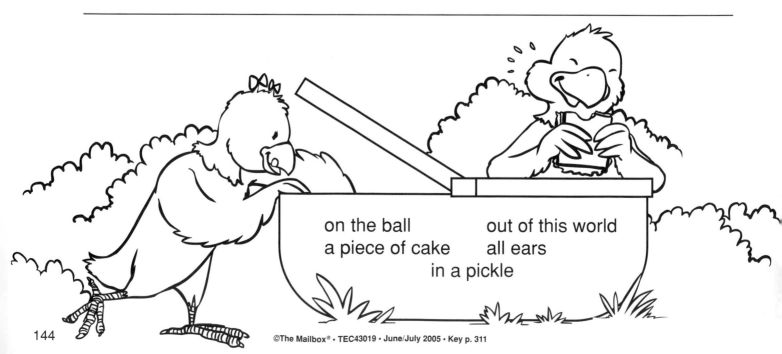

on the ball   out of this world
a piece of cake   all ears
          in a pickle

What a Ride!

Taking a Trip Through the Writing Process

HIGH-FLYING STORIES
Publishing

Students have reached their final destinations! To publish a magic carpet story, a child copies his edited and revised draft onto story paper and illustrates his work. Next, he glues his story on a 12" x 18" sheet of construction paper. He decorates the construction paper border with crayon details that suggest a magic carpet. Then, for fringe, he punches a series of holes along opposite ends of the construction paper and loops individual lengths of yarn through the holes as shown. Invite students to share their work with the class; then showcase the stories with the title "Writing Is Magical!"

My Magic Carpet Ride

One day I found a magic carpet. I climbed onto the carpet and told it to take me to Hawaii. After a couple of hours we got there.

First, I went surfing. The water was really warm and the waves were high. I surfed a wave or two and I did really good. Then I saw a monster wave. I got up on my board and started riding it.

All aboard for a fun-filled writing jaunt! This quick excursion ends with each writer having a published souvenir of his trip!

ideas contributed by David A. Green, North Shore Country Day School, Winnetka, IL

WHERE, OH WHERE?
Brainstorming

Authors begin their writing adventure here! Invite each child to close her eyes and imagine she's riding on a magic carpet. Ask her to think about different places she'd like to visit. Then have each student divide a sheet of blank paper into fourths and in each box, name and illustrate a different destination she's considering.

THIS IS THE PLACE!
Choosing a writing idea

During this leg of the writing excursion, a writer decides where he will travel by magic carpet. Ask each child to cut apart the illustrations he made during "Where, Oh Where?" Then have him choose one illustration, glue the picture near the top of a sheet of blank paper, and list on the paper what he hopes to see and do in this location. Challenge him to note five or more things. Then have him choose a second picture and repeat the activity in a similar manner. Last, ask him to review both pages of ideas and choose the story idea he's most eager to develop. Have him draw a star in a bottom corner of this paper and save his other story ideas for later use.

STEP BY STEP
Completing a plan

Now writers are ready to decide how their stories will unfold. Ask each author to review his starred set of notes from "This Is the Place!" on page 146 and decide what will happen first, next, and last in his story. Have him describe (or illustrate) the three main events on a copy of page 148 and list details about each event in the provided space. It's a plan!

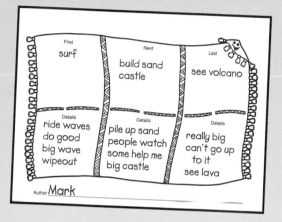

WORD CHOICE
Revising

What a difference a word makes! Ask each author to silently read her story draft. Then challenge her to find and circle words she could replace to make her story clearer or more interesting. Also encourage her to draw a caret (or an arrow) in each place she thinks an added word will increase clarity or interest. Next, have students work with partners to brainstorm substitutions and additions for their writing. Then provide time for each student to complete her revision.

THE FIRST TRY
Drafting

It's time to put the stories on paper! Instruct each child to use a colorful crayon to title his work "DRAFT." Then remind him to follow the plan he completed in "Step by Step" as he writes. When he's finished, ask him to use a different color of crayon to star the three main events of his story.

LAST LOOK
Editing

Give this step of the process a colorful twist! First, label each of several different-colored flags, construction paper circles, or markers with a different editing reminder (see the illustration). Then ask students to use the matching color of crayon or pencil to edit for each reminder and to dot the bottom of their papers to confirm the edit. This colorful and systematic approach promotes thorough editing!

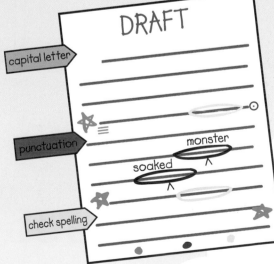

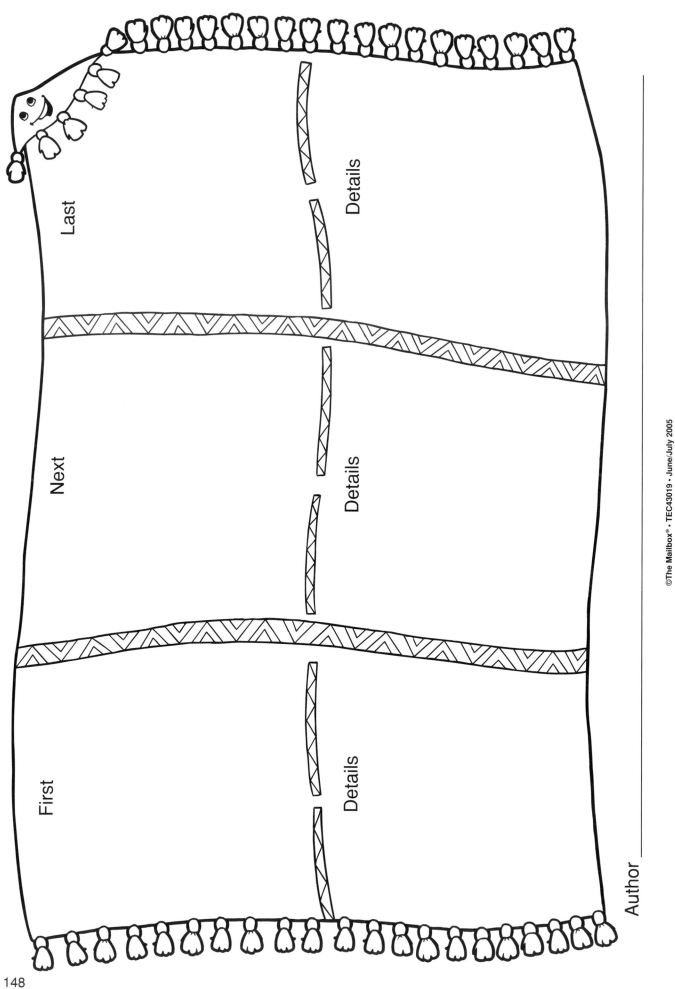

Last

Details

Next

Details

First

Details

Author _____

©The Mailbox® • TEC43019 • June/July 2005

Note to the teacher: Use with "Step by Step" on page 147.

Literature Units

Miss Nelson Is Missing!

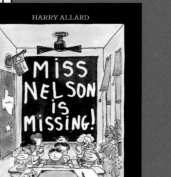

Written by Harry Allard • Illustrated by James Marshall

A group of misbehaving students takes sweet-natured teacher Miss Nelson for granted—until the no-nonsense Miss Swamp takes over. Loaded down with rules and homework, the students search for their beloved teacher. Miss Nelson returns as suddenly as she left, creating a new mystery—the disappearance of Miss Swamp!

ideas contributed by Laura Wagner, Raleigh, NC

A Class Act

Skill: exploring a story's theme

Get students thinking about their own behavior by taking a closer look at the antics in Room 207! Divide a sheet of chart paper into two columns. Label the left column "Miss Nelson's Students" and the right column "[Your name]'s Students." Prompt students to recall ways that Miss Nelson's students misbehave. List their examples in the left column. Then ask students to consider how they should behave in your classroom. List their ideas in the right column. Display the chart in a prominent location to remind students of appropriate ways to behave!

Miss Nelson's Students	Ms. Wagner's Students
make spitballs	are respectful
toss paper airplanes	listen
squirm	do their homework
make faces	work quietly
refuse to do their lessons	are kind to one another

Missing!

Miss Nelson

Miss Nelson has blond hair and pink cheeks.

She was last seen wearing a pink dress and pink shoes.

She has left because her students have been misbehaving again.

Reward: The students in Room 207 will do their work. They will be polite during storytime.

Finding Miss Nelson

Skill: recalling story details

Miss Nelson's mysterious absence prompts several students to seek help from the police. Suggest to students that a missing persons poster may be helpful in their search. To make a poster, give each child a 9" x 12" sheet of white construction paper. Tell students to include in their posters the elements below, as well as any other desired details. Display students' work on a bulletin board titled "Missing!"

Poster Elements
- an illustration of Miss Nelson
- a description of what she looks like and what she was last seen wearing
- why she has disappeared
- a reward for her return (good behavior from the students in Room 207)

Maybe Miss Nelson is at home with the flu.

Maybe Miss Nelson ran away to join the circus.

What Are the Chances?
Skill: responding to literature

When the students in Room 207 speculate about Miss Nelson's whereabouts, their imaginations run wild! Revisit this part of the story with your students. Prompt them to discuss the likelihood of each child's speculation. (For example, it is impossible that Miss Nelson has been carried off by a swarm of butterflies.) Next, tell each child to think of two new explanations for Miss Nelson's absence: one probable, such as being away on vacation, and one outlandish, such as the ones in the story. Have her divide a sheet of drawing paper in half as shown. Tell her to follow the book's format to write about a different idea on each half. Then ask her to illustrate her writing. As she shares her ideas with the class, challenge the remaining students to determine whether the explanation is likely.

Two of a Kind
Skill: analyzing characters

By the end of the story, readers are given the impression that Miss Nelson and Miss Swamp are the same person. Nonetheless, their personalities are vastly different! Miss Nelson is sweet and patient, while Miss Swamp is strict and short-tempered. To assess students' understanding of the two characters, have each child complete a copy of page 152. Discuss the answers as a class. Then prompt youngsters to discuss what their experience with Miss Swamp taught them about good behavior and teacher appreciation!

Follow the Clues
Skill: making inferences

Students are sure to agree—Detective McSmogg is not much of a detective! Point out to students that the author provides several clues about Miss Swamp's identity throughout the story. Then, to help students track down these clues, have each child glue a provided foil-covered tagboard circle to a craft stick to make a magnifying glass. Reread the story aloud. When a student hears a clue, have her raise her magnifying glass. List the clues on the board as they are found, asking students to explain each one. Then tell students to save their magnifying glasses to look for specified details in later read-alouds. **To boost writing skills,** have each child pen a letter to Detective McSmogg to inform him about the clues. Mystery solved!

Dear Detective McSmogg,
   You should have known that Miss Swamp is really Miss Nelson. When the class doesn't behave, Miss Nelson says that something must be done. Miss Swamp is near Miss Nelson's house. There is an ugly black dress in Miss Nelson's closet. I hope that you solve your next case.

Your friend,

Jamila

Miss Nelson

Name _____

Miss Nelson Is Missing!
Analyzing characters

Who's Who?

Read each statement.
Decide if it is talking about Miss Nelson or Miss Swamp.
Cut and glue.

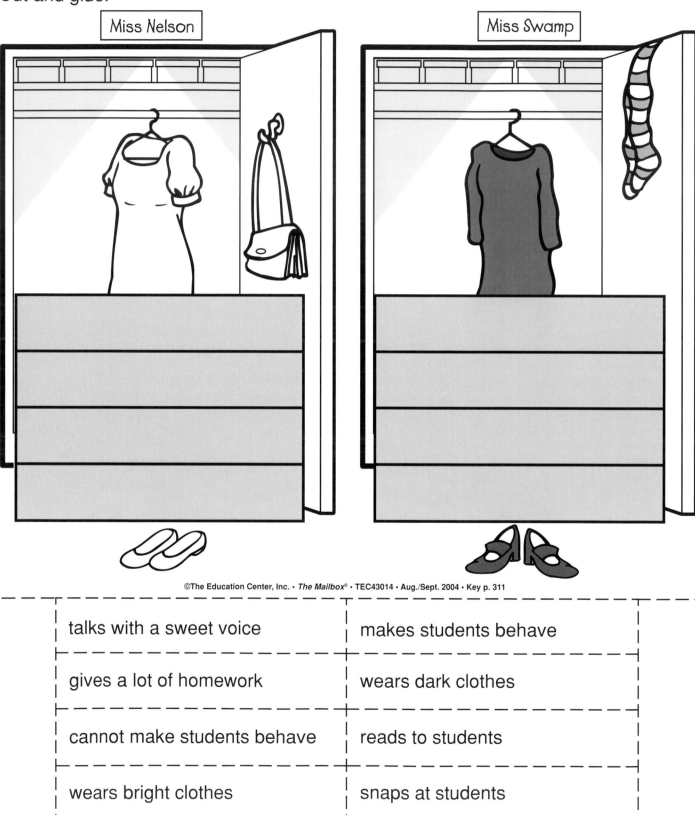

Miss Nelson

Miss Swamp

©The Education Center, Inc. • *The Mailbox*® • TEC43014 • Aug./Sept. 2004 • Key p. 311

talks with a sweet voice	makes students behave
gives a lot of homework	wears dark clothes
cannot make students behave	reads to students
wears bright clothes	snaps at students

152   **Note to the teacher:** Use with "Two of a Kind" on page 151.

Whodunit?
Using Nate the Great Mysteries

PANCAKES, ANYONE?
Analyzing characters

This character investigation really stacks up—just like Nate's favorite food! Have each student trace a five-inch circle on manila paper and cut out the tracing. Ask her to draw a box near the top of her cutout and inside the box illustrate a story character, such as Nate, Rosamond, or Annie. Below the box have her write the character's name and her observations about the character. Provide time for each child to investigate three or more characters in a similar manner.

To make a booklet, a student stacks her cutouts. Next, she cuts a five-inch circle from manila paper and a slightly smaller circle from light brown construction paper. On one side of the manila cutout she writes "A Stack of Characters by [student's name]" and on the other side she glues the light brown cutout. She staples the resulting cover to her stack, keeping the programming to the inside. Then she glues the back of her booklet in the center of a paper dessert plate and adds desired decorations to the top of the stack. Nate would be very impressed!

A Stack of Characters

by Liza

Nate the Great
He is a detective who is good at finding things. He works alone or with his dog. He is a good writer.

Bring literacy skills into focus! Use these suggestions to complement any book in Marjorie Weinman Sharmat's delightful detective series.

by Beth Romie, New Albany-Plain Local Elementary, New Albany, OH

HOT ON THE TRAIL
Word analysis

At this literacy center, students track down vowel sounds, compound words, suffixes, and more! Stock the center with white construction paper copies of the magnifying glass pattern on page 155, some Nate the Great books, crayons, and scissors. Assign a case, such as compound words, to each student using the center. A student chooses a book and then labels a magnifying glass with the book's title and the assigned case. He writes his findings on the pattern, colors the pattern to his liking, and cuts it out. If he needs additional writing room, he writes on the back of his cutout or he continues on a second pattern.

Compound Words

outside   anyone
pancakes   somebody
himself   nightshirt
saleslady   inside
anymore   nobody

Nate the Great and the Big Sniff

HERE'S THE SCOOP
Writing messages

Set the stage for this activity by reminding the class that Nate often writes his mother a short note telling her of his whereabouts. Invite students to explain how this action shows that Nate is responsible. Next, ask them to brainstorm opportunities they have to write notes for their family members. Suggestions might include notes similar to Nate's, reminder notes, and feel-good notes. Involve students as you write on the board a sample note that includes a greeting, a closing, and a signature. Then ask them to follow the format of your note as they each write a note to a family member. For extra writing motivation, have an assortment of notepad papers on hand!

Dear Dad,
   I have a soccer game on Saturday. I sure hope you can come! It starts at 11:00.

   Love,
   Nigel

CASE SOLVED
Identifying story elements

Reviewing a case is an important part of detective work! To prepare for the job, have each child staple several copies of the form on page 155 between two construction paper covers. Then have her personalize the front cover of her notebook and decorate it to her liking. Have students complete a form for every Nate the Great story they read. Encourage your sleuths to compare notes and look for similarities and differences in Nate's cases. Hey, Sludge helped solve this case too!

Karen Pavlosky
Woodbrook Elementary
Charlottesville, VA

Case Solved!
Nate the Great and the Monster Mess
name of case

- This case takes place ___ in Nate's home and neighborhood.
- The main characters are ___ Nate and Sludge.
- Nate is asked to find ___ his mom's recipe for monster cookies.
- Nate solves the case when ___ he finds "Lemfan" scribbled on a paper.
- One clue that helps Nate solve this case is ___ that his mom was seen writing on a long piece of paper.

154

Form
Use with "Case Solved" on page 154.

Case Solved!

name of case

- This case takes place

- The main characters are

- Nate is asked to find

- Nate solves the case when

- One clue that helps Nate solve this case is

©The Mailbox®

Marvin Redpost
Class President

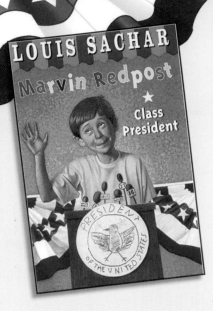

by Louis Sachar

Today is no ordinary Thursday! It's Hole Day and everyone, including Marvin's teacher, is wearing clothes with holes. But that's not the only excitement of the day! Marvin's teacher suddenly announces that a special visitor is on his way—the president of the United States! Soon the classroom fills with news reporters and television cameras. When the president arrives, Marvin and his classmates have the opportunity to ask questions. Surprisingly, Marvin's question lands him a spot on the evening news!

with ideas by Peggy Morin Bruno—Language Arts Consultant
Squadron Line School, Simsbury, CT

Presidential Predictions

Making, revising, and confirming predictions

Use the book's title to inspire wonder about the story! Announce the title and ask students why the author might have chosen it. Next, give each child a copy of page 158 and ask him to write his favorite explanation for the title under "Before Reading." Then collect the papers, making sure each has a name. After chapter 5 is read, have each child revisit his prediction and either confirm or revise it in the section labeled "During Reading." Repeat the activity at the completion of the book. When students are finished writing, have them color and cut out their hats. Encourage students to use the hats to tell their families about Marvin Redpost's extraordinary day at school!

Telling It to a T
Summarizing significant story events

Hole Day at Dogwood Elementary School grows more eventful by the minute! This ongoing idea is a "T-riffic" way for students to summarize the main event of each story chapter. For each child, precut nine three-inch white paper squares to be used during the reading of the book. Then have each child make a construction paper T-shirt by gluing two 4" x 4½" rectangles to a 9" x 12" sheet. Next, have her trim a neckline in the shirt shape and use a marker to add neckline and sleeve details and her name. Post the projects on an easily accessible display titled "Hole Day Happenings."

After each chapter is read, have each child write on a precut paper square the chapter number and a sentence that describes the chapter's main event. Then have her trim the edges of the cutout to resemble a hole and use a glue stick to attach the cutout to her T-shirt project. There's a "hole" lot happening at Marvin's school!

Got a Question?
Questioning, using information resources

Marvin has trouble coming up with a unique question for the president. Would your students? To find out, pair students at the end of chapter 3 and ask the partners to brainstorm questions they would like to ask the current president of the United States. Next, ask each pair to share with the class the question it would most like to have answered. After you've determined that each pair has a different question, have each twosome write its question on a precut speech bubble. Display the speech bubbles with the title "Mr. President,…"

Next, invite the class to find the answers to the posted questions during their free time. Make available age-appropriate print and Internet resources about the current U.S. president. Every few days, set aside time for students to share their findings. When a question is answered, add a foil star to the corresponding cutout.

Stellar Citizens
Understanding responsibilities of a good citizen

In chapter 6, the president asks the students in Marvin's class to think of ways to be good citizens. Ask students to recall the good citizen behaviors mentioned in the story. Write this information on the board and then add to the list your youngsters' suggestions for how to be good citizens. For a well-rounded list, guide students to contribute behaviors such as voting, recycling, being a leader, following rules, and solving problems. Then point out to students that the behaviors listed describe a responsible person! Remind students of the importance of practicing these behaviors each and every day. To inspire stellar citizenship in your classroom, each day ask students to describe how good citizens would respond to one of the provided scenarios.

Scenarios
- A classmate has a really hard time with reading or math.
- A classmate makes up jokes about other students and wants you to laugh.
- The teacher gives your group craft materials for a project. Some students in the group use more of the supplies than are really needed.
- A new student in your class is from another country. He doesn't speak much English.
- Your teacher asks students to vote on the best group's project. Your group's project is not the best, but you want to win the prize.
- Another student teases you and calls you names. She sometimes takes your lunch money.
- Your best friend wants to copy your homework.
- You see a student throw something out of the bus window, but the bus driver doesn't notice.

News 2 film coverage at 6:00 and 11:00…

Hat Pattern

Use with "Presidential Predictions" on page 156.

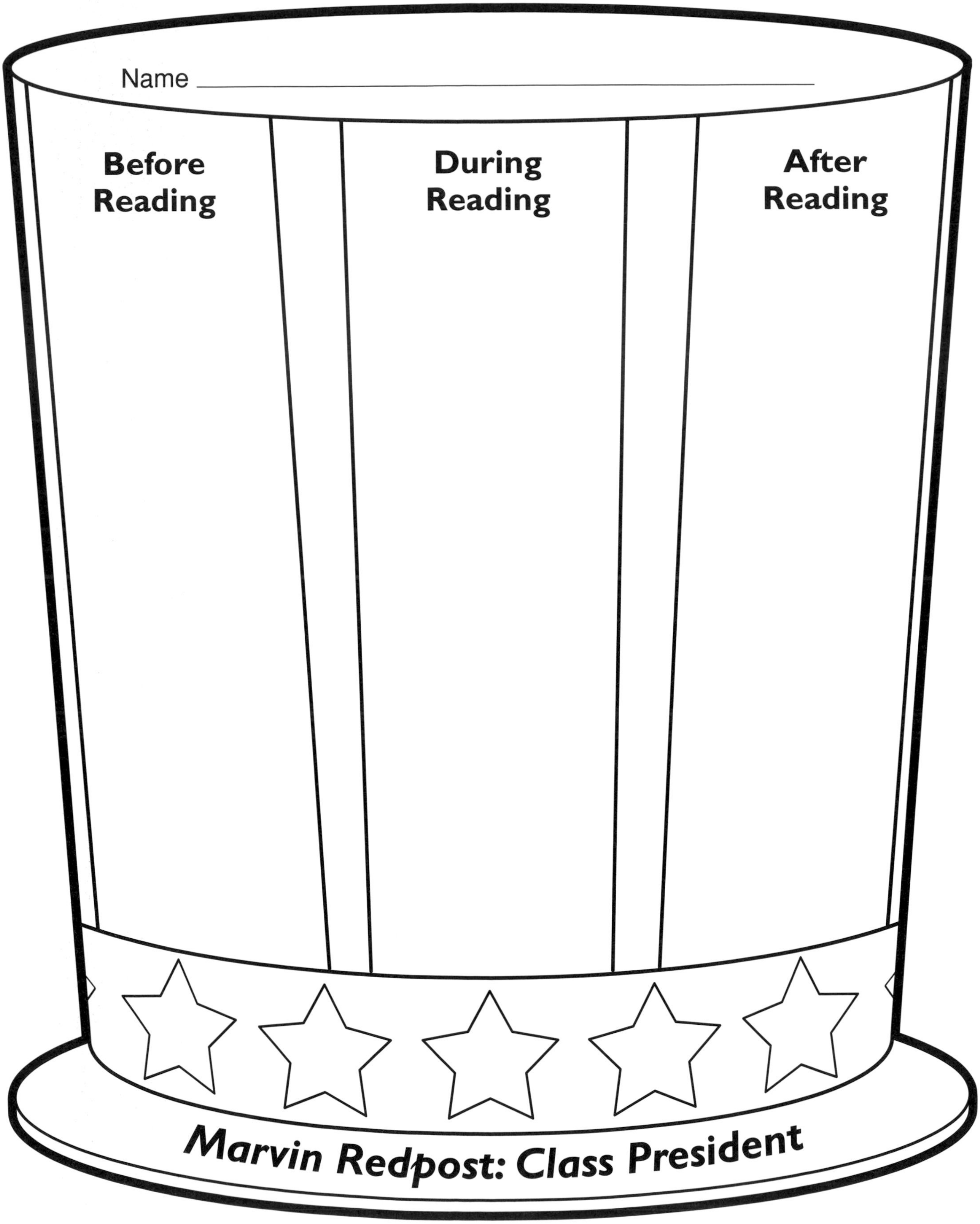

Name _____

Before Reading

During Reading

After Reading

Marvin Redpost: Class President

Character Close-Ups

Cross out two statements about each character that are not true.
Then complete the sentence about the character.
Use the word bank to help you.

Marvin Redpost

- thinks other people have good ideas
- tries hard at school
- says mean things to his classmates
- gets embarrassed sometimes
- remembers everything
- thanks others for their help

I think Marvin is _____

because _____

_____

_____

Word Bank

shy	brave	caring
friendly	smart	curious
kind	talented	helpful
bossy	selfish	clever

Mrs. North

- never gets excited
- wears a shirt with a hole on Hole Day
- reminds her students how to behave
- tells the TV crew to wait quietly
- takes up a lot of the president's time
- fills the marble jar

I think Mrs. North is _____

because _____

_____

_____

The President

- remembers many students' names
- shakes a lot of hands
- is very quiet
- tries to hurry people
- praises the students
- likes to answer questions

I think the president is _____

because _____

_____

_____

Note to the teacher: Use after reading *Marvin Redpost: Class President* by Louis Sachar.

The Legend of the Indian Paintbrush

Retold and illustrated by Tomie dePaola

A Native American boy uses berries and horsehair brushes to dutifully paint the stories of his people. But he is dissatisfied with his colors until the evening that his faithfulness is rewarded. He finds the blazing colors of the sunset and unintentionally plants them in the earth. Legend has it that because of his perseverance, Indian paintbrush flowers blanket the countryside with vibrant colors each spring.

ideas contributed by Julie Douglas, St. Louis, MO

Legend Has It

Skill: understanding the characteristics of a legend

If you've been looking for an easy way to introduce your children to a variety of story types, get off to a fine start by pulling *The Legend of the Indian Paintbrush* from a shelf. Then let the legend telling begin! Display the book's cover, read the title, and ask children what a legend is. Guide the conversation to establish that a legend is a folk story told as though it is a true account of someone's deeds or of something that happened. Find out which legends your children are already familiar with and what attributes they believe legends have in common. Discuss the cover. Have your students predict what the legend will be about as you note their thoughts. After reading the book, return to the predictions to discuss how accurate they were.

Flowery Descriptions

Skill: using descriptive language

Indian paintbrushes fill meadows and hills with the glowing colors of the sunset. What better invitation do you need to put your children's imaginations and descriptive language to work? Prepare for this activity by having volunteers cut pictures of flowers from catalogs or magazines. Ask each child to select one flower cutout and glue it to a sheet of paper. Then remind children that the author uses very vivid language when he describes Indian paintbrushes. Ask them to use vivid phrases to describe their flowers too. Hole-punch the pages and place them in a notebook. As you flip through the book with your students, talk about their word choices and how they trigger the reader's imagination.

lily

A lily brings snow white to a deep green day.

iris

dripping with purple and mist

Ablaze With Meaning

Skill: exploring vocabulary

There are two reasons your students will love this vocabulary-enhancing activity—choice and collaboration! Before rereading the story, provide two paper strips for each child. Ask that he jot down two words from the story that seem unusual, intriguing, or especially important. Afterward, place all the slips on one tabletop; then have volunteers sort them, discard the duplicates, revise spellings, and add additional words if necessary so there's one unique word for each student. Have each group of four children select four word strips. Provide each group with a copy of the book and a dictionary (or access to one), a glue stick, markers, four index cards, scissors, and a 6" x 18" tan strip of construction paper accordion folded at four-inch intervals to create a booklet.

Ask children to work cooperatively to locate each selected word in the story and read it in context before discussing its meaning. To confirm the definitions they deduce, have students refer to the dictionary; then have each of them write the definition of one of the words on a card using his own phrasing. Have the members of each group glue their cards into the folded booklet, fringe the extended strip, and decorate the cover. Close the activity by asking each group to meet with two other groups to discuss their words.

> When you **struggle** you have trouble with something.
>
> A **custom** is something people do to remind them of something they don't want to forget.
>
> When you **prove** something you show you can do it.
>
> A **deed** is something a person does.

> Words From
> The Legend of the Indian Paintbrush

> custom
> struggle

Dreaming of Tomorrow Today

Skill: making connections

Perhaps, like Little Gopher, your students are sensing that they have special talents. Help children connect the book's message to their own lives by inviting them to make dream vision shields and write about their future contributions. Begin by having each child think about what her talents are and how she's likely to use them. Provide water, a watercolor paint set, and a paper plate for each child. Then ask her to paint the back of the plate to represent one of her talents. When the artwork is dry, provide an additional paper plate half for each child and then either have her glue them rim to rim (and attach yarn for hanging) or use a hole puncher and yarn to stitch the rims together and create a hanger. Tissue paper strips or other embellishments may be added. Ask each child to write about her dream vision. How might she use her talents and what might result? When each child has finished writing, have her share it with her classmates before tucking it inside her shield for display.

> This is me with a bunny I know. His name is Thumper. I am good with animals. I have fixed a bird's wing and helped a squirrel get back to its mother. My dream is to be a veterinarian one day. I would like to help all kinds of animals. It would make me happy to make them well again.
> Sarah

About Little Gopher and Me

Complete each sentence about Little Gopher.
Use the word bank below.
Then write about yourself.

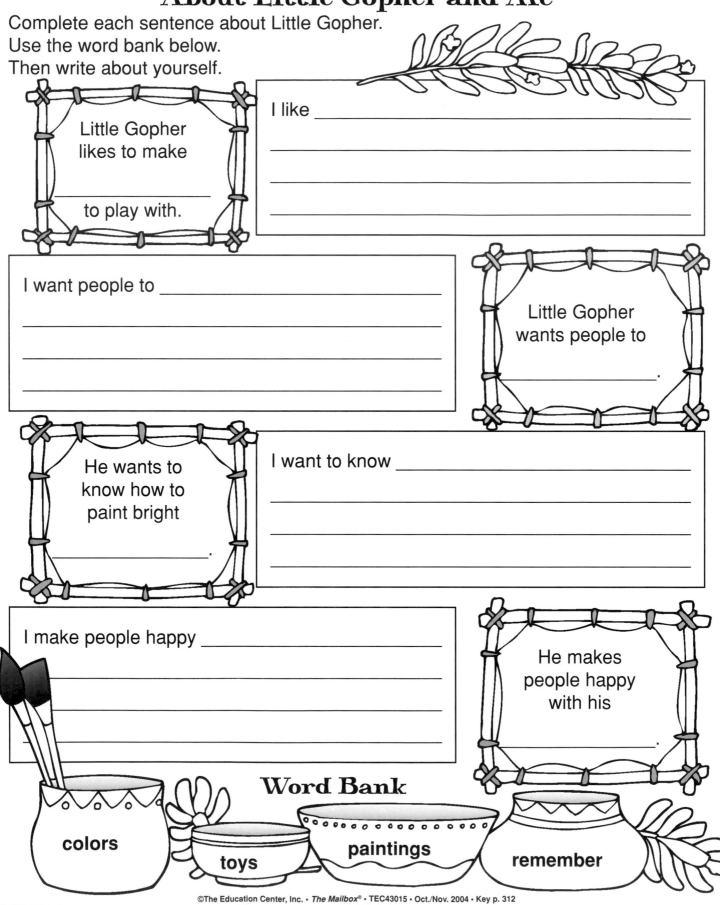

Little Gopher likes to make _____ to play with.

I like _____
_____
_____
_____

I want people to _____
_____
_____
_____

Little Gopher wants people to _____.

He wants to know how to paint bright _____.

I want to know _____
_____
_____
_____

I make people happy _____
_____
_____

He makes people happy with his _____.

Word Bank

colors   toys   paintings   remember

TACKY THE PENGUIN

Written by Helen Lester
Illustrated by Lynn Munsinger

He's a peculiar penguin, a bizarre bird, an interesting individual. All the other penguins cringe over Tacky's differences. He has odd ways of saying hello, of diving, of singing, and of dressing. But that slouching, leaping, flip-flopping march of his might be the oddest thing of all. Yep, everyone agrees that Tacky is truly tacky! That is, until the day the hunters come. That's when it becomes clear that an odd bird can be a great one to have around.

ideas contributed by Stacie Stone Davis—Lima, NY

Tacky	His Companions
Wears bright clothing	Wear regular penguin outfits
Doesn't care that he is different	Always want to be like one another
Likes to do cannonballs	Dive gracefully
Is interesting	Are sort of boring

jennifer tipton cappoen

ODDLY APPEALING

Skills: making predictions, comparing characters

Is it time your children had a gentle reminder that individual differences are cause for celebration? Then you'd better dive into the library and pick up a copy of *Tacky the Penguin*. Before reading, explain that Tacky is considered by his companions to be more than a little bit odd. Find out what your children know about penguins and penguin behavior. Then ask them to define the word *odd*. Guide the conversation to help them understand that odd things differ from the ordinary, usual, or expected. Then have them predict how an odd penguin might behave.

Read *Tacky the Penguin* aloud; then invite students to comment on how Tacky is different from his companions. As the children describe the differences between Tacky and the others, write their observations on chart paper. When the list is complete, review it aloud. Is Tacky odd in the predicted ways? Guide students to understand that Tacky's unusual behavior causes no problems and ultimately helps him—and his companions—survive. What a penguin!

163

TOTALLY TACKY TIMES
Skill: making text-to-self connections

There's a little bit of Tacky in each of us. Sometimes it just feels good to be a little different from our friends, but other times we like going with the flow. Use this writing activity to bring students' thoughts about similarities and differences to the forefront in an eye-appealing tabletop display. On a five-inch white paper square, have each student write about one of her Tacky times—a time when she thought, acted, or looked different from her friends. (Provide additional squares as necessary.) On one or more additional squares, have each child write about a time when it felt good to blend in with the crowd. Staple together any work that requires more than one square per topic.

And now for the penguin panache! Provide each student with a 6" x 22" strip of black poster board marked as shown. Then demonstrate how to round the ends, fold along the parallel lines, and tape to make a self-standing penguin form. Also have each child glue her two writing samples on opposite sides of the form. Provide pom-poms, markers, scissors, and scraps of poster board and construction paper; then encourage each child to complete her penguin so that the side describing a time she was different from her peers is the most flamboyant, while the other side is more conservative like Tacky's companions. When all the projects have been completed, have children meet in small groups to share their writings. Afterward, arrange the penguins on a tabletop where others can waddle by to read them too!

It felt good to be different last week on the bus. I was the only one who stood up for Sammy. One of the big kids bothers him every day. I told the kid to stop. No one else would.

It felt good that my friends and I were thinking alike when we wrote our science report. We all wanted to do a report on monkeys. It was fun. We all liked it so much that the time just flew by.

TACKY BY ANOTHER NAME
Skill: changing story elements

Get the overhead projector ready. Your students will soon be needing it to share their stories. Begin by discussing with students story elements in *Tacky the Penguin* such as the characters, setting, and problem. Then enlist students' help in brainstorming alternate settings and characters that could be used with a similar story line. Afterward, have children form small groups. Provide each group with six transparencies and several colors of transparency pens. Ask each group to create an original story (with a plot similar to *Tacky the Penguin*) using one of the brainstormed settings and corresponding characters. Have each group of children use the supplies to illustrate its story. When all groups have finished their work, ask each group to share its original story using the overhead projector. You just may be surprised at what colorful storytellers there are in your class.

	Tacky	Story A	Story B
setting	icy island	jungle	ocean
characters	penguins	lions	fish
problems	one is different	one is different	one is different

164

A Penguin With Dazzling Effects

Cut out the sentences below the dotted line.
Read each cause.
Glue its effect beside it.

Cause	Effect
Tacky slapped a penguin on the back.	
Tacky made a splashy dive.	
The hunters came with traps.	
Tacky did not run from the hunters.	
Tacky marched and flopped down.	
Tacky sang to the hunters.	
Tacky made the hunters leave.	

The hunters ran away.	The hunters were puzzled.
The other penguins hugged Tacky.	The hunters walked up to Tacky.
The other penguins got very wet.	The other penguins ran and hid.
	The penguin nearly fell.

165

Amazing Grace

Written by Mary Hoffman • Illustrated by Caroline Binch

Grace wouldn't know how not to perform. This little story lover brings one tale after another to life with a few household props and a generous helping of imagination. When the opportunity arises to try out for the lead role in the class play, Grace has some moments of self-doubt thanks to the stereotypical thinking of her classmates. But in the satisfying finale, Grace's indomitable spirit triumphs.

by David Green—North Shore Country Day School, Winnetka, IL

You Can!

Skill: understanding a story's theme

Spotlight comprehension with lively conversations about this story's central theme. To prepare, locate a die and two copies of the book. Write questions like the ones shown on star-shaped notepad sheets and attach the stars to the corresponding pages of one copy of the book. Next, read *Amazing Grace* aloud from the unstarred book. Then divide your children into six groups, assigning each a number from one to six.

Reread the story, using the starred book. Pause on each starred page to read the question aloud; then have each group discuss answers to the question. After a while, signal for the conversation to stop as you roll the die to determine which group will respond. Ask a representative to share his group's thoughts. Roll again before continuing the story, to involve more children. Continue through the book in this way, reading and pausing for reflection and conversation. Make sure each group gets a chance to share. Conclude this activity by mentioning that the part of Peter Pan has often been performed by women and by emphasizing that we need not be limited by others' perceptions of what we can do.

Why do Grace's classmates think she can't be Peter Pan?

Why does Nana take Grace to the ballet?

What things helped Grace get the role?

What things were unimportant?

What does Grace learn because of this experience?

Peter Pan Starts Tonight 7:00

Star Performances
Skill: recall and making a text-to-self connection

Grace's nonstop imagination shifts into high gear as she acts out first one famous story character and then another. After reading *Amazing Grace* to your students, ask them to recall characters that Grace pretends to be. Then find out what roles they have acted out (or would enjoy acting out). On one side of a sheet of paper, have each student complete and illustrate the sentence starter "Grace pretends to be…" On the other side have her complete and illustrate "I pretend to be…" Provide markers, adhesive foil stars, stamp pads, and star-shaped rubber stamps, if desired, so students can embellish their illustrations with stars before you staple the pages between construction paper covers. Tuck this booklet into your reading corner and encourage children to read about the stage and screen aspirations of their classmates. It's easy to see that you have students with star quality too!

Amazing Myself
Skill: recall and making text-to-self connections

Amazing Grace reminds readers that goals are reached by setting our sights on what we'd like to accomplish and then taking each of the necessary steps to be successful. Discuss with students the factors that make Grace successful in getting the role she wants. Emphasize that Grace doesn't become Peter Pan just because of a wish. She gets the role because she prepares by practicing the movements and dialogue of Peter Pan. Discuss with students the kinds of goals different people have and then ask each child to complete a copy of page 168. Afterward, ask volunteers to talk about Grace's goals and their own. With a little encouragement, each of your students can be just as amazing as Grace!

Casting Call
Skill: identifying similar character traits

Encourage a little typecasting with this story extension activity. Choose a familiar story that your class knows well, such as a fairy tale, a folktale, or a favorite class picture book. Ask each child to design a promotional poster, like the one Nana shows Grace, announcing the story as an upcoming play. To plan the poster, have each child think of each of the story's main characters and someone he knows that has many of the personality characteristics represented by that character. Provide large sheets of art paper and let the promotions begin! When the posters are complete, give children opportunities to explain who they chose to cast as each of the characters and why he or she fit the role perfectly. Perhaps you should close the door. For a few minutes it's bound to sound like a comedy club in there!

Name

Amazing Myself

Read *Amazing Grace*. Complete one side for Grace and one side for yourself.

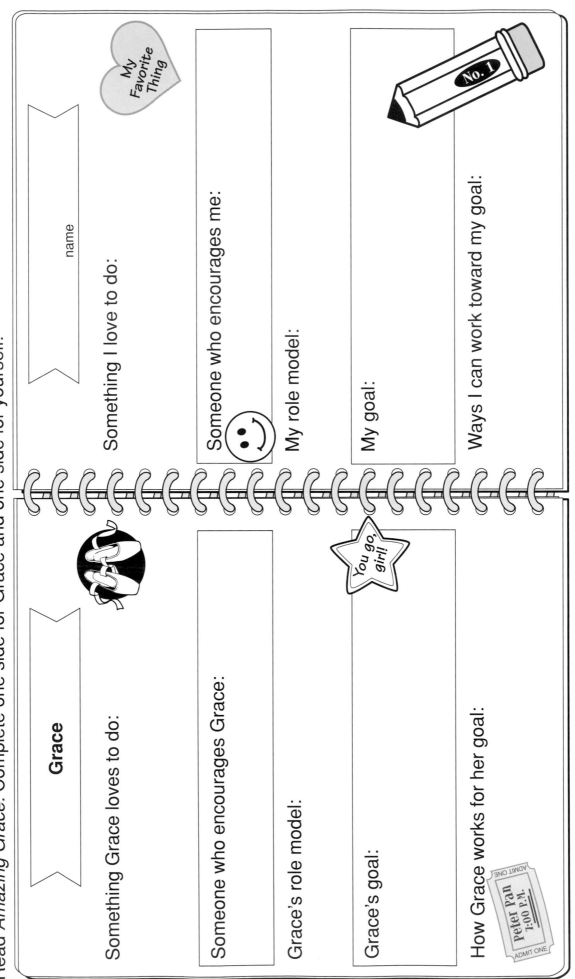

Grace

Something Grace loves to do:

Someone who encourages Grace:

Grace's role model:

Grace's goal:

How Grace works for her goal:

My Favorite Thing

name

Something I love to do:

Someone who encourages me:

My role model:

My goal:

Ways I can work toward my goal:

©The Mailbox® • TEC43017 • Feb./Mar. 2005

Note to the teacher: Use with "Amazing Myself" on page 167.

The Lorax

by Dr. Seuss

The Lorax pleads on behalf of the Truffula Trees, the Brown Bar-ba-loots, and the Swomee-Swans. But the Once-ler just continues to crank out more thneeds, destroying the scenery and polluting the water and air. The story could end on that low note UNLESS Dr. Seuss plants seeds of hopeful inspiration within your students. He—and *The Lorax*—surely will.

by David A. Green, North Shore Country Day School, Winnetka, IL

Lerkim   snergelly
gruvvulous
snarggled   slupps
cruffulous

Froobulous Words
using context to determine word meanings

Since *The Lorax* is loaded with nonsense words, its language is just perfect for helping children understand how context can support their understanding of unknown words. Before reading aloud the book, flag a few of the nonsense words using large, bright sticky notes. Then, as a prereading activity, have a child choose a sticky note and read the word it is marking. Find out what he thinks the word means. Then read the word in its two- or three-sentence context. Allow plenty of time for him to confer with some classmates on several things that the nonsense word might mean. When he has determined the word's meaning and shared it, have him explain how the context helped him conclude something about the meaning. Repeat the process with the other sticky-note words before reading the story aloud.

It all
started...

by Ben

The trees were tall and bright. They looked like furry lollipops and they were everywhere.

unless...

The Once-ler's Story
identifying changes in a story's setting, writing descriptions

After reading aloud *The Lorax* and discussing the story's conservation message with your students, give each child three sheets of paper. Ask her to pay close attention to the environment, or the setting of the story, as she hears it a second time. Instead of starting at the beginning of the story, begin reading where the Once-ler begins telling his tale. Stop reading when the Once-ler has made the first thneed. Ask each child to use an entire sheet of paper to draw and color the setting as described at the beginning of the Once-ler's story. Repeat the read-and-draw cycle, stopping again before the Lorax brings up the plight of the Swomee-Swans and after the Lorax flies away.

Show students how to fold the scenes in half and glue them together to transform the pictures into a booklet. Have each child write a short description of each of the three scenes and attach it to the corresponding page. Then have children take turns sharing their writing and their pictures as classmates listen for vivid descriptions of the changing landscape. To remind them of the story's ending, provide seeds and encourage each child to tape one to the outside back cover of his booklet as a reminder that he can make a positive difference.

I Speak for the...
determining an author's purpose, making connections

After reading *The Lorax* to your children, ask them what message Dr. Seuss wanted his readers to get from the story. Have them explain how they know. Then ask your children to name some environmental concerns, particularly ones in your area that involve plants, animals, or parts of the environment negatively impacted by people. Help children form several small groups. Ask each group to choose a plant, animal, or setting on which to focus and then to draw or locate a picture of it. Have the group's members draw and cut out an imaginary Lorax-like creature, write its concerns on a speech balloon cutout, and attach both pieces to the first picture. Ask each group to share its environmental concerns with the other groups; then attach all the projects to a bulletin board.

I speak for the lake! Do you know what people are doing to my crystal clear waters? Do you know what they leave behind on the shores or floating in the current? What they put in the water oozes, seeps, and smells. It makes some animals sick and smothers the fish. How I wish people would clean up their act before it's too late!

Name _____

How Do You See It?

Cut out the sentence strips below the dotted line.
Glue them to contrast the characters' views.

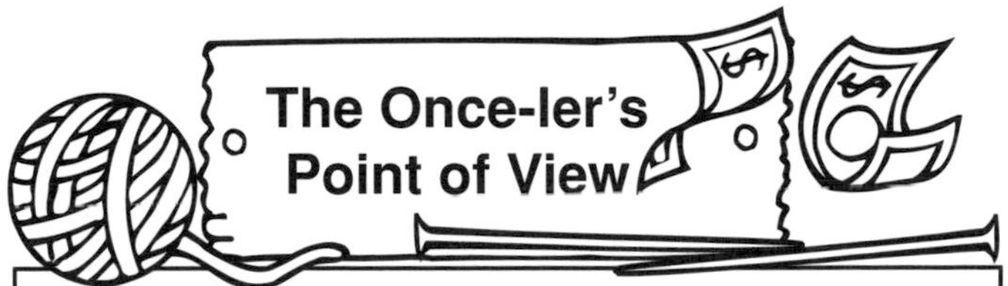

The Once-ler's Point of View

I thought people needed Thneeds.
I liked chopping down four trees at a time.
My factory needed to be bigger to make more Thneeds.
My machines needed to run all day and night.
When the last tree was gone, I was lonely.
Maybe the Lorax was right.

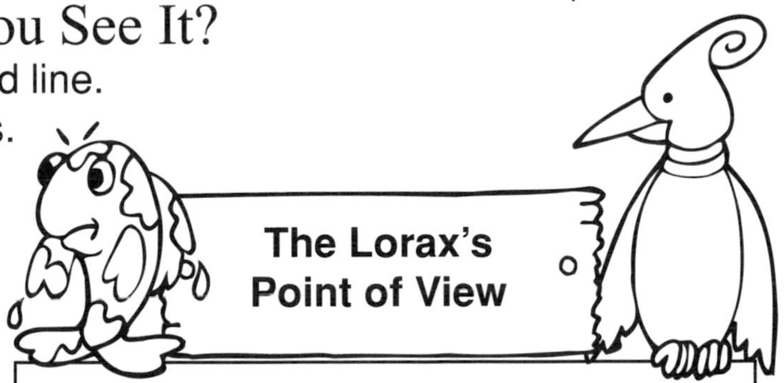

The Lorax's Point of View

©The Mailbox® • TEC43018 • April/May 2005 • Key p. 312

I thought Thneeds wouldn't sell.

I was sad the trees were all gone.

I hated that the factory's smoke stopped the birds from singing.

I was mad that the Bar-ba-loots were hungry for tree fruit.

I was mad that machine goo went into the pond.

_____'s
name

Point of View

Glue this square on another sheet of paper. On the paper write your thoughts about the story.

Was one character right and one wrong? Explain.

Take a Spin in a Magic Tree House

It doesn't matter which books your students are reading from the Magic Tree House series by Mary Pope Osborne. Why? Because these suggestions are designed to use with any of Jack and Annie's adventures! Simply choose your favorite activities and use them to grow reading enthusiasm and skills.

ideas contributed by Beth Romie, New Albany Elementary, New Albany, OH

A Classroom Tree House

A tree house in the classroom! Why not? It's the perfect setting for reading books from the Magic Tree House series. To make a tree house, cut away the top and one side of a large appliance box. Flip the box over and cut a window opening in one side. Involve students in decorating the box to resemble a tree house. Also cut a large treetop shape from green bulletin board paper. Mount the cutout on a wall and slide the back of the decorated tree house up against it. Post a schedule or a sign-up sheet for tree house visits. The tree house in Frog Creek woods won't be the only tree house that's buzzing with excitement!

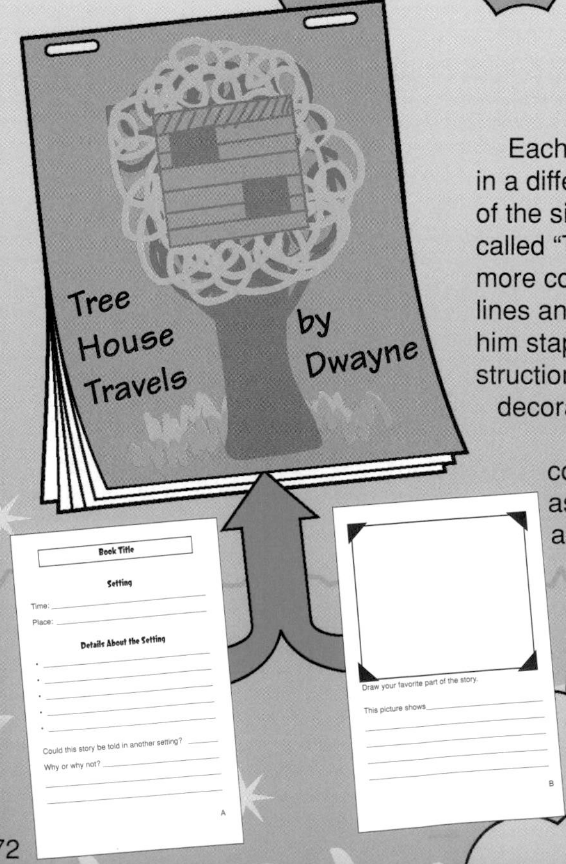

Tree House Travels
Exploring the significance of a setting

Each time the siblings take a spin in the tree house, they land in a different setting. To increase your students' understanding of the significance of a setting, have each child keep a notebook called "Tree House Travels." Copy page 175 to make three or more copies per child. Next, have each child cut along the dotted lines and stack the pages (alternating page A and B). Next, have him staple the stack of pages between two half sheets of construction paper as shown. Then have him title, personalize, and decorate the front cover of the resulting booklet.

During the reading of a Magic Tree House book, a child completes a consecutive page A and B. Periodically set aside time for students to share their setting-related notes and pictures. Jack would be so impressed!

Tree House Travels by Dwayne

Book Title
Setting
Time:
Place:
Details About the Setting

Could this story be told in another setting?
Why or why not?

A

Draw your favorite part of the story.

This picture shows

B

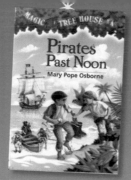

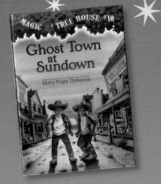

Reading Recommendations
Responding to literature

Keep sprouting interest in tree house mysteries by inviting students to post their opinions of the adventures they've read. Design a leaf form like the one shown and then make copies of the page on light green construction paper. A student fills in the number and title of the book she read. Next, she describes the setting and the purpose of the adventure. Then she writes her opinion of the book, signs her work, and cuts out the shape. Showcase the leaves on a large treetop shape like the one described in "A Classroom Tree House" on page 172.

Magic Tree House # __4__

Title: Pirates Past Noon

Setting of adventure: a sandy beach in the time of pirates, about 300 years ago

Purpose of adventure: They want to get away from the rain. Then they have to find gold for some pirates.

Opinion of books: I think the story is good. The pirates are scary. The storm is scary too!

by __Meredith__

The Titanic was a big ship.

Most people thought the Titanic could not sink.

The Titanic hit an iceberg at 11:40 P.M.

A band played.

Tonight on the Titanic	**Beginning** Jack and Annie find a small dog in the tree house. The dog is under a magic spell. It needs four gifts to be set free.
Middle	**Ending**

Adventure After Adventure
Identifying parts of a story, recalling facts

Students are never quite sure what's going to unfold as they read Magic Tree House mysteries, and the same is true for this nifty project. Have each child divide a sheet of paper into four quadrants, write the title of a recently read mystery in the top left quadrant, and then label the remaining sections as shown. After he describes each story part, he cuts along the fold lines. Then he stacks the cutouts in sequential order (title page on top) and staples the stack in the middle of a 9" x 12" sheet of green construction paper. He scallops the edges of the green paper, making a treetop shape. Then he decorates a 4½" x 6" rectangle of brown paper to resemble a tree house and staples it atop his stack of papers.

Next, give each child a 6" x 12" strip of brown paper for a tree trunk. Have him glue his treetop to the tree trunk. To make a ladder, the student writes facts he learned in the story on precut rectangles. He glues the rectangles on the tree trunk and uses a crayon to add rope details. Encourage each child to embellish the project to his liking.

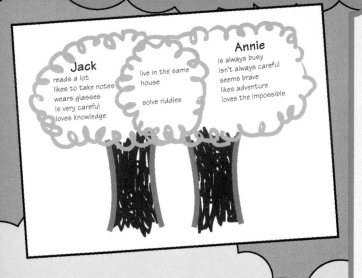

Jack and Annie
Analyzing main characters, supporting an interpretation

Take a team approach to investigating the characters of Jack and Annie! Ask the boys to learn about Jack's character including his likes and dislikes. Ask the girls to do the same for Annie. Allow time for students to read a few chapters from their books. Then invite members of each group to tell, and verify with evidence, what they have learned so far about the siblings. List the discoveries about each character on a separate sheet of chart paper labeled with that character's name. Then have students continue their investigations. When students finish the books they're reading, list any new information on the character charts. Next, have each student use the charts as she draws, labels, and programs a Venn diagram that compares and contrasts the two siblings. Be sure to demonstrate how to add treelike details to the projects!

In Search of Solutions
Identifying the problem and solution, making a prediction

Jack and Annie routinely set off on an adventure in search of a solution. This scenario creates a "tree-rific" opportunity for reinforcing story elements and thinking skills. Before a child begins a Magic Tree House mystery, have her stack two 7" x 12" pieces of paper, slide the top sheet upward about one inch, and then fold the papers forward to create four graduated layers. Staple the child's project near the center of the fold. Next, have her write the book title on the top layer and program the remaining layers "Problem," "My Prediction," and "Solution." Then instruct her to trim the project into a treetop shape and use crayons to add foliage details.

When the problem Jack and Annie face is described, the student explains it on her first booklet page. On the second booklet page, she predicts a solution and explains her thinking. Later, she describes the solution Jack and Annie discover and compares it with her prediction. Then she mounts her completed project at the top of a 9" x 12" sheet of brown construction paper. She trims the paper into a tree trunk and embellishes it as desired.

Jack and Annie must build a special kind of ship to find a special kind of magic.

Problem

My Prediction

Solution

Draw your favorite part of the story.

This picture shows _____

_____

_____

B

Book Title

Setting

Time: _____

Place: _____

Details About the Setting

_____
_____
_____
_____

• _____
• _____
• _____
• _____
• _____

Could this story be told in another setting? _____

Why or why not? _____

A

Note to the teacher: Use with "Tree House Travels" on page 172.

Julian's Stories

In Ann Cameron's delightful books *The Stories Julian Tells* and *More Stories Julian Tells,* readers pal around with two spunky brothers. The older brother, Julian, has a wild imagination that frequently leads to trouble. And most of the time his gullible little brother, Huey, tags right along! Use the following activities with either story collection (or both!).

ideas contributed by Julie Douglas, St. Louis, MO

I Wonder...
Establishing a purpose for reading

Titles can be great reading motivators. Before launching into one of Julian's tales, display the story's title and then write your students' questions about it. Next, circle one question and ask students to read (or listen to) the story for the purpose of answering that question. After discussing the answer to the circled question, ask students how they might find answers for the remaining questions *(recall details from the story, reread the story, look for clues in the pictures, apply personal experiences, and so on).* Challenge students to find the answers, reinforcing, when appropriate, that another resource may be needed.

"Because of Figs"

What happens because of figs?

What is a fig?

Is a fig an animal?

Do the brothers get in trouble because of figs?

Is a fig big or little?

Quite a Character!
Analyzing a character

Julian is quite a character, but then so is his father. To explore Julian's characteristics, first have students describe feelings Julian displays. Write the words on the board in a list titled "Feelings." Next, have students recall things that Julian does. Write these suggestions in a list titled "Actions." Then have each child use the format provided to compose a character poem about Julian. If time allows, have each child create a construction paper cutout that reminds him of Julian and display his edited poem on it.

Julian

Happy, hopeful, silly, sorry
Hides under the bed
Eats too many figs
Tricks his brother
Makes a new friend
He has lots of imagination!

Title:	Name of character
Line 1:	Three or more ways the character feels
Lines 2–5:	Four phrases that tell what the character does
Line 6:	A summarizing thought about the character

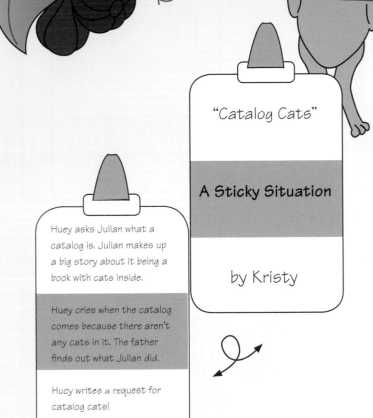

"Catalog Cats"

A Sticky Situation

by Kristy

Huey asks Julian what a catalog is. Julian makes up a big story about it being a book with cats inside.

Huey cries when the catalog comes because there aren't any cats in it. The father finds out what Julian did.

Huey writes a request for catalog cats!

Sticky Situations
Exploring cause and effect

Julian's talent for telling stories can sure land him in trouble! When students evaluate Julian's actions, they realize that it is his behaviors that get him into sticky situations. To make a paper glue bottle, have each child fold in half a 3" x 12" strip of colorful construction paper, sandwich a half sheet of white paper between the folded paper, and glue the construction paper to the white paper as shown. Next, have her trim off excess construction paper and round each corner of the white paper. Then have her fashion a bottle top from scrap paper and glue it in place.

Ask each child to select a Julian story—one in which Julian gets into mischief—and label her project with the story title, "A Sticky Situation," and her name. On the opposite side of her project, have her describe the sticky situation Julian gets into and what causes it, followed by the effect the situation has on Julian and/or others and how the situation is resolved. Lead students to conclude that when Julian finds himself in a heap of trouble, it's usually because of something he's done.

Here's What Happened...
Writing a personal story

Julian's tales describe ordinary events in an imaginative way, and that makes them wonderful writing inspiration. For a prewriting activity, give each child a copy of the writing rubric from page 178. Review the rubric. Then have students listen carefully for the characteristics listed as you read aloud a single-chapter Julian tale. Invite students to share what they learned. Next, give each child a copy of the story planner from page 178 and ask her to plan a personal story that describes an ordinary event in her life, such as walking the family pet, feeding a younger sibling, doing homework, or playing with a friend. When a child has her story planned, have her write a draft and use the rubric to evaluate it. Then have her complete the writing process as is customary in your classroom. Publish the students' final drafts in a class book titled "The Stories We Tell."

The
Stories
We
Tell

Writing Rubric and Story Planner

Use with "Here's What Happened…" on page 177.

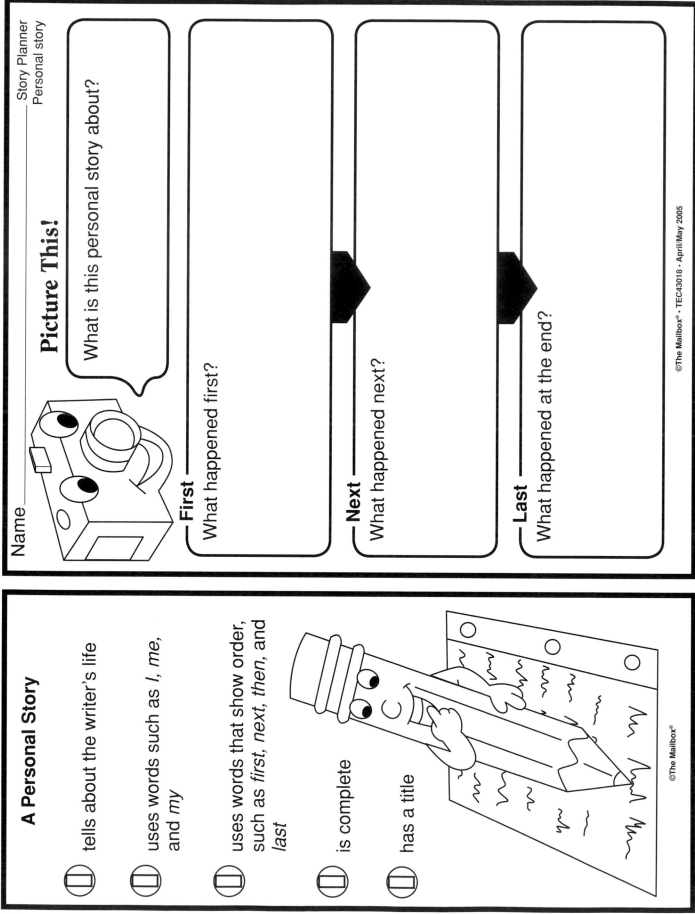

Story Planner
Personal story

Name _____

Picture This!

What is this personal story about?

First What happened first?

Next What happened next?

Last What happened at the end?

©The Mailbox® • TEC43018 • April/May 2005

A Personal Story

- ⊖ tells about the writer's life
- ⊖ uses words such as *I, me,* and *my*
- ⊖ uses words that show order, such as *first, next, then,* and *last*
- ⊖ is complete
- ⊖ has a title

©The Mailbox®

178

Ramona Quimby, Age 8

by Beverly Cleary

In this Newbery Honor book, Ramona is pleased as punch that she's eight years old and starting third grade. Now that she's old enough for her family to depend on, she's determined to not let them down—at least not if she can help it! Being a responsible eight-year-old isn't always easy for this spunky heroine, but that's not going to stop her. After all, she's Ramona Quimby, and she is eight years old!

ideas contributed by Julie Douglas, St. Louis, MO

First-Day Feelings
Using prior experiences to relate to a character

Like Ramona, your students have anticipated and experienced first days of school. At the end of chapter 1, invite students to share some first-day memories. List on the board feelings youngsters describe, such as excitement, nervousness, and hopefulness. Then ask volunteers to circle the feelings that could cause a tummy to quiver (like Ramona's).

Remind your students that new children enter their school all year long, and suggest that your class create a welcome display. Ask each child to describe in a sentence or two something she thinks a new enrollee would like to know about the school. Have her sign her writing and then turn it into a speech bubble by cutting around it. Next, provide time for each child to make a self-portrait. Mount each child's portrait and speech bubble together around the door to the school office. Even returning visitors are sure to enjoy this warm welcome!

You will love our library. It is packed with great books! Becky

Chapter by Chapter
Recalling story events, summarizing

Keeping up with Ramona and her family isn't easy. After all, their lives are anything but dull! To maximize your students' understanding of the story and nurture their summarizing skills, approach this task chapter by chapter. First, have each child make a summary sheet like the one shown that includes the book's title and author, a numbered 3 x 3 grid, and his name and the date. At the conclusion of each chapter, prompt students to recall the main events. Then provide time for each child to write a summary of the chapter in the corresponding space on his summary sheet.

Before each day's reading, ask a volunteer to use his summary sheet to recap the last reading. The sheet can also be used to help students who have been absent catch up with the Quimbys!

Ramona Quimby, Age 8
by Beverly Cleary

1	2	3
Ramona begins third grade. She almost gets in trouble, but she doesn't!	After school, Ramona has to play with Willa Jean. She hates it, but her family is counting on her.	
4	5	6
7	8	9

Leon Green   January 11, 2005

Desiree

| I do my homework. | I feed Missy the cat. |
| I make my bed. | I help with my little sister. |

Medal of Responsibility

Being Counted On
Making text-to-self connections

Ramona quickly discovers that being eight *and* being responsible is a lot of work! Have students recall ways in which Ramona's family depends on her. Then have students think about the ways in which their families count on them. To applaud their responsible actions, give each child a white construction paper copy of the medal on page 181. Instruct her to write her name in crayon or marker at the top of the medal. Then, in each remaining box, have her describe and illustrate one way she helps her family. When she has completed this part of the project, have her cut out the shape, glue the cutout onto colorful construction paper, and then trim the colorful paper to make a border. Press a strip of magnetic tape to the back of every project so students can proudly display their medals on their families' refrigerators.

Mrs. Quimby loves her family very much. She keeps the house neat and clean.
Mrs. Quimby

Mr. Quimby

Picky-picky

Beezus

Ramona

Introducing the Quimbys
Analyzing characters

Introductions, please! This booklet project prompts students to share what they know about each member of the Quimby family. To make the booklet shown, have each child stack three half-sheets of blank paper, fold the papers forward to create six graduated layers, and staple the stack near the fold. Instruct each child to title his booklet "Meet the Quimbys" and label one page for each family member, saving the last (and largest) page for Ramona. Then, on each page, have the child illustrate the family member who is named and write a brief introduction that tells what he likes most about this member of the family. Students may enjoy this project so much they'll ask to make booklets to introduce their families too!

Medal of
Responsibility

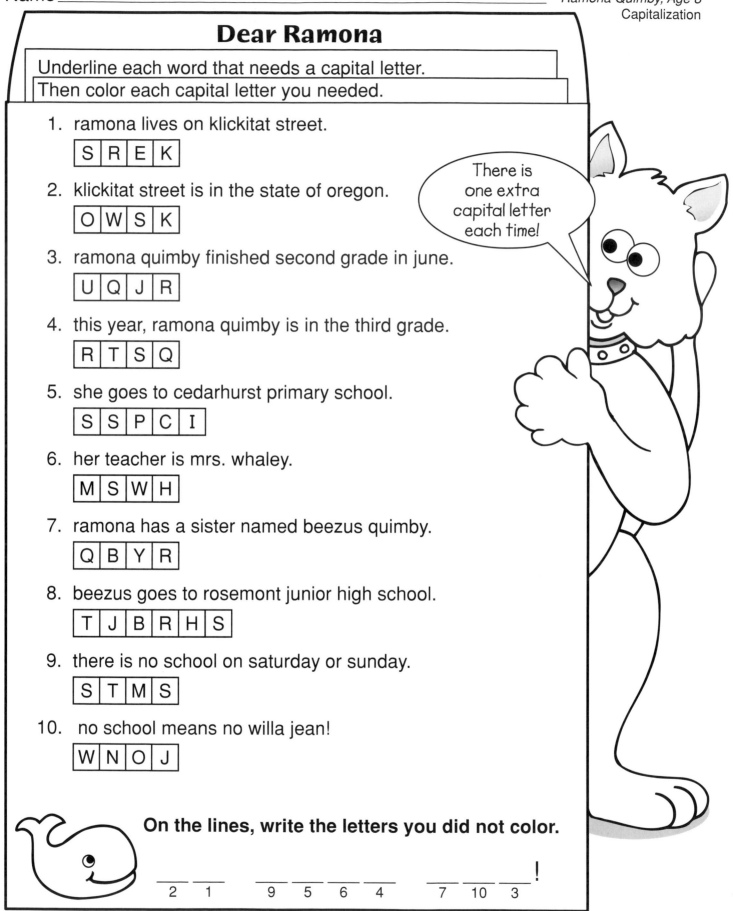

Dear Ramona

Underline each word that needs a capital letter.
Then color each capital letter you needed.

1. ramona lives on klickitat street.

   | S | R | E | K |

2. klickitat street is in the state of oregon.

   | O | W | S | K |

3. ramona quimby finished second grade in june.

   | U | Q | J | R |

4. this year, ramona quimby is in the third grade.

   | R | T | S | Q |

5. she goes to cedarhurst primary school.

   | S | S | P | C | I |

6. her teacher is mrs. whaley.

   | M | S | W | H |

7. ramona has a sister named beezus quimby.

   | Q | B | Y | R |

8. beezus goes to rosemont junior high school.

   | T | J | B | R | H | S |

9. there is no school on saturday or sunday.

   | S | T | M | S |

10. no school means no willa jean!

   | W | N | O | J |

There is one extra capital letter each time!

On the lines, write the letters you did not color.

___ ___   ___ ___ ___ ___   ___ ___ ___!
 2   1   9   5   6   4   7 10   3

MATH UNITS

From Place to Place
Activities to Reinforce Place-Value Skills

Use the following ideas to unpack students' understanding of place value!

ideas contributed by Laura Mihalenko, Holmdel, NJ

Bunches of Beans
Skill: counting sets of tens

This idea helps students feel right at home with place value! Give each child a cup containing 50 to 100 beans. Invite students to brainstorm ways to find the total number of beans without losing count. Suggest that they start by dividing the beans into groups of ten. After each child has done this, have him write the amount in place-value format. (For example, he might write "five tens and nine ones.") Tell him to count the beans by tens and ones to find the total. **For a greater challenge,** divide students into teams and tell them to combine their beans. Have them repeat the process to find the total, this time grouping sets of hundreds. Now that's an idea students can count on!

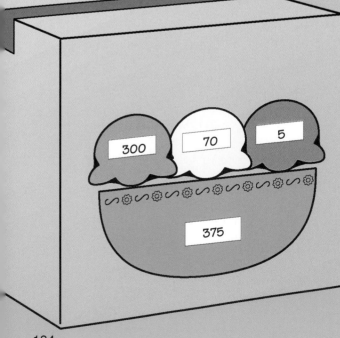

What's the Scoop?
Skill: identifying standard and expanded forms

This student-made center leads to cool and creamy practice with expanded form! Give each child one bowl pattern and three ice-cream scoop patterns (page 186). Tell the child to program his bowl with a three-digit number and then write the value of each digit on a different scoop. Have him color each cutout around the box. To make the set self-checking, instruct him to write the expanded form of the number on the back of the bowl. Check the cutouts for accuracy. Then place several sets of cutouts in a plastic resealable bag. Place the bags at a center.

A child removes the cutouts from a bag and places them faceup. He studies the number on each bowl and then positions the corresponding scoops above it. He flips the bowls to check his work. What a "scooper" review!

More or Less
Skill: interpreting place value

Students will have place-value skills covered when they use this hands-on strategy! Give each child three plastic chips and a copy of the grid on page 186. Have him divide a sheet of paper into three columns. To begin, describe a chosen three-digit number by naming each digit's value. (For example, 238 would be announced as two hundreds, three tens, and eight ones.) Have each child use his chips to cover the corresponding place values on his grid. Then ask him to write the resulting number in the middle column of his paper. Confirm the correct number.

Next, challenge each student to determine the number that is ten more than the designated number by moving one chip. Have him write the new number in the left column and then return the chip to its original grid space. In a similar manner, have him write in the right column the number that is ten less than the original number. Repeat this process with additional numbers as desired. **To vary the activity,** have students find numbers that are one hundred more and less than the originals.

Poppin' Place Value
Skill: interpreting place value

Here's a mouthwatering partner review of place value! Obtain popcorn in three different flavors. Give each student a small paper plate and a plastic resealable bag containing at least nine pieces of popcorn for each flavor. List the value of each flavor for student reference. Then pair students. In turn, have each partner use his popcorn pieces to represent a chosen number for his partner to identify. Conclude the activity by giving each child some fresh popcorn for munching!

Popcorn Place Values
Caramel = hundreds
Cheese = tens
Butter = ones

Pick a Place
Skill: comparing numbers

Challenge students to rise to the challenge of comparing numbers! For each of two teams, use blank cards to label a floor space with place values as shown. Place a set of numbered construction paper sheets (1–9) facedown beside each set of labels. Then divide students into two teams.

Next, tell each team that its goal is to make the largest possible three-digit number. To begin, one student from each team takes a number without revealing it to the remaining students. She stands in a chosen place-value position. Teams repeat this process until each one has formed a three-digit number. Then, on your signal, the standing members of each team reveal their digits. The remaining team members state the number. The team that formed the greater number receives a point for the round. Additional rounds continue in this manner. The top-scoring team at the end of the game wins!

hundreds   tens   ones

Grid
Use with "More or Less" on page 185.

	Hundreds	Tens	Ones
9			
8			
7			
6			
5			
4			
3			
2			
1			

Bowl and Scoop Patterns
Use with "What's the Scoop?" on page 184.

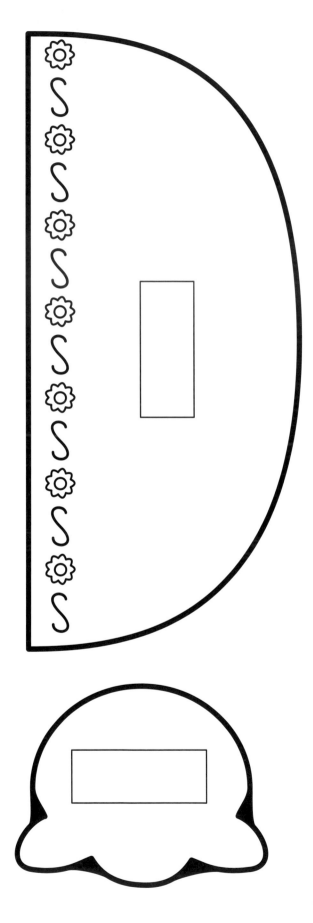

Time to Clean Up!

Count the blocks.
Write the number.
Write the matching
room.

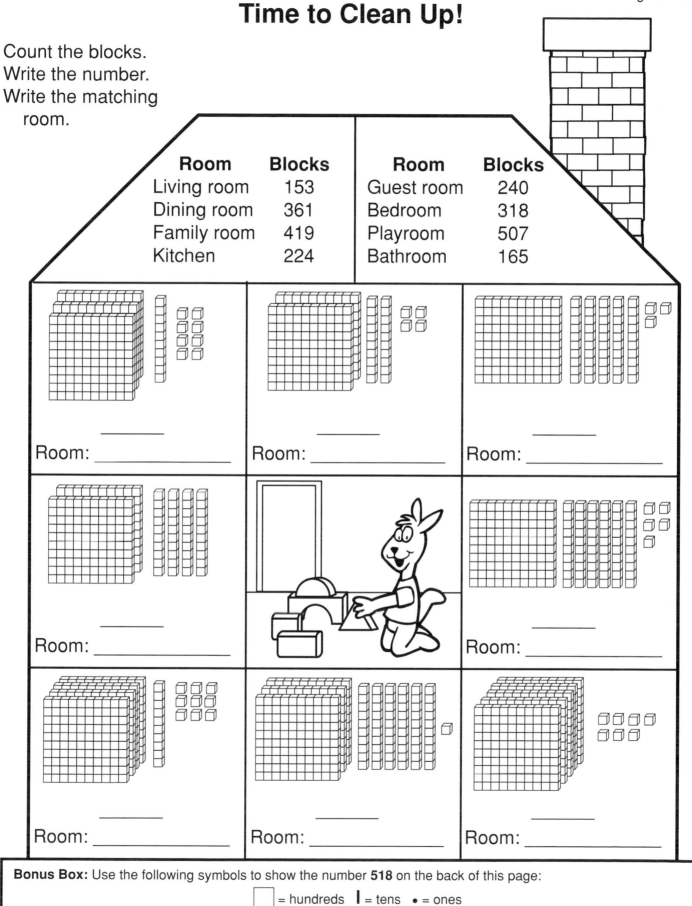

Room	Blocks	Room	Blocks
Living room	153	Guest room	240
Dining room	361	Bedroom	318
Family room	419	Playroom	507
Kitchen	224	Bathroom	165

_____
Room: _____

_____
Room: _____

_____
Room: _____

_____
Room: _____

_____
Room: _____

_____
Room: _____

_____
Room: _____

_____
Room: _____

Bonus Box: Use the following symbols to show the number **518** on the back of this page:

☐ = hundreds   **l** = tens   • = ones

Making Sense of Numbers

Bearboro Population: 51 bears

Bear Bungalow 22 miles

Looking to increase your youngsters' number sense? Of course you are! Check out these engaging activities, bearing in mind that providing fun experiences with numbers is a fantastic way to promote number sense!

ideas contributed by David A. Green—Gr. 3
North Shore Country Day School, Winnetka, IL

One More, One Less

Counting forward and backward by one

Number sense is in the cards during this small-group game. Divide students into groups of three, and give each group a deck of playing cards from which the tens and face cards have been removed. Explain that aces represent the digit 1. To play, one child in the group draws up to four cards from the deck. She arranges the cards in any order to make a number. Next, she reads the number for her opponents and says the numbers that are one more and one less. If her answers are correct (as confirmed by her opponents), she keeps the cards and her turn is over. If she makes a mistake, she returns the cards to the bottom of the deck. Players in the group rotate turns until no cards remain in the deck. The child with the most cards at the end of the game wins.

Team Scores

Grizzly Bears 13
Black Bears 20

124

Park closes at 11 P.M.

In the News

Identifying and reading whole numbers

Your mathematicians may be surprised by how many numbers are in the news! Give each child a highlighter (or crayon) and a newspaper page. Instruct him to scan the newspaper page for numbers and circle each one he finds. Challenge him to find five or more numbers, if possible. Next, have students describe the kinds of numbers they found, such as times, temperatures, team scores, prices, addresses, and ages. Add these headings to a display titled "Numbers in the News." Invite students to cut around the numbers they circled and the words that describe them and post each one under the corresponding category. Make sure students have numerous opportunities to read the display and make additions to it!

Build a Number

Reading whole numbers

Here's a perfect warm-up to any math lesson. Write a random digit on the board (or on a transparency) and ask students to read it. Next, write another random digit to the left of the previous one, and ask students to read the resulting number. Keep repeating the procedure until a number with a desired number of digits has been built. Wow! That's a big number!

Rebecca Heikes
Horizon School
Johnston, IA

3
73
273
4,273
54,273
254,273

Name the Symbol

Comparing numbers

Students stay on the edge of their seats during this large-group game! In advance, make a transparency of a page like the one shown. To begin play, display the transparency on an overhead projector, and divide the class into two teams. Alternate play between the teams. For each team's turn, write a different number to the left and to the right of the circle. Team members compare the numbers, ask you to add the greater than or less than symbol, and then read the number sentence aloud in unison. Next, one team member comes to the overhead and spins the spinner. (Provide a paper clip and a pencil for this purpose.) If the spinner stops on the sign used in the team's number sentence, the team earns one point. If it does not, no point is earned. The first team to earn ten points wins!

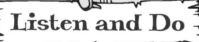

Listen and Do

Identifying, reading, and writing whole numbers

Give this large-group activity a different look each time you present it! Outline a simple shape (or photocopy a pattern) on 9" x 12" paper, write a set of numbers inside the outline, and then copy the programmed page to make a class supply plus one. Give students oral directions that ask them to complete a variety of number-related tasks like the ones provided. Simultaneously complete each task on your copy and you'll have a ready-to-use answer key!

A sampling of oral directions:
Find the number 4,231 and circle it.
X out the number 1,090.
Underline the number 2,099.
Find the number 399. Below it, write the number that is one more.
Draw a box around the largest number inside the shape.
Find the number 631. Draw a triangle around it.

Count On!

Counting forward and backward

Keep your students' counting skills in shape by giving them a workout every few days! Remove the tens and face cards from a deck of playing cards and explain that aces will represent the digit 1. Have two students each draw a card. Write the two digits on the board in the order they were drawn. Below the digits, write another two-digit number that is identified in the same manner. Have students determine whether they must count forward or backward to get from the starting number to the ending number. Then have students take turns counting in a large group, in small groups, or with partners. To increase the challenge, add a hundreds digit to each number before students determine the counting direction. Ready? Count!

Honey

7 5 4

754

745

574

547

475

457

Honey

Filling Orders

Identifying, writing, and ordering numbers

A student's number sense is sure to increase when she fills number orders. For an independent activity, display three different digits from 0 through 9. Have each child fold a 4½" x 12" strip of blank paper in half three consecutive times and then unfold her paper to show eight rectangles. Have her write her name in the first rectangle, copy the three numbers from the board in the second rectangle, and then circle each number with a crayon. To fill her number order, a student uses the three circled numbers to write six different numbers in the empty rectangles on her paper. Next, she cuts along the fold lines. She stacks the three-digit numbers in numerical order, places her name cutout on top of the stack, and staples the left edge of the resulting booklet. Suggest that each child take her booklet home and read the numbers she made to a family member.

For a more challenging class activity, display four different digits, and challenge students to identify the 24 four-digit numbers that can be made using them. Write the student-suggested numbers in a list. Then, for an independent task, have each child sequence the four-digit numbers on a sheet of paper.

Name ______________________________

Number Sense
Comparing two-digit numbers

Finding Cub Club

Compare the numbers.
Write > or < in the circle.

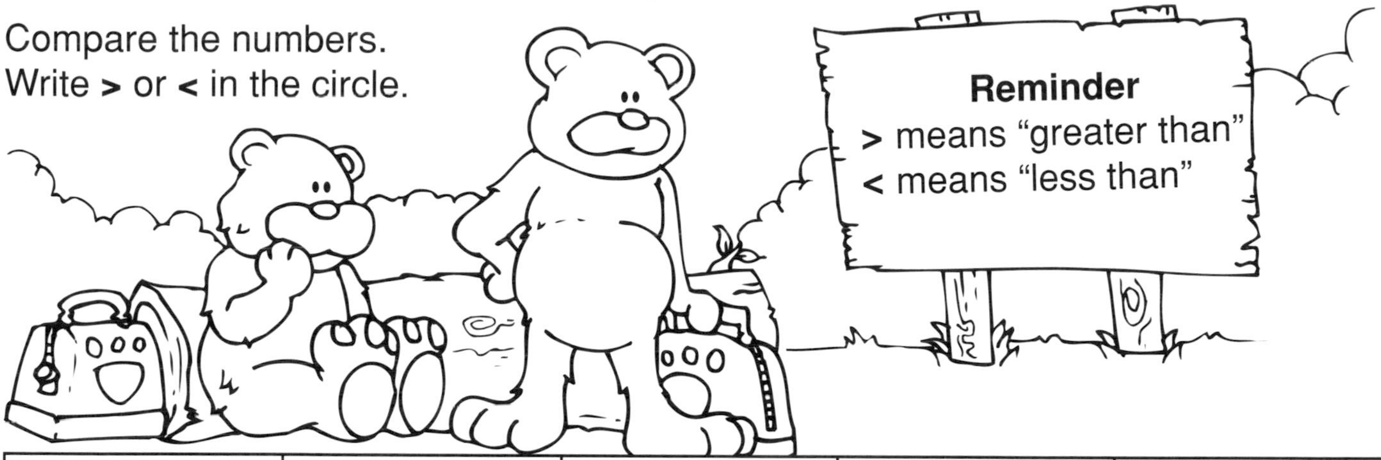
Reminder
> means "greater than"
< means "less than"

38 ◯ 25	41 ◯ 46	76 ◯ 72	19 ◯ 18	59 ◯ 49
27 ◯ 11	82 ◯ 88	92 ◯ 86	33 ◯ 35	74 ◯ 69
54 ◯ 50	75 ◯ 63	28 ◯ 21	91 ◯ 92	44 ◯ 28
90 ◯ 99	46 ◯ 49	71 ◯ 84	16 ◯ 61	32 ◯ 15
43 ◯ 62	33 ◯ 32	84 ◯ 58	13 ◯ 11	56 ◯ 23
17 ◯ 71	58 ◯ 47	23 ◯ 39	89 ◯ 98	29 ◯ 39
82 ◯ 97	64 ◯ 60	75 ◯ 59	57 ◯ 49	73 ◯ 65

Show the path the cubs took.
Color the boxes.
Use the color code.

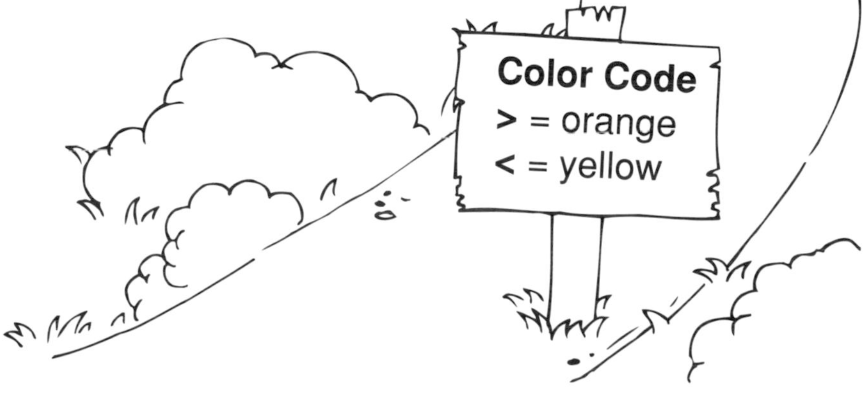
Color Code
> = orange
< = yellow

Rare Bears

Write each number.
Use a comma when one is needed.

nine hundred ninety-four **A**	one thousand, four hundred twenty **N**
one hundred fifty-five **T**	four thousand, six hundred twenty **R**
six hundred seventy-two **W**	eight hundred fifteen **C**
two thousand, two hundred ten **O**	two thousand, forty-seven **H**
one thousand, three hundred one **E**	nine thousand, eight hundred **A**
four hundred thirty-four **I**	four thousand, five hundred fifteen **U**
nine hundred thirty-five **G**	six hundred ninety-five **Y**

Solve the riddle.
Match the letters to the
numbered lines below.

What do you call bears that wear earplugs?

____ ____ ____ ____ ____ ____ ____ ____   ____ ____ ____   ____ ____ ____ ____ .
9,800 1,420 695 155 2,047 434 1,420 935   695 2,210 4,515   672 994 1,420 155

,

____ ____ ____ ____   ____ ____ ____ ____   ____ ____ ____ ____   ____ ____ ____ !
155 2,047 1,301 695   815 994 1,420 155   2,047 1,301 9,800 4,620   695 2,210 4,515

Name _____

Bears in Hiding

Numbers tell about many things.
Draw a line to connect each number to a phrase that describes it.

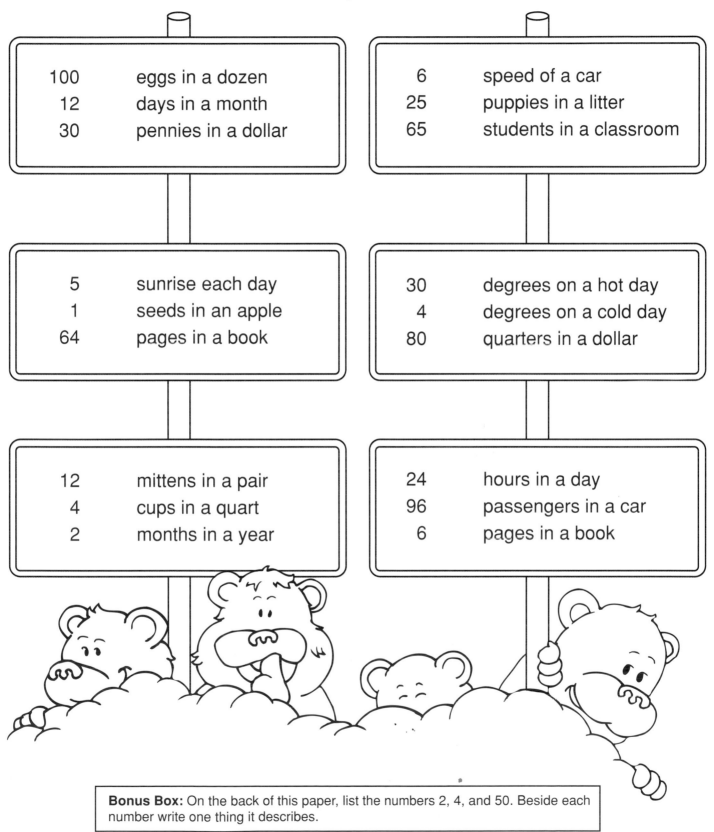

100	eggs in a dozen
12	days in a month
30	pennies in a dollar

6	speed of a car
25	puppies in a litter
65	students in a classroom

5	sunrise each day
1	seeds in an apple
64	pages in a book

30	degrees on a hot day
4	degrees on a cold day
80	quarters in a dollar

12	mittens in a pair
4	cups in a quart
2	months in a year

24	hours in a day
96	passengers in a car
6	pages in a book

Bonus Box: On the back of this paper, list the numbers 2, 4, and 50. Beside each number write one thing it describes.

To the Tune of Addition and Subtraction

Take note of these stellar suggestions—they're perfect for keeping students in tune with adding and subtracting larger numbers.

ideas contributed by Stacie Stone Davis
Lima, NY

One Hand Down!

Adding larger numbers

Fine-tuning addition skills is twice the fun with a partner! Prepare a gameboard for each child by writing five different two-digit numbers on a 9" x 12" sheet of construction paper. Laminate the gameboards (for repeated use) and hand them out. Then pair students, making sure each child has blank paper and a pencil.

To begin play, use the command "One hand down!" to signal each child to cover one number on her gameboard. Next, ask each student to show her partner the number she covered. Then have each partner write the two selected numbers on her paper in the form of an addition problem, solve the problem, and compare her sum to her partner's. If the sums match, each partner draws a star beside her sum. If the sums do not match, the partners recheck their calculations until they agree upon a sum. Use the command "One hand down!" to begin each new round of play. To keep interest high, occasionally invite students to switch gameboards and/or partners.

Additional playing options:
- **For practice adding three addends,** have students play in groups of three.
- **For practice subtracting,** ask partners to subtract the smaller number from the larger number.
- **For an individual activity,** ask each child to write and solve ten different addition (or subtraction) problems using the numbers on her gameboard.

Four Corners

Subtracting larger numbers, checking subtraction with addition

Add this stellar suggestion to your repertoire of independent activities. In advance, copy a hundred chart onto colorful paper, cut apart the numbered squares, and store the cutouts in a container. (If desired, discard the single-digit numbers.) Instruct each student to take four cutouts from the container and glue each number in a different corner of his paper. Next, challenge him to use the glued numbers to write six different subtraction problems, remembering to place the larger number in each pair on top. After he solves each problem, have him use addition to check his work. Now there's an activity that's sure to receive a standing ovation!

194

1,000 or Bust!

Adding and subtracting larger numbers

Strike up a chorus of computation and problem-solving practice using a deck of shuffled cards. Write "Teacher" and "Students" on the board and award each team 100 starting points. Tell students that the goal of the game is to be the first team (Teacher or Students) to earn 1,000 points!

To begin play, a student draws two cards from the deck and uses them to make a two-digit number. Clarify that an ace represents the numeral 1 and that a face card is wild and can be assigned any numeral from 0 through 9. Further explain that when both cards are the same color, the two-digit number is added to the team score. When the cards are different colors, the two-digit number must be subtracted from the team score. When the students agree that the best number for the corresponding operation has been made, write the number below their current team score. Allow time for the students to solve the problem on their math papers. Then update the team's score accordingly. Next, take your turn and invite students to check your calculations. Continue alternating turns as described. If 1,000 points is not reached by the end of math time, simply continue the game on another day. If a team loses all its points, the game is over.

COOL!

Students

$$
\begin{array}{r}
100 \\
+\ 86 \\
\hline
186 \\
-\ 15 \\
\hline
171 \\
+\ 94 \\
\hline
265
\end{array}
$$

?

Twinkle

46 99 ~~64~~ 10 27

$$
\begin{array}{r}
{}^{7}\cancel{8}{}^{13}\cancel{3} \\
-\ 19 \\
\hline
64
\end{array}
\qquad
\begin{array}{r}
{}^{5}\cancel{6}{}^{17}\cancel{7} \\
-\ 28 \\
\hline
39
\end{array}
$$

ROCK STAR

Five in a Row

Adding or subtracting larger numbers

An element of chance makes this computation practice especially engaging! On the board, randomly copy the answers from a page of computation practice. Ask each child to draw a long rectangle at the top of his math paper. Then have him use a crayon or marker to write five different answers (from the board) inside the rectangle.

Next, read aloud the first problem on the practice page and allow a set amount of time for students to write and solve the problem on their math papers. If the answer to the problem is listed in the rectangle at the top of the child's paper, he crosses it out. If it is not, he scans the board to be sure it is there. Repeat the procedure for each succeeding problem on the practice page. The first child to cross out all five answers in his rectangle declares, "Five in row!" If the child correctly verifies five problem-and-answer matches, computation practice for the class is over! If not, practice continues until a student achieves this goal. Tra la la!

Sing and Shine!

Add or subtract to solve each problem.
Show your work.

1.
Red sings 44 minutes.
Blue sings 23 minutes.
How many minutes do
they sing in all?

2.
Yellow knows 26 songs.
Green knows 12 songs.
How many more songs
does Yellow know?

3.
Blue has 16 hats.
Orange has 12 hats.
How many hats do they
have in all?

4.
Red claps 33 times.
Pink claps 56 times.
How many more times
does Pink clap?

5.
Orange knows 47 dances.
Yellow knows 25 dances.
How many more dances
does Orange know?

6.
Pink counts 54 full chairs.
Green counts 15 empty
chairs.
How many chairs in all?

7.
Red sings 20 minutes.
Yellow sings 37 minutes.
How many more minutes
does Yellow sing?

8.
Blue taps his foot 31 times.
Pink taps her foot 38 times.
How many taps in all?

Name_____

Addition and Subtraction
With and without regrouping

Stars on Stage

Write an addition and a subtraction problem in each box.
Use the numbers in the circles.
The answers in each box must match.

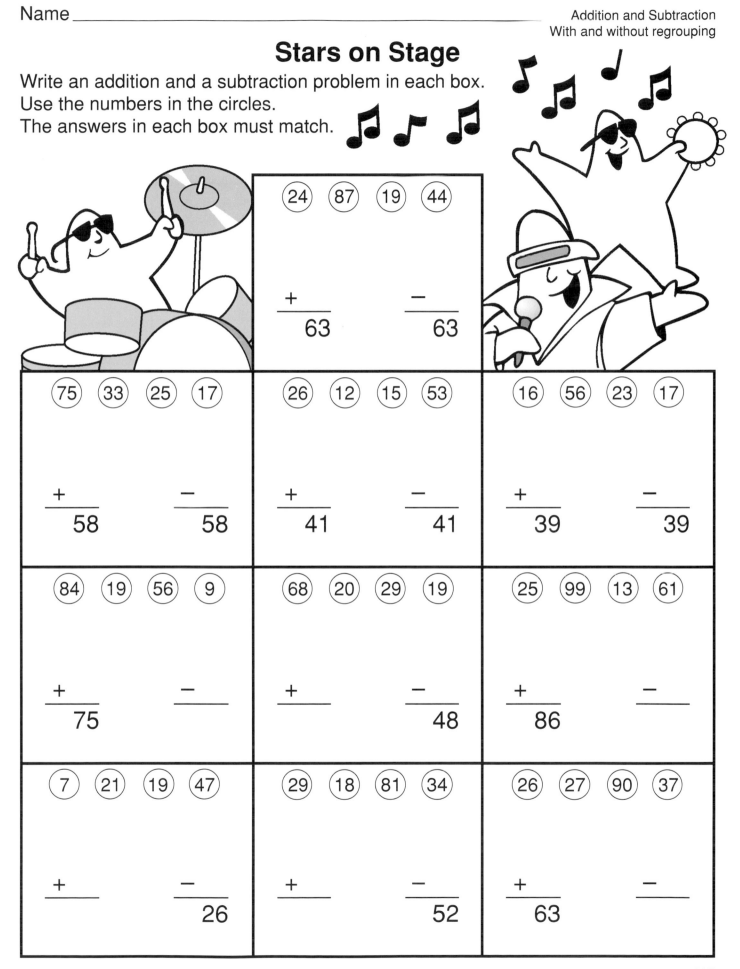

(24) (87) (19) (44)

$+$ _____ $-$ _____
63   63

(75) (33) (25) (17)

$+$ _____ $-$ _____
58   58

(26) (12) (15) (53)

$+$ _____ $-$ _____
41   41

(16) (56) (23) (17)

$+$ _____ $-$ _____
39   39

(84) (19) (56) (9)

$+$ _____ $-$ _____
75

(68) (20) (29) (19)

$+$ _____ $-$ _____
              48

(25) (99) (13) (61)

$+$ _____ $-$ _____
86

(7) (21) (19) (47)

$+$ _____ $-$ _____
              26

(29) (18) (81) (34)

$+$ _____ $-$ _____
              52

(26) (27) (90) (37)

$+$ _____ $-$ _____
63

CA$H ONLY!

When it's time to reinforce your students' money skills, there's no room for bank cards, credit cards, or checks. It's strictly cash on the table—or something that closely resembles cash! Invest in these ideas and reproducibles and quickly turn a profit on your time and your students' understanding of money!

ideas contributed by David A. Green, North Shore Country Day School, Winnetka, IL

COUNT AND COMPARE
Counting coins, comparing amounts of money

Counting money is so much fun! For this partner center gather eight empty 35 mm film canisters with lids. Secure an assortment of real or plastic coins inside each one and then place the canisters and copies of the recording sheet on page 200 at a center. Each partner chooses a canister and records its cash value. He also confirms and records the value of his partner's coin set. Then together the classmates determine and record which set has the greater value and the sum of the two coin sets. The coins are then returned to the canisters and the process is repeated with two different canisters of coins. When all eight coin sets are counted, the center is completed.

To encourage return visits to the center, redistribute the coins in the canisters every few days.

Quick Coin Sets

Cash in on these quick and easy coin sets! Copy the coin patterns on page 200 to make a class supply. Ask each student to color a set of coins and then have her cut out the coins and store them in a personalized envelope. What a deal!

TRADE ONE
Making equivalent coin sets

You can bank on this activity to expand your students' understanding of coin equivalencies. Make available an assortment of coin manipulatives or have students use personalized coin sets. (See "Quick Coin Sets" on this page.) First, have each child fold a sheet of blank paper in half lengthwise and then repeat the fold two more times. After she unfolds the paper, instruct her to title the top row "25¢" and in the second row trace a quarter, labeling the tracing "25¢." Or she can label the tracings of two dimes and one nickel. For each succeeding row, she trades one coin for an equivalent coin set. She traces each new coin set, labels her tracings, and verifies that the set's value equals 25 cents. If desired, have students use crayon lines to separate their coin sets. This is especially helpful when a set expands beyond a single row. Hey, let's try 50 cents!

SALE SHOPPING
Identifying coins needed for specific purchases

This spontaneous shopping spree is full of surprises! Cut individual items from pharmacy and grocery store flyers, making sure each cutout includes a single item price. Store the cutouts in a container. Each child pulls out three cutouts. He glues each one on his paper and beside it draws and labels the coins (and bills) he needs to make the purchase. Potato chips, hair gel, and a notebook—what a shopping spree!

...43, 44, 45, 50, 75...

CHANGE IS GOOD
Making change by counting on

Sometimes a picture is worth a thousand words. During this large-group activity, a picture means change is due. Cut out pictures of catalog merchandise and glue each picture to an index card. Label each card with a purchase price less than 75 cents. Prepare one card for every two students. Then pair students, making sure each twosome has access to a coin supply such as the one described in "Quick Coin Sets" on page 198. One partner uses a pretend dollar bill to make the purchase and one partner calculates the change due by counting on. Then, upon a signal from you, each pair hands its card to the right. The partners switch roles and repeat the activity. Continue until each partner has had several chances to make change. For additional practice, have students complete the activity on page 201. Count on!

Jessie Chun, PS 88 The Seneca School, Ridgewood, NY

TAG SALE
Estimating and computing costs

Reinforce everyday money skills with a faux tag sale. For quick and easy preparation, purchase a pack of string tags (available at office supply stores). Have each child personalize a tag and select an item from his desk to "sell." Then have him label his tag with the name of the item and his asking price. Establish a price range, if desired. Next, have each child tag his item and display it atop his desk. Open the sale by appointing a "buyer" to choose three items and bring them to the board. Post the price of each item. Then challenge students to estimate the total cost by rounding the individual prices and then adding them together. After writing a sampling of student estimates on the board, engage students in calculating the total cost, evaluating the estimates, and brainstorming strategies for improved estimates. Continue the process described until all items are purchased. Then return the goods to their original owners and plan to repeat the sale on another day!

Coin Patterns

Use with "Quick Coin Sets" on page 198 and "Remember Your Change!" on page 201.

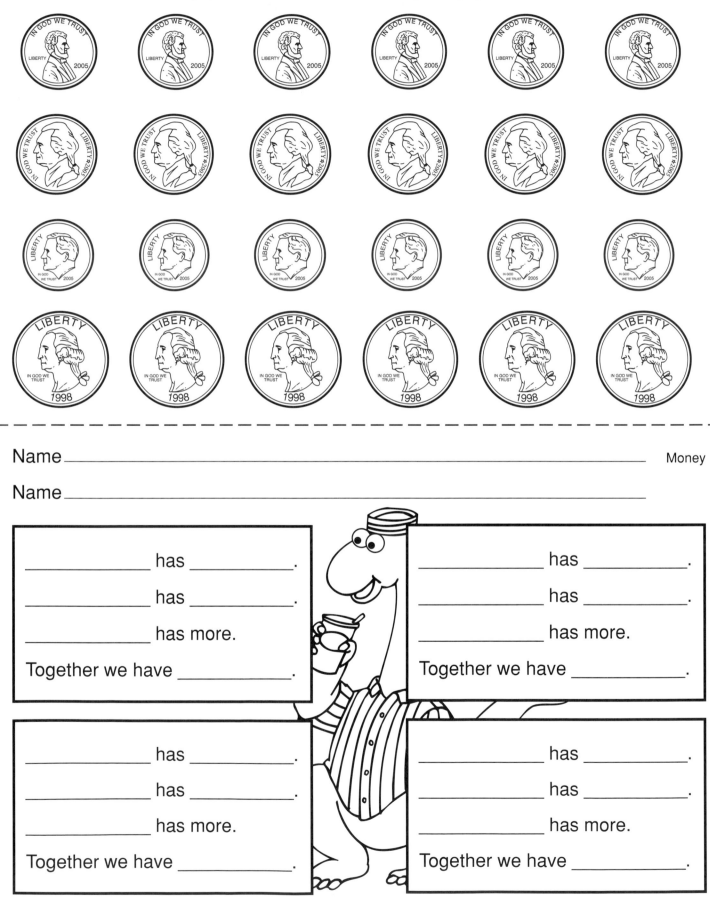

Name _____ Money

Name _____

_____ has _____ .

_____ has _____ .

_____ has more.

Together we have _____ .

_____ has _____ .

_____ has _____ .

_____ has more.

Together we have _____ .

_____ has _____ .

_____ has _____ .

_____ has more.

Together we have _____ .

_____ has _____ .

_____ has _____ .

_____ has more.

Together we have _____ .

Name_____

REMEMBER YOUR CHANGE!

Count on to find the change due from $1.00.
Glue a coin on each ●.
Write the amounts.
The first one has been started for you.

When you finish, count the coins you have left. You should have 56¢!

DINO POP $0.78	● $0.79	● $0.80	● _____	● $1.00
Fossil Fizz $0.60	●	●	● _____ $1.00	
Fern Juice $0.93	●	●	● _____ $1.00	
Fruity Spikes $0.45	●	●	● _____ $1.00	
$0.34	●	●	●	● ● _____ $1.00

Note to the teacher: To complete this page a child will need a copy of the coin patterns on page 200.

201

Get Rolling With Computation!

What teacher doesn't need a few extra ideas for jazzing up computation practice? Roll out these games and activities and watch your students' interest in adding, subtracting, and multiplying skyrocket. Dice and computation practice—now that's a winning combination!

ideas by David A. Green, North Shore Country Day School, Winnetka, IL

Sum It Up!

Two-digit addition with regrouping

Students who add together learn together! For this partner activity, students alternate rolling a die until together they have rolled four different numbers and written each number at the top of both of their papers (see the illustration). Then each child uses the four numbers to write and solve 12 different two-digit addition problems. When both partners finish the task, the students compare their calculations. If any sums differ, they work together to find and make each needed correction. Addition is awesome!

Alec

| 1 | 5 | 2 | 6 |

15	15
+ 26	+ 62
41	77

J. T.

| 1 | 5 | 2 | 6 |

62	62	25
+ 51	+ 15	+ 61
113	77	86

Tara

III

0
+ 41
41
+ 23
64
+ 33
97

Ten Rolls

Three-digit addition with regrouping

You can sum up this partner game in one word—fun! The object of the game is to be the player who, after rolling two dice a total of ten times, has the sum closer to 300. To begin play, each partner draws a rectangle at the top of her paper in which to tally her dice rolls and writes "0" below it for her current sum. Then, alternating turns, the players roll the dice. Each player uses the numbers she rolls to form a two-digit number (for example, 32 or 23 from a roll of 2 and 3). Then she announces her number and writes it on her paper so that she can add it to her current sum. When she announces her new sum, her partner may take his turn. When the tenth round is complete, the partners evaluate their sums and determine who is closer to 300. Being close counts in this game!

Quick Drop
Two-digit subtraction with regrouping

Two or more youngsters can drop in to play this exciting subtraction game. A group needs two dice. The object of the game is to have the score closest to, but not below, zero. What's the catch? Each player begins with only 99 points! Players alternate rolling the dice in an established order for three turns each. After each roll, a player announces the points he will use for the roll (for example, 42 or 24), then he subtracts the points from his score. An opponent must verify his subtraction before play continues. If a player's score goes below zero, he is no longer in the game; however, he can continue to check the subtraction of others. Quick drop!

Max

$$
\begin{array}{r}
99 \\
-26 \\
\hline
73 \\
-44 \\
\hline
29 \\
-13 \\
\hline
16
\end{array}
$$

Secret Numbers
Checking addition with subtraction

It takes two partners, Agent Add and Agent Subtract, to make a list of secret numbers. To begin, each agent rolls a different die. Then the two partners combine their rolls to make a two-digit starting number. Each agent writes the number on her paper. Next, Agent Add privately adds a secret number from ten to 99 to her starting number. She passes the sum of the two numbers to Agent Subtract, who subtracts the starting number from the sum. Agent Subtract then shares her difference with Agent Add. If the difference is Agent Add's secret number, the number becomes the first number on the agents' list of secret numbers. Instruct each pair of agents to collect five secret numbers and then switch roles and collect five more. Shhh! It's a secret!

Secret
Numbers

54
61

Agent Add

$$
\begin{array}{r}
45 \\
+54 \\
\hline
99
\end{array}
\qquad
\begin{array}{r}
45 \\
+61 \\
\hline
106
\end{array}
$$

Agent Subtract

$$
\begin{array}{r}
99 \\
-45 \\
\hline
\star\,54
\end{array}
\qquad
\begin{array}{r}
106 \\
-45 \\
\hline
\star\,61
\end{array}
$$

Roll 'em!
Computation

Whether your youngsters need extra practice adding, subtracting, multiplying, or dividing, this partner game delivers it in style! In advance, make a copy of page 205. Program the page with 11 computation problems; then make one copy of the page for every two students. Pair students and give each pair two dice and a copy of the page. Or put two dice and the prepared pages at your math center. Students alternate taking turns until all 11 problems are solved. Roll 'em!

Roll 'Em!

Dice Math Game for Two
Computation

Score Box	Score Box
IIII	╫╫
Player 1 Hope	Player 2 Sarah

To take a turn
1. Roll two dice and say the sum.
2. Solve the math problem in the matching box.
   (If the problem is already solved, your turn is over.)
3. Have your partner check your work.
4. If your answer is correct, draw two tally marks in your score box.
   If not, rework the problem with your partner.
   Draw one tally mark in each score box.

	2	3	4
	$\begin{array}{r}621\\-410\\\hline 211\end{array}$	$\begin{array}{r}587\\-432\\\hline\end{array}$	$\begin{array}{r}291\\-151\\\hline 140\end{array}$
5	6	7	8
$\begin{array}{r}488\\-214\\\hline\end{array}$	$\begin{array}{r}989\\-685\\\hline 304\end{array}$	$\begin{array}{r}897\\-597\\\hline 300\end{array}$	$\begin{array}{r}753\\-110\\\hline\end{array}$
9	10	11	12
$\begin{array}{r}695\\-510\\\hline\end{array}$	$\begin{array}{r}365\\-122\\\hline 243\end{array}$	$\begin{array}{r}488\\-214\\\hline\end{array}$	$\begin{array}{r}939\\-533\\\hline\end{array}$

Cross Out!
Multiplication facts 1–6

This large-group dice game gives multiplication practice an exciting twist! Display a transparency of a multiplication table from 1 x 1 through 6 x 6 like the one shown. Have each child draw a ten-box grid near the bottom of his paper and then, in each box, use a crayon to write a different product from the fact table. To play, roll two dice on a child's desktop and ask him to name the factors rolled. Instruct students to multiply the factors at the top of their papers and then, if the resulting product is on their grids, cross it off. Continue play in this manner, rolling the dice on the desktops of different students. When a player has crossed off every product on his grid, he declares, "Cross out!" Then enlist your students' help in verifying his claim.

For a center activity, provide blank paper, two dice, and a copy of the multiplication table. Students prepare their grids and play in the manner described, except the players take turns rolling the dice.

X	1	2	3	4	5	6
1	1	2	3	4	5	6
2	2	4	6	8	10	12
3	3	6	9	12	15	18
4	4	8	12	16	20	24
5	5	10	15	20	25	30
6	6	12	18	24	30	36

Cole

$$\begin{array}{r} 5 \\ \times 2 \\ \hline 10 \end{array} \quad \begin{array}{r} 3 \\ \times 1 \\ \hline 3 \end{array} \quad \begin{array}{r} 4 \\ \times 6 \\ \hline 24 \end{array} \quad \begin{array}{r} 1 \\ \times 1 \\ \hline 1 \end{array}$$

X̶	12	20	30	X̶
2	15	18	4	9

Math is fun!

It sure is!

"Sum" Products
Multiplication facts 2–12

Roll out this partner game for your multiplication aficionados! Place four dice, a multiplication table through 12 x 12, scrap paper, and 20 counters at a center. To begin play, each partner rolls two dice and finds the sum of her rolled numbers. Next, the partners combine their sums to make a multiplication fact. The player who contributes the larger sum earns the chance to answer the multiplication fact. If her answer matches what is on the multiplication table, she earns one counter. If her answer does not, her turn is over. The game continues in this manner until one partner earns ten counters. Your students' fact knowledge is sure to multiply!

Player Monica
Player Nigel

Dice Math Game for Two
Basic Facts

Four in a Row

To take a turn
1. Roll two dice.
2. Add, subtract, multiply, or divide the numbers on the dice.
3. Find a matching box and color it. (If there is no matching box, your turn is over.)
4. If the box you color touches an uncolored , color it!

	18	8	20	12	5
4	9	2	0	36	
30	1	10		4	16
15	25	12	11	3	24
0		5	6	2	7

Four in a Row
Basic facts

This partner game reviews basic math facts and promotes strategic thinking. Make one copy of page 206 for every two students. Pair students and give each pair two dice and a copy of the page. Each partner also needs a different-colored crayon. Students alternate taking turns until one player has four in a row.

If students are not yet multiplying and dividing, white out any number larger than 12 on a copy of page 206 and change the second direction to allow only addition or subtraction. Program each empty box with a number 12 or lower and then make a desired number of copies.

Roll 'Em!

<table>
<tr><td>**Score Box**

Player 1 _____</td><td>**Score Box**

Player 2 _____</td></tr>
</table>

To take a turn

1. Roll two dice and say the sum.
2. Solve the math problem in the matching box.
   (If the problem is already solved, your turn is over.)
3. Have your partner check your work.
4. If your answer is correct, draw two tally marks in your score box.
   If not, rework the problem with your partner.
   Draw one tally mark in each score box.

2	3	4
5	6	7	8
9	10	11	12

Four in a Row

To take a turn

1. Roll two dice.
2. Add, subtract, multiply, or divide the numbers on the dice.
3. Find a matching box and color it. (If there is no matching box, your turn is over.)
4. If the box you color touches an uncolored , color it!

	18	8	20	12	5
4	9	2	0	36	
30	1	10		4	16
15	25	12	11	3	24
0		5	6	2	7

Note to the teacher: Use with "Four in a Row" on page 204. Each student pair needs two dice, two crayons (different colors), and one copy of this page.

Building Measurement Success

Check out this blueprint for reinforcing customary and metric units while measuring length and perimeter! You'll find activities for individuals, partners, and groups. There's even a homework project! So grab an assortment of measurement tools and start measuring!

Laura Wagner, Raleigh, NC

For Good Measure
Reinforcing linear measurement

A measurement task each day keeps a student's skills as sharp as a tack! Each morning assign students a task (see the suggestions shown). Then, at a designated time, invite students to share their measurement solutions. To encourage a variety of answers, award one tally point for every unique answer. On days that the class earns a specified number of tally points, award one letter toward the spelling of a measurement term such as *inches* or *centimeters*. When the measurement word is spelled, award the class ten minutes of free time.

Name three classroom items that have a combined length of 16 inches.

- Name a classroom item that is five inches long and another that is five centimeters long.
- Name three classroom items that have a combined length of one meter.
- Name two objects, one of which is three inches longer than the other.

Mile			Yard	
	hiking trail		football field	driveway
				school track
river		ocean	parking lot	
	highway			

Inch		
	CD	key
		eraser
chalk	worm	

Foot		
pillow		
	window	chair
		arm

Tooling Up
Naming uses for specific measurement tools

Build a foundation of vocabulary and critical-thinking skills during this group project. For a review of inches, feet, yards, and miles, divide the class into groups of four and have each group member title a grid like the one shown for a different measurement unit. Explain that each group's goal is to fill every space on each grid with an appropriate item for that unit of measure. For example, a crayon is a suitable item for measuring in inches, but it is not suitable for measuring in feet, yards, or miles. Then allot one minute for each child to work on the grid she titled. Next, direct group members to rotate their cards to the right. Allot another minute for grid work before asking group members to rotate the cards again. Continue this process until each group member has worked on every grid. Then provide time for group members to review the grids and collaborate on any empty spaces. Encourage plenty of thinking out loud as group members work together and as teams share their work with the class.

To reinforce the metric units of centimeter and meter, pair students and follow a similar procedure.

A Mixed Bag
Estimating and measuring length

The only one who knows what's really in this bag isn't telling! (That would be you!) Select several lightweight items that can be stored inside a large paper bag with handles. Measure each item and write its length on a blank card. Then, on each of two or more blank cards, write a random measurement. Place the cards in an envelope and place the items, the envelope, and a measurement tool (such as a ruler or tape measure) in the bag. A student takes the bag to a desired classroom location and empties it. He estimates the length of each item. Next, he matches a card to each item based on its estimated length. Then he uses the measurement tool to check his work. Change the bag's contents frequently or create additional bags. Hey, these measurements are metric!

Room by Room
Choosing appropriate measurement tools

Making a house call is all in a day's work for a measurement inspector! Officially proclaim your students to be measurement inspectors and give each child three sheets of blank paper to stack and fold in half. Staple each inspector's resulting booklet near the fold. Then have her write "Measurement Inspector" on the front cover and add a self-illustration and her name. To ready each booklet page, she draws an oval near the center and then divides the page into quadrants.

A child takes her booklet home and, after receiving a parent's permission, she proceeds to inspect each of four different rooms for a variety of measurements. She completes one booklet page per room. To do this, she writes the name of the room in the oval. In each quadrant she writes a different item she will measure along with the unit of measure she will use. Then she completes the measurement task and records the outcome. Most likely this homework assignment will be completed and returned with a smile!

Students may also complete the project at school by measuring items in the lunchroom, library, school office, and so on.

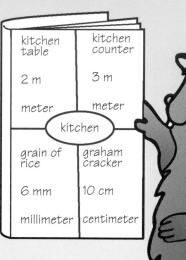

kitchen table	kitchen counter
2 m	3 m
meter	meter
kitchen	
grain of rice	graham cracker
6 mm	10 cm
millimeter	centimeter

One Time Around
Measuring perimeter of plane figures

Partners who enter this construction zone practice measuring perimeter! Use a paper cutter to cut a variety of straight-edged shapes from construction paper scraps. Cut the shapes on the inch unless your students have practice adding fractions. Each partner chooses two or three shapes. He measures and labels each straight edge of a shape and then tallies the measurements and writes the perimeter near the center of the shape. Next, the partners combine their shapes to form one single shape and glue the shape on provided paper. Then they work together to determine the perimeter of the new shape. Very fun!

Perimeter = 46 inches

Name_____

Daily Delivery

Read the packing list.
Write each item on the chart.
Choose the length that best describes the item.

one inch	one foot	one yard

Packing List

nail	hammer	umbrella
paintbrush	shovel	ladder
paper clip	safety pin	broom
lunchbox	ruler	button
screwdriver	thumbtack	mop
bucket	key	rug

Busy Beaver Hardware

For "Chew-sy" Shoppers

Math Is in the Air!

A Fresh Collection of Springtime Activities

This year when spring sweeps in and awakens wintertime sleepers and spurs new growth, count on these teacher-tested activities to reenergize your youngsters' enthusiasm for math. Each activity reinforces a core math skill and is guaranteed to put a little spring in your required curriculum!

ideas contributed by David A. Green, North Shore Country Day School, Winnetka, IL

A High-Flying Affair
Fact families

The sky's the limit for this review of addition and subtraction (or multiplication and division). On the board, write 12 numbers that can be used to create four different fact families. Ask each child to make a kite shape by cutting the corners from a colorful quarter sheet of construction paper and drawing lines on the cutout as shown. Have her repeat the process with a second piece of construction paper. Then, using the numbers on the board, she writes in each top section of each kite three numbers of a different fact family. In the section directly below the number set, she writes the related addition and subtraction facts. Then she incorporates her high-flying fact kites into a springtime scene.

Cleaning Up 100s
Estimation, two-digit addition

Like most spring cleaning, this activity involves "sum" elbow grease! Near the top of the board, write and circle the number 100. Then program the board with several pairs of addends that equal 100, making sure to separate the addends in each pair. Next, invite a child to read two numbers from the board that he thinks have a sum of 100. Ask each student to write the addition problem on his own paper and solve it. If the sum of the problem is 100, the student who chose the numbers erases them from the board. If not, the numbers remain. Continue the process until every number pair is wiped clean! The next time you plan a similar cleaning spree, consider using a sum that's another multiple of 100.

210

What's the Likelihood?

Probability

Hatch this review of probability terms, and a nifty springtime display is certain! Use lengths of yarn to divide a bulletin board into four sections and then add four nest cutouts and the probability terms shown below. Also prepare a title strip and a class supply of large egg patterns. Ask each child to describe on an egg pattern an activity she especially enjoys. Then have her illustrate herself engaged in the activity. Next, have each child share her project with the class and enlist her classmates' help in deciding whether it is *certain, likely, not likely,* or *impossible* that the activity she described can be enjoyed in spring. Post each egg in the appropriate nest and add the title to complete the display. For another "eggs-traordinary" review of probability terms, title the display for a different season and engage the students in reorganizing the eggs!

Blooms and Buddies

Multiplication

Cultivate a bouquet of fact recall at this center for two. Make several colorful construction paper copies of the flower and flower center patterns on page 213. For a review of multiplication, program each flower center for a different factor, cut it out, and glue it to a flower of a different color. Then laminate the flowers, cut them out, and punch a series of holes around each one where indicated. Next, program the back of each flower for self-checking. To do this, label each hole with the product that corresponds to the programming on the front. Then place the flowers and pencils (or coffee stirrers) at a center.

Partners sit facing each other. Then, in turn, each child puts his pencil in a hole in his cutout, reads aloud the corresponding problem, and answers it. His partner, who is looking at the back of the cutout, gives a thumbs-up for a correct answer or a thumbs-down for an incorrect one. Partners continue in this manner until each has completed a desired number of blooms.

Gear Up!
Number sense

Pump up number skills and promote bike safety! Use the pattern on page 213 to make a class supply of construction paper bike helmets. Program each pattern with a different three-digit number and then laminate the patterns and cut them out. Periodically, hand out the bike helmets and direct students to perform number-related tasks. For example, have students line up numerically from the smallest number to the largest. Or have students use their numbers to form different groups, such as even numbers and odd numbers or numbers with five or more tens and numbers with less than five tens. Or challenge groups of four to use the numbers on their cutouts to make and solve different addition (subtraction) problems. There "wheelie" are a lot of possibilities!

Having a Ball!
Telling time

A review of A.M. and P.M. fits nicely into this time-telling activity. Have each child decorate both sides of a six-inch construction paper circle to resemble a soccer ball or baseball. Next, have her cut out six copies of the booklet page on page 213, stack the pages, and staple the stack atop her decorated cutout. Remind students that the idiom "having a ball" is an expression of fun. Challenge each child to record in her booklet over the next few days six different times that she has fun. To do this she writes the day and the time and circles A.M. or P.M. Then she draws hands on the clock and describes what she was doing at that time. On a predetermined day, provide time for each child to share her booklet with a partner. Time sure flies when you're having a ball!

Pool Designers
Area

The guess-and-check strategy comes in handy during this measurement activity! Hand out individual copies of centimeter paper and remind students that the arrival of spring means summer isn't far away. Then challenge each child to design several different pool shapes on his paper, making sure that the area of each pool is exactly 30 square centimeters. Invite students to color and name their pool designs too. How refreshing!

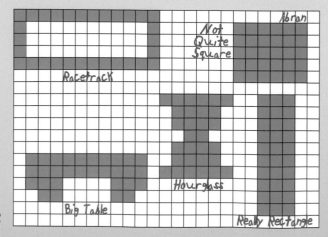

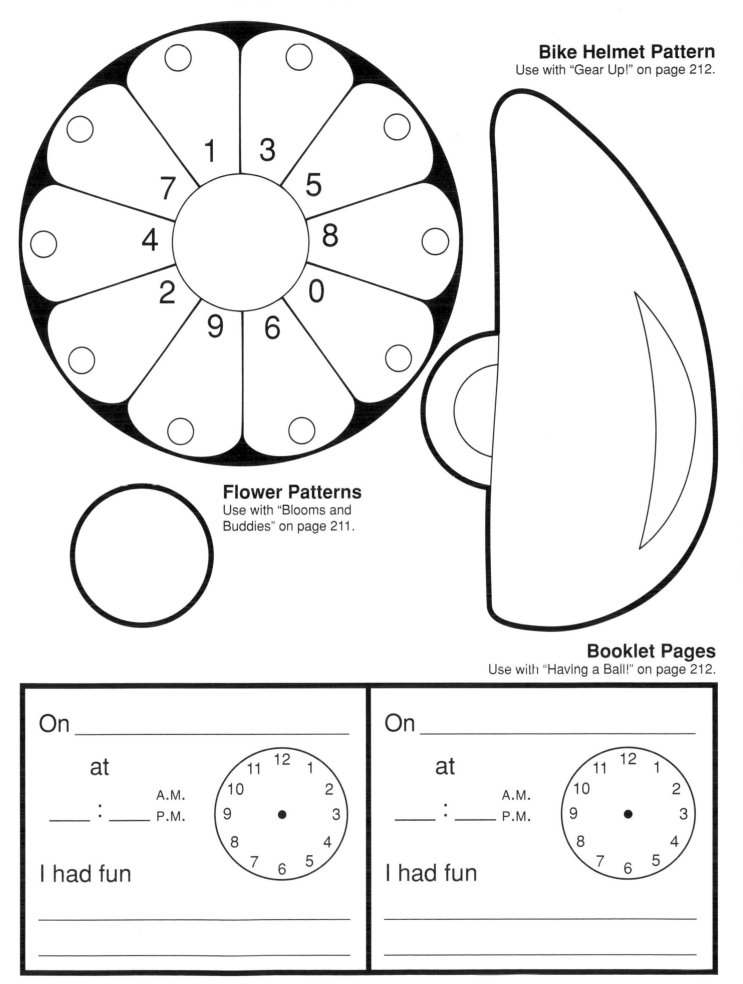

Bike Helmet Pattern
Use with "Gear Up!" on page 212.

Flower Patterns
Use with "Blooms and Buddies" on page 211.

Booklet Pages
Use with "Having a Ball!" on page 212.

On _____

at

____ : ____ A.M.
         P.M.

I had fun

_____
_____

On _____

at

____ : ____ A.M.
         P.M.

I had fun

_____
_____

Spring Training

To fill in the chart below, measure the length of
each hit to the nearest half inch.
Use the code to change each distance into feet.

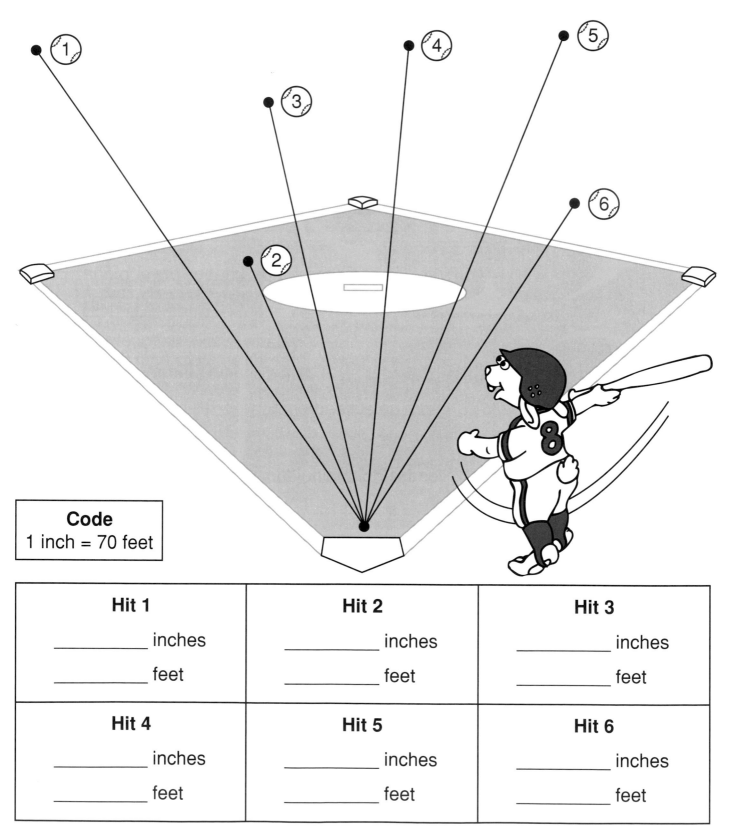

Code
1 inch = 70 feet

Hit 1	Hit 2	Hit 3
_____ inches	_____ inches	_____ inches
_____ feet	_____ feet	_____ feet
Hit 4	**Hit 5**	**Hit 6**
_____ inches	_____ inches	_____ inches
_____ feet	_____ feet	_____ feet

Funny Flowers

Name_____

Add or subtract.
Show your work.

68 + 23 I	25 + 79 A	92 − 41 P	32 + 56 L	83 − 47 E
54 − 19 R	85 − 16 T	17 + 43 S	75 − 28 M	44 + 54 F
			68 + 22 C	57 − 26 G

If an April shower brings a May flower, what does a May flower bring?

To solve the riddle, match the letters to the numbered lines below.

___ ___ ___ ___ ___ ___ ___ ___ ,
104 47   36   35   91   90 104   60

___ ___ ___ ___ ___
98   91   35   60   69

___ ___ ___ ___ ___ ___ ___ ___
51   91   88   31   35   91   47   60

A GALLERY OF PLANE FIGURES

Step inside this art gallery, and you'll quickly discover that it's quite unique! After all, how many art galleries encourage patrons to touch artwork, reorganize artwork, and create artwork for display? These quick and easy hands-on activities will supplement your study of plane figures beautifully!

ideas contributed by Stacie Stone Davis, Lima, NY

NEW EXHIBITS

Identifying characteristics of plane figures

Organizing exhibits of plane figures is just plain fun! Have each child color the artwork on a construction paper copy of page 218 and then cut out the cards. Give her a zippered plastic bag in which to store her artwork collection. Then, on each of several days, challenge students to identify artwork (from their collections) for specific displays that include open figures; closed figures; artwork having curved, straight, or both curved and straight lines; congruent artwork; artwork with corners; and symmetrical artwork. Students can even find artwork that shows a flip, a turn, and a slide!

> Today's exhibit is artwork with curved lines.

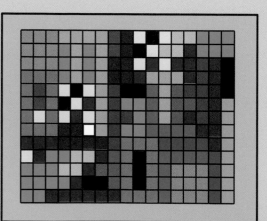

IT TAKES TWO

Creating congruent figures

The result of this partner activity is a masterpiece loaded with congruent figures. Each student pair begins with a half sheet of centimeter paper and crayons. Partner 1 colors a desired figure on the paper and then he hands the crayon to Partner 2, who uses the same crayon to color a congruent figure on the paper. Partner 2 then selects another crayon and colors a different figure on the paper. He hands the crayon to Partner 1, who uses it to color a congruent figure. The partners continue in this manner until their masterpiece is complete. Mount each piece of artwork on construction paper and exhibit the collection with the title "Colorful Congruency."

square

↓

rectangle

↓

triangle

A NEW LOOK
Rearranging shapes to make new shapes

For this special exhibition, a square gets a make-over—twice! First, have each child fold a four-inch colorful square into fourths by folding on each diagonal. Ask her to cut on the fold lines and reassemble the square. Next, challenge her to arrange the four cutouts to form a rectangle with two long sides and two short sides. When every student has a rectangle, ask students to re-create their squares. Then challenge each child to arrange her cutouts to form a triangle that has three equal sides. Very nifty!

To extend the fun, ask students to combine their cutouts and work together to create figures of any size and shape. If desired, invite groups to glue the shapes they make onto construction paper and add scenic details. Hey, check out that lighthouse!

Symmetry, symmetry, symmetry! See "Designer Wings" on page 281 for an activity that reinforces symmetry.

SHAPELY SOUVENIRS
Classifying plane figures

A souvenir booklet is the perfect place for students to show off their knowledge of plane figures. Give every child a multi-page booklet of blank quarter-size pages and a copy of the cards from page 218. (Or have each child use the card set she prepared for "New Exhibits" on page 216.) Have her title the booklet "Plane Figures" and add her name and desired decorations to the front cover. Next, instruct each child to glue one or two specified cards to a blank booklet page and list on the page all that she knows about the figure(s). Repeat the process until the pages of the souvenir booklets are filled.

- open figure
- straight lines
- three corners
- not symmetrical

- octagon
- straight lines
- eight corners

- closed figure
- eight sides
- symmetrical

Plane Figures by Melissa

Plane Figure Cards

Use with "New Exhibits" on page 216 and "Shapely Souvenirs" on page 217.

"Cow-pacity"

Filling Up on Customary Units of Capacity

I can produce up to 14 gallons of milk a day.

That's 56 quarts,

112 pints,

or 224 cups!

HOW MUCH MILK?
Relating customary units

Use manipulatives to help students see the relationship between cups, pints, quarts, and gallons! Gather 14 empty gallon-size containers. Show the containers to the class and ask students how long they think it would take a cow to produce this amount of milk. Share with students that a dairy cow can produce that amount of milk (14 gallons) in one day. Then, as a group, calculate the number of quarts, pints, and cups in 14 gallons of milk. If desired, have each child make a booklet containing these facts. To make the cover, a student folds a 6" x 18" piece of construction paper in half. He rounds the bottom corners of the front cover to make the nose. The child fashions eyes and ears from construction paper scraps and uses crayons to add desired facial details. On each of four quarter sheets of writing paper, he writes a fact. Then he staples the pages in order between the covers.

adapted from an idea by Lisa Strieker, St. Paul Elementary, Highland, IL

Fill up your capacity files with these "moo-velous" ideas!

Two cups equals how many pints?
Four pints equals how many quarts?
Two pints equals how many cups?
One quart equals how many cups?

Come rap with me about capacity!
Come rap with me about capacity!
Two cups in a pint, two pints in a quart,
Four quarts in a gallon—let's keep this short!
Come rap with me about capacity!
Come rap with me about capacity!

A GALLON OF FUN
Comparing customary units

Finding equal measures is the trick to winning this group game! Divide students into small groups. Give each group a copy of the gallon pattern on page 223 and a wipe-off board. State a capacity-related question (see samples above) and have the team work together to answer it. After a preset amount of time, one team member writes the answer on the board and then holds it up for checking. If the group has the correct answer, a team member colors one cup on its gallon pattern. To increase the difficulty of the game, challenge groups to answer multiple-step questions that earn two cups when answered correctly. The first team to earn a gallon by coloring all 16 cups wins!

Beth Romie, New Albany Elementary, New Albany, OH

LINING UP
Comparing customary units

Get students on their feet to put capacity units in order! In advance, program a class supply of index cards with different units of capacity. Explain that each student will receive a card with a capacity amount written on it. The class will be divided into teams that will work together to order themselves from the smallest amount to the largest within each team. (If two cards show equal amounts, then the students holding those cards stand beside each other.) Then distribute the cards. Divide students into two teams and signal the teams to begin. The first team to line up correctly wins. To play again, simply shuffle the index cards and repeat the process. On your mark, get set, go!

Beth Romie

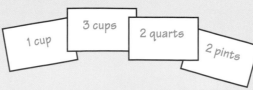

CAPACITY "RAP-SODY"
Relating customary units

"Rap" up your unit with a catchy rhyme that helps students remember the relationship between units of capacity! If desired, have students create additional verses using different equivalencies.

Amy Barsanti, Pines Elementary, Plymouth, NC

Name _____

Moo for Milk

Finish each math sentence.

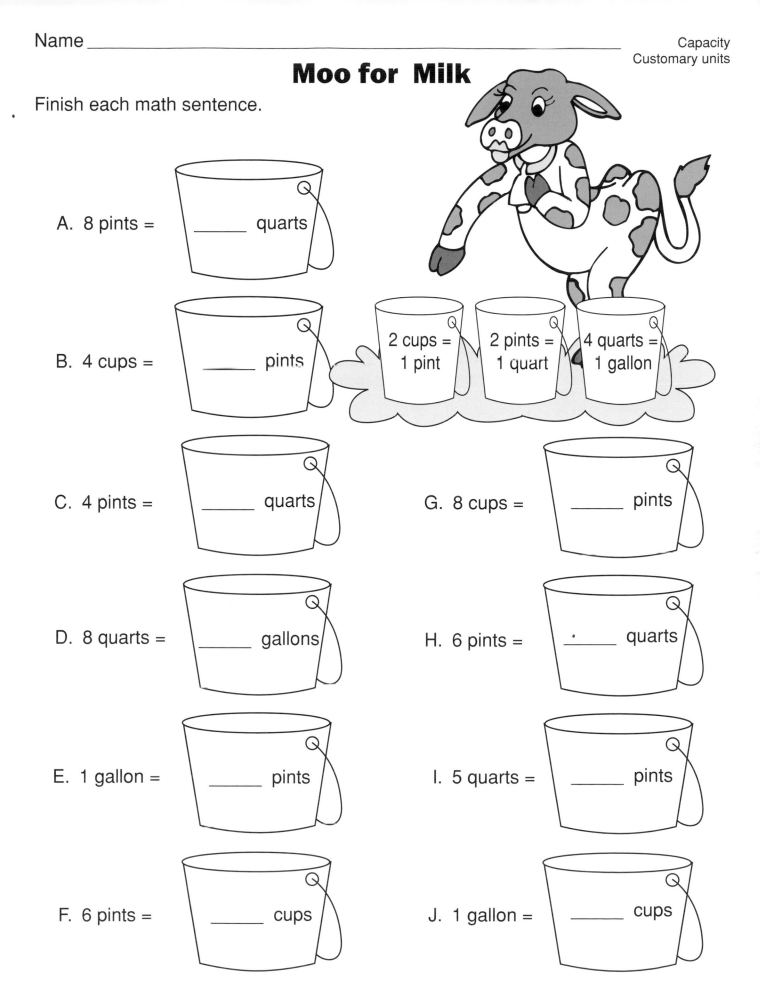

A. 8 pints = _____ quarts

B. 4 cups = _____ pints

2 cups =
1 pint

2 pints =
1 quart

4 quarts =
1 gallon

C. 4 pints = _____ quarts

G. 8 cups = _____ pints

D. 8 quarts = _____ gallons

H. 6 pints = _____ quarts

E. 1 gallon = _____ pints

I. 5 quarts = _____ pints

F. 6 pints = _____ cups

J. 1 gallon = _____ cups

Which One?

Circle the best unit to measure the capacity of each item.
Color the glass by the key.

1 | **bathtub**
gallons   cups

2 | **coffee mug**
quarts   cups

3 | **water bottle**
pints   gallons

4 | **soup pot**
cups   quarts

5 | **cereal bowl**
pints   quarts

6 | **pitcher of milk**
quarts   cups

7 | **bucket**
pints   gallons

8 | **coffee pot**
pints   gallons

9 | **swimming pool**
quarts   gallons

Check it out! You should have 2 green glasses, 3 yellow, 2 purple, and 5 blue.

10 | **fish tank**
gallons   cups

Key
cups = green
pints = yellow
quarts = purple
gallons = blue

11 | **drinking glass**
cups   quarts

12 | **large can of paint**
pints   gallons

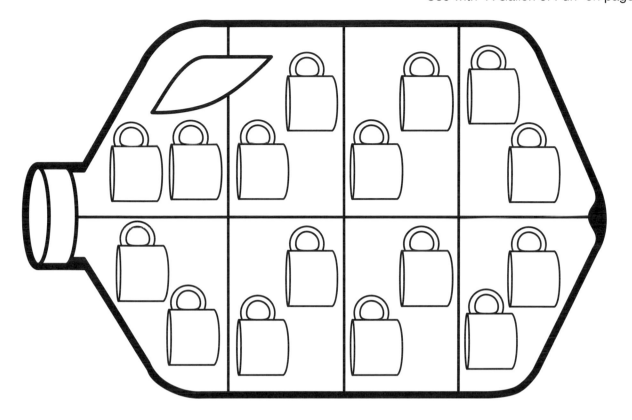

Hat Pattern
Use with "Hats Off!" on page 224.

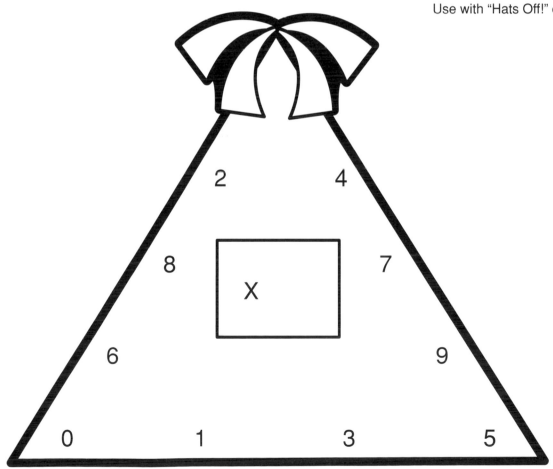

Party ★ Time!

A Multiplication Celebration!

HATS OFF!
Basic facts

This festive center is the
perfect place for mathematicians to showcase their skills.
Make ten copies of the party hat
pattern on page 223. Program
each hat with a different digit
from 0 to 9. Laminate the hats for
durability, cut them out, and then
use a permanent marker to program
the answers on the back of each one
for self-checking. Place blank paper,
pencils, and crayons in a center. To
solve a factor hat, a student traces a hat
shape on his paper and writes an answer
for each fact as shown. Then he flips the
hat over and checks his work. If his calculations are correct, he decorates his hat
tracing. He continues in this manner until he's
solved every factor hat or time runs out.

adapted from an idea by David Green
North Shore Country Day School
Winnetka, IL

20

10

35

40

25

30

45

15

5

0

2   4

8   7

x 5

6   5

0   1   3   9

Factor in these ideas for a festive review of basic facts!

Five times seven equals 35!

GET THE SCOOP!
Fact families

The relationship between multiplication and division takes center stage during this large-group activity. Make a class supply of construction paper ice-cream cones and program each one with a different multiplication product. Laminate the cones for durability and cut them out. Begin by handing out the cutouts and instructing each child to trace her cone onto a blank sheet of paper. Also have her copy the product from inside the cone inside her tracing and list the two factors that equal the product when they are multiplied. To make a fact family, the student draws a colorful ice-cream scoop above the cone and uses the three numbers to write two multiplication and two division facts as shown. After finishing, the child trades cones with a classmate and repeats the process. Have students continue scooping up fact families in this manner for as long as desired.

David Green
North Shore Country Day School
Winnetka, IL

IN THE CARDS
Basic facts

An element of chance multiplies the fun of this review game! Remove the face cards (and tens if desired) from three card decks and divide the class into four teams. Keep one card deck for yourself and give each team half of a deck. Explain that all cards are to be stacked face-down and aces equal one.

For each round of play, display for the teams the top card in your deck. Each team then turns over its top card and multiplies the two numbers together. One member from each team states her team's math sentence for the round. The team that has the highest product earns one point, and the team that has the lowest product earns one point. In the event of a tie, both teams earn points. The first team to score 15 points wins!

adapted from an idea by Laura Wagner, Raleigh, NC

Name _____

Party Game

Multiply.

E. 7 x 2	**D.** 9 x 4	**G.** 8 x 8	**K.** 5 x 7	**Y.** 6 x 9	**U.** 2 x 4
W. 3 x 5	**N.** 8 x 6	**Q.** 7 x 7	**I.** 4 x 3	**A.** 3 x 6	**P.** 8 x 5
		T. 4 x 4	**S.** 6 x 5	**H.** 9 x 7	**V.** 5 x 4

What game do mice like to play at parties?

To solve the riddle, match the letters to the numbered lines below.

___ ___ ___ ___ - ___ ___ ___ - ___ ___ ___ ___ ___ ___ ___ !
63 12 36 14   18 48 36   30 49 8 14 18 35

SCIENCE &
SOCIAL STUDIES UNITS

Then and Now

Exploring the Past and Present

The first Sunday after Labor Day marks Grandparents Day, the perfect springboard for exploring changes in the community over the years. Use the following ideas, and students are sure to have a grand ol' time!

ideas contributed by David Green—Gr. 3
North Shore Country Day School, Winnetka, IL

Sign of the Times
Comparing past and present

This idea prompts students to take a peek into the past! Modifying the provided sentence starters for the past tense, list them on the board. Have each child copy the list on a sheet of paper, leaving writing space after each phrase. Challenge each student to use the sentence starters to interview a grandparent or older friend to find out how life was different for her when she was a child. Ask students who completed the assignment to share their findings with the class.

Next, have each child staple a few half sheets of drawing paper between two construction paper covers. Post the sentence starters shown. Have each student complete each sentence starter and illustrate her writing. Instruct her to title the front cover "My Life in [current year]" and add any desired illustrations. Invite students to share their booklets with the class. Prompt them to compare their childhoods with those of their grandparents. (For example, a grandparent may have taken the bus to school but probably didn't play video games.) My, how times change!

Sentence Starters
I travel to school by...
For fun, I like to...
My favorite book is...
A famous person is...
My family buys food at...

Movie Ticket Prices

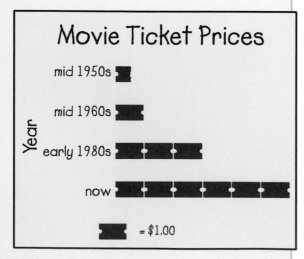

Tickets, Please!
Exploring price changes

Skyrocketing movie ticket costs provide the perfect opportunity for students to explore how prices have changed over time! Obtain a roll of raffle tickets for the activity. Give each child a 9" x 12" sheet of construction paper and a strip of 15 tickets. Tell students that in this activity, each ticket represents one dollar.

Next, explain to youngsters that prices were much lower when their grandparents were children. Inform them that in the mid 1950s, a movie ticket might have cost about 50 cents. Lead students to conclude that they should tear a ticket in half to represent this price. Then tell youngsters that in the mid 1960s, a movie ticket cost about one dollar. Have students tear off the appropriate number of tickets to represent this price *(one)*. Repeat this process to show three dollars, the average movie ticket price in the early 1980s *(three tickets)*, and six dollars, the average current price *(six tickets)*. Then have each child label his paper and glue the tickets in place to make a pictograph. Encourage him to share his display with a grandparent or older friend and then ask about price changes for other items. Interesting!

Remember When...
Understanding the importance of an invention

After this activity, students are less likely to take modern conveniences for granted! List the provided information on the board. Divide students into ten small groups and give each group a half sheet of drawing paper. One group member illustrates an assigned invention. A second member labels it with the year and name. The group members predict whether the invention existed while their grandparents were children. Then a third member works with members of the remaining groups to display the illustrations on a bulletin board to create a timeline. Prompt youngsters to discuss how the absence or introduction of selected inventions might have impacted their grandparents' lives.

Next, give each child a copy of the form below to take home. Have him find out when a grandparent or older friend was born and write it in the space provided. Upon returning to school, he completes the form using a selected invention from the timeline. Mount students' work around the timeline and title the display "Timely Inventions."

Inventions
1906 Zipper
1918 Three-color traffic light
1950 Credit card
1955 Home microwave oven
1955 LEGO toys
1972 Video game
1972 Pocket calculator
1977 First popular personal computer
1980 Compact disc
1996 DVD Player

1977

First Popular Personal Computer

Name __Marshall__

The Good Ol' Days

Year grandparent/older friend was born ___1940___

I don't know how ___Grandpa Seydou___

without ___a computer___ (grandparent/older friend) lived
(invention) ! He must have had to go to the library to find things out. Maybe he called people on the phone. Now Grandpa uses his computer. We email each other all the time!

- -

Name _____

The Good Ol' Days

Year grandparent/older friend was born _____

I don't know how _____ lived
(grandparent/older friend)

without _____ ! _____
(invention)

_____

_____

_____

A Habitat Is a Must!

Where's an owl's favorite place to hang out? Its habitat! After all, where else in nature can an owl find food and shelter? Use the following activities to strengthen your students' understanding of the importance of animal habitats and adaptations.

ideas contributed by Stacie Stone Davis, Lima, NY

"Whoooo" Lives Where?
Identifying the needs of animals

Ask students whether a whale can live in a forest, and you'll receive immediate and animated responses. You can count on a similar level of enthusiasm when you introduce this kid-pleasing habitat handbook! For each student, staple an even number of blank pages (four or more) between two construction paper covers. Ask him to title his handbook "Here's Why!" and number the pages. Next, have each child write the following sentence starter on page 1: "A whale can't live in a forest because..." Then, on page 2, have him write two or more reasons why a forest is an unsuitable habitat for a whale. To complete his handbook, a child programs each remaining odd-numbered page with a sentence starter that's similar to the one on page 1 except that it pairs a different animal to an unsuitable habitat. Then he uses each even-numbered page to explain why the named habitat is unsuitable. Be sure to set aside time for students to illustrate their handbooks and then share them with the class.

Here's Why! by Ricki

A whale can't live in a forest because...

a whale needs saltwater to swim in and lots of food to eat!

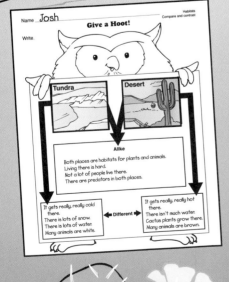

Give a Hoot for Habitats!
Comparing and contrasting

The graphic organizer on page 233 is just the tool you need to engage students in a variety of compare-and-contrast activities. Students can illustrate in the provided boxes two habitats or animals they wish to compare and contrast. Other options include gluing cards from page 232 onto a copy of page 233 before making a class set of the page. Or students can color, cut out and glue cards from page 232 onto their own copies of page 233. Whatever option you choose, students can apply their knowledge of habitats and/or animal adaptation as they note similarities and differences between the pictured subjects. No doubt they'll have a hoot of a time!

Staying Alive
Recognizing adaptations

This nifty picture reference shows students how animals adapt to their environments. Give each child a copy of page 232 and ask her to color the cards that show scenery and animals from the Arctic tundra. (See "Tundra Animals" below for helpful information.) As students color, encourage them to share their observations. In a similar manner, have each child color and share her observations about the cards that show desert scenery and animals. (See "Desert Animals" below.) Then have her cut out her cards.

To make the picture reference, give each child a 6" x 18" sheet of construction paper that has been prefolded and prepunched as shown. Instruct her to first glue the four habitat cards in place. Then have her unfold the paper and glue the animal cards to the paper so that each row features animals from the same habitat and each column shows a similar animal in a different habitat. (See below.) When the glue dries, have her refold her project, thread a length of yarn through the holes, and tie the yarn ends into a bow. (If desired, use a length of clear tape to secure the yarn to the back of the reference.) A better understanding of adaptations is sure to unfold.

Tundra Animals

Snowy Owl
mostly white feathers
some brown markings
nests on the ground
heavily feathered legs
   and feet

Arctic Fox
short, furry ears
thick, white winter coat
short tail

Arctic Hare
white winter fur
short ears with black tips
large hind feet that work
   as snowshoes
short tail

Tundra Vole
gray fur
plump body
short legs and tail
tiny ears

Desert Animals

Elf Owl
smallest owl
keeps cool inside a cactus
large yellowish eyes
gray, brown, and white
   feathers
lightly feathered legs

Kit Fox
small
yellow-gray fur, black tip on tail
large ears (help it cool off)
cools off in a cave or burrow

Jack Rabbit
brownish-gray fur
white belly
long hind legs
large eyes
long thin ears (help it cool off)

Kangaroo Rat
plump little body
long, bushy tail
tan or cream in color
strong hind legs for jumping
small ears
large eyes

Habitat and Animal Cards

Use with "Give a Hoot for Habitats!" on page 230 and "Staying Alive" on page 231.

The Desert · **Elf Owl**

Kit Fox · **Jack Rabbit** · **Kangaroo Rat**

The Arctic Tundra · **Snowy Owl**

Arctic Fox · **Arctic Hare** · **Tundra Vole**

Name _____

Give a Hoot!

Write.

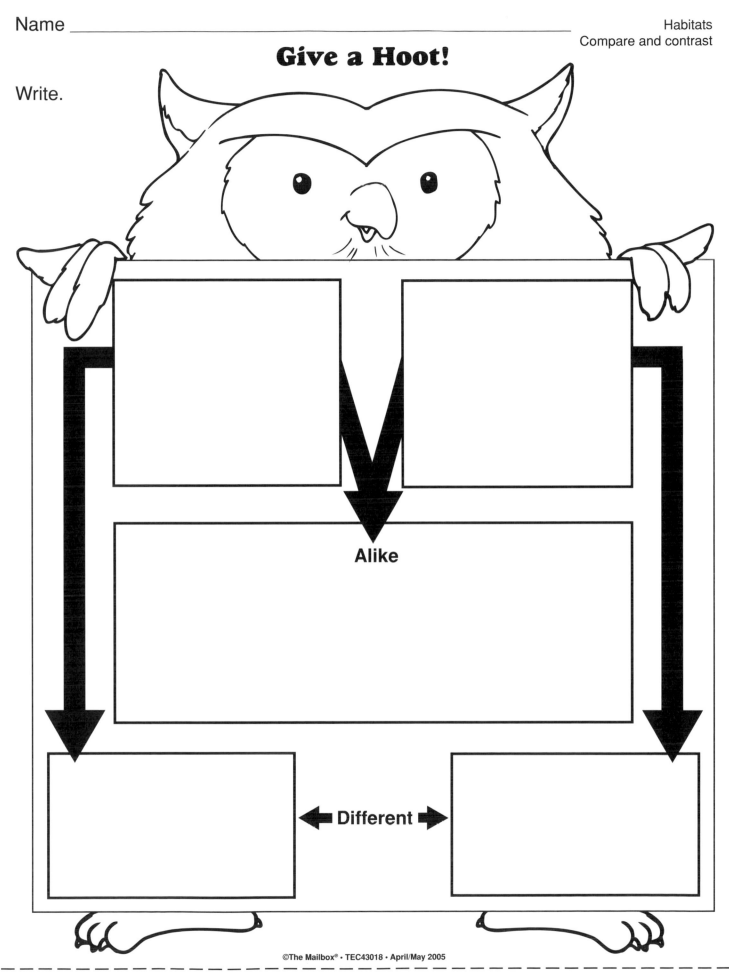

Alike

◀ **Different** ▶

Thinking *Like a* Scientist

Whoa! Hold on! Stop! This science dude is certain you don't want to pass by these hands-on experiments! Each investigation promotes scientific inquiry and only requires easy-to-find materials such as pennies or plastic straws. That means in a matter of minutes you can have your students actively thinking like scientists. Now that's a scientific discovery!

ideas by Stacie Stone Davis, Lima, NY

Pennies and a Paper Towel

Purpose:
To discover how many pennies a wet paper towel can hold

Materials for each small group:
paper towel
2 tbsp. water
pennies (approximately 50)
wide-mouth nonbreakable container (to catch pennies)
individual copies of a recording sheet from page 236

Procedure:
1. Have each group member write his name and the date on a copy of the recording sheet.
2. Provide time for group members to observe the supplies. Then ask each child to write on his recording sheet a hypothesis for the question "How many pennies can a wet paper towel hold?"
3. Invite one child in each group to grab opposite edges of the paper towel and hold it taut over the container for the duration of the experiment.
4. Ask another group member to pour the water near the center of the paper towel.
5. Have group members take turns placing one more penny on the dampened towel until the towel tears.
6. Have each child describe on his recording sheet the data his group collected.
7. Instruct each group to collectively draw a conclusion based on its data.
8. Have each child write the group's conclusion on his recording sheet.

Follow-Up:
Have members of each group explain how their group reached its conclusion. Facilitate a class discussion that addresses differences in collected data or the conclusions that were reached. Also invite youngsters to tell the class what most surprised them about this experiment.

Extension:
Invite students to form new hypotheses, such as "A wet paper towel holds fewer pennies when the pennies are stacked on the towel." Then replenish the supplies as needed so students can test the hypotheses.

Pennies and a Paper Towel
Investigation

Scientist _____ Sammy
Date _____ Nov. 11, 2004

Hypothesis
I think a wet paper towel can hold ten pennies.

Data Collected Cool!
The towel held 35 pennies!

Conclusion
A wet paper towel is very strong!

Paper Loops and a Plastic Straw

Purpose:
To discover how far an airplane made from two paper loops and a plastic straw can fly

Materials for each student:
plastic drinking straw
½" x 4½" paper strip
1" x 6" paper strip
clear tape
access to a tape measure
copy of a recording sheet from page 236

Procedure:
1. Have each student write her name and the date on her recording sheet.
2. Have each child make a plane. To do this, have her slightly overlap the ends of each paper strip to form a loop and tape the ends together. Next, have her slip each paper loop under an opposite end of her straw and tape each loop to the straw. (See the illustration for clarity.)
3. Provide time for each child to observe her plane. Then ask her to write on her recording sheet a hypothesis for the question "How far can an airplane made from two paper loops and a plastic straw fly?"
4. Pair students and have each partner take a turn flying her plane from a designated start line. Then direct the partners to measure the distance from the start line to the front end of each plane (the smaller loop). Have each child write on her recording sheet the distance her plane flew.
5. Have each pair repeat Step 4 two more times.
6. Instruct each student to draw a conclusion based on the data she collected and then write it on her recording sheet.

Follow-Up:
Have students compare and contrast their conclusions. Facilitate a class discussion that addresses differences in collected data or the conclusions that were reached. Also invite youngsters to tell the class what most surprised them about this experiment.

Extension:
Invite students to form new hypotheses, such as "The placement of the paper loops affects how far a plane will fly," and use their planes to test them.

Recording Sheets

Use with the science investigations on pages 234 and 235.

Investigation _____

Scientist _____

Date _____

Hypothesis _____

Data Collected _____

Very interesting!

Conclusion _____

Investigation _____

Scientist _____

Date _____

Hypothesis _____

Data Collected _____

Cool!

Conclusion _____

A Visit With Penguins

They're always decked out in tuxedos but seem to avoid weddings. They waddle and hop but are rarely seen at dances. They are birds, but they do not fly in the sky. No wonder penguins are such a curiosity! Pair your students' interest in these one-of-a-kind birds with the following activities, which reinforce your science curriculum. It's a winning combination!

ideas contributed by Stacie Stone Davis, Lima NY

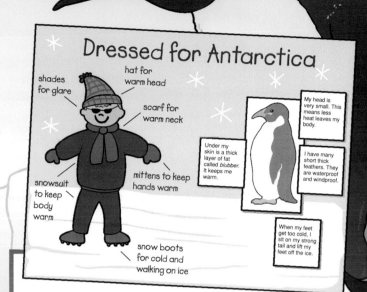

Dressed for Antarctica

shades for glare

hat for warm head

scarf for warm neck

snowsuit to keep body warm

mittens to keep hands warm

snow boots for cold and walking on ice

My head is very small. This means less heat leaves my body.

Under my skin is a thick layer of fat called *blubber*. It keeps me warm.

I have many short thick feathers. They are waterproof and windproof.

When my feet get too cold, I sit on my strong tail and lift my feet off the ice.

Well Suited
Identifying adaptations

Not only do penguins survive in what is known to be the coldest and iciest region of the world, but they also thrive there! How can that be? That's what students discover during this investigation of penguin adaptations. Have each child title a 9" x 12" sheet of light blue construction paper "Dressed for Antarctica." After a brief discussion of the cold conditions on the continent, instruct each child to illustrate himself on the left half of his paper dressed for a visit. Ask that he label each article of cold weather attire he's wearing and write a phrase that explains its purpose.

Next, show students magazine photographs of adult penguins. (Ranger Rick magazine is a good source.) Invite them to contemplate why penguins seem comfortable in the cold. Then share the provided information about penguin adaptations, using the penguin photos as visual aids. Follow up by giving each child a copy of the penguin pattern and caption cards from page 239. Ask each child to cut out the pattern and glue it to the right half of his project. Then have him cut out the captions and glue each one near a corresponding part of the penguin. Encourage students to add scenery to their projects.

Penguin Adaptations
- thick layer of fat for warmth
- windproof and waterproof feather coat
- small feet, wings, and heads to conserve body heat
- strong tail that supports body so feet can be raised off ice

Down South
Identifying habitats, using a map key

To see penguins in their natural environment, a trip south of the equator is necessary, but a trip to Antarctica is not. Use the mapping activity on page 240 to introduce students to a variety of penguin habitats with one thing in common—each is near water!

Beverly C. Lee, Greensboro, NC

Pint-Size Penguins

Comparing offspring to their parents

What do adult penguins have that no other animal has? Baby penguins, of course! During this activity, students identify similarities and differences between adult penguins and their pint-size offspring. Give each child pieces of construction paper in the following dimensions and colors: 9" x 12" light blue, 4" x 6" dark blue, 6" x 6" white. Have her scallop a short edge of the dark blue paper to represent water and trim one edge of the white square to represent ice-covered land. Instruct her to glue the rectangles side by side along the bottom edge of the light blue paper. Then provide a large index card for her to trace in the center of her paper as shown.

Next, give each child a copy of the penguin cards from page 239 to cut out. Help students identify the three cards that are category titles and have them glue these cards onto their projects as illustrated. Invite students to work alone or with partners to sort the cards into the three categories. Set aside time for students to share the results of their sorts. If opinions differ, guide the discussion to a correct conclusion. When students agree on a final sort similar to the one shown, have them glue the cards in place and add penguin illustrations to complete their projects. Cool!

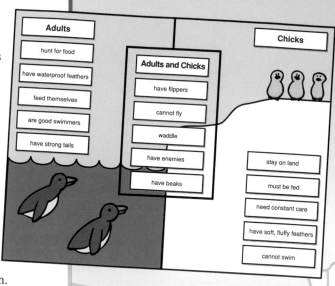

Gone Fishin'!

Exploring interdependency

This quick demonstration shows students that penguins depend on the ocean for food. Cut out a class supply of construction paper cards. Cut half the cards from one color of paper and the other half from another. Shuffle the cards and give one to each student. Explain that one color of card stands for penguins and the other stands for squid, small fish, shrimp, and other ocean life that is food for penguins. Designate one side of the room as ice and the opposite side of the room as ocean. Send the penguins to the ice and the food into the ocean.

First, have each penguin enter the ocean and find food. When every penguin is paired with a food, send the penguins back to the ice (with full tummies). Have the food stay in the ocean. After repeating this scenario a time or two, play the role of a commercial fishing boat. Enter the ocean, catch some food, and leave the ocean with your catch. (Ask the "caught" students to sit out of the game.) Then once again send the penguins into the ocean for food. When students realize that there isn't enough food for every penguin, ask them what could happen to penguins that cannot find food in the ocean. Students quickly understand how important the ocean is to the survival of penguins.

My head is very small. This means less heat leaves my body.	I have many short thick feathers. They are waterproof and windproof.
Under my skin is a thick layer of fat called *blubber.* It keeps me warm.	When my feet get too cold, I sit on my strong tail and lift my feet off the ice.

Penguin Cards
Use with "Pint-Size Penguins" on page 238.

Adults	Adults and Chicks	Chicks
need constant care	feed themselves	hunt for food
have waterproof feathers	have flippers	have strong tails
cannot swim	are good swimmers	have soft, fluffy feathers
have enemies	cannot fly	have beaks
stay on land	must be fed	waddle

Where Do Penguins Live?

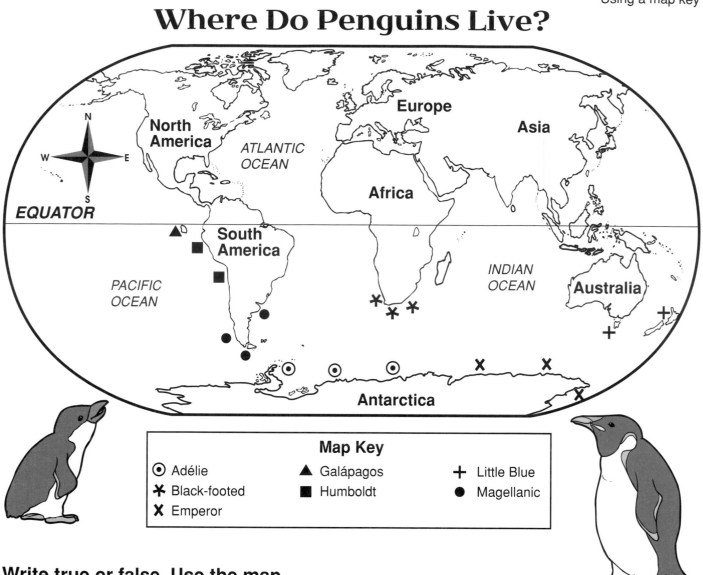

Map Key

⊙ Adélie   ▲ Galápagos   + Little Blue

✳ Black-footed   ■ Humboldt   ● Magellanic

✖ Emperor

Write true or false. Use the map.

_____ 1. Galápagos penguins live on an island east of South America.

_____ 2. Black-footed penguins live at the southern tip of Africa.

_____ 3. Humboldt and Adélie penguins live close to the equator.

_____ 4. Galápagos penguins swim in the Atlantic Ocean.

_____ 5. Adélie and Emperor penguins live along the coast of Antarctica.

_____ 6. Little Blue penguins live on an island north of Australia.

_____ 7. Magellanic penguins live on the southern shores of South America.

_____ 8. No penguins live south of the equator.

Bonus Box: In each false sentence circle the one word that makes the sentence false.

©The Education Center, Inc. • *The Mailbox*® • TEC43016 • Dec./Jan. 2004–5 • Key p. 313

240   **Note to the teacher:** Use independently or with "Down South" on page 237.

Dig In!

Getting the Scoop on Soil

GOTTA HAVE IT!
Connecting soil and food supply

So what's the big deal about dirt? Students are reminded during this activity! Ask each child to choose a favorite meal and list on paper the foods in it. If a food has more than one ingredient, have her write them to the best of her knowledge. Next, challenge each child to choose several ingredients in her meal and show how each one depends on soil. To do this, she colors a soil line across the bottom of a sheet of light blue construction paper. Then she uses lines, captions, and illustrations to diagram the connections. Invite students to share their work with the class, or showcase it on a bulletin board titled "We Sure Depend on Dirt!"

From Dirt to Tacos

taco shells are made
hamburger is made
milk is used to make cheese
corn grows
cow is sold
cow makes milk
tomatoes grow
cow eats grass
cow eats grass
lettuce grows
grass grows
grass grows

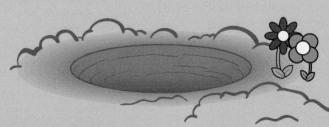

Cultivate core science standards and unearth learning enthusiasm when you incorporate this rich collection of activities into your study of soil.

ideas contributed by Liz Harrell, Sacred Heart School, Highland Falls, NY

A COMMUNITY DIG
Observing differences in soil

For an intriguing soil investigation, send each student home with an empty zippered bag and a parent note similar to the one shown. Use white bulletin board paper to cover a large tabletop and then glue a simple map of your community on the paper. When a student brings a soil sample to school, help him locate on the map where the sample was gathered. Then tape the soil sample to the table near the location and use a marker to visually connect the two. Engage students in comparing and contrasting the colors and textures of the gathered soil. Very interesting!

Dear Parent,
We are studying soil. I am asking each student to bring to school a small sample of soil on or before Tuesday, June 7. A zippered bag is provided. Please include with the soil sample a brief note that explains where the soil was collected. We are hoping to gather soil from different places in the community.

Thank you!
Ms. Harrell

Name Sofie

Protect the soil.

AN IMPORTANT RESOURCE
Identifying human actions as helpful or harmful

What surfaces during this partner game are different ways that human behavior affects soil. For a center activity, make a class supply of the gameboards on page 243 and make one construction paper copy of the game cards. Laminate the cards for durability and then cut apart the cards and the gameboards. Place the cards in a clean flowerpot. Then store the flowerpot, the gameboards, and crayons at a center.

To play, partners take turns drawing cards. Each player reads her card aloud and identifies the action as helpful or harmful. (Each helpful action is marked with a flower.) If the action is helpful, she colors a section of soil and its flower on her gameboard. Then she returns the card to the flowerpot and her turn is over. If the action is harmful, she returns the card. The first child to color her entire garden plot wins.

CHECK IT OUT!
Naming parts of soil

This catchy song, sung to the tune of "Do Your Ears Hang Low?" reminds students that soil is a mixture of weathered rock, humus, water, and air.

Soil Song

Have you checked out soil?
Have you held it in your hand?
Did you see the weathered rock
Or find humus mixed with sand?
Did you notice any water?
Did you feel a bit of air?
Have you checked out soil?

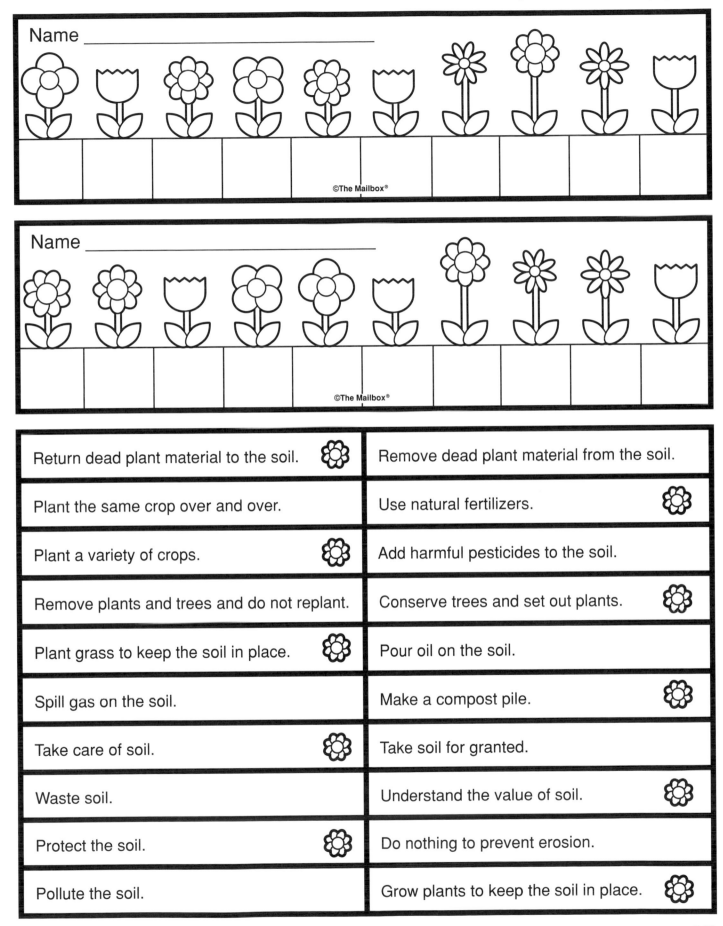

Name _____

Name _____

Return dead plant material to the soil.	Remove dead plant material from the soil.
Plant the same crop over and over.	Use natural fertilizers.
Plant a variety of crops.	Add harmful pesticides to the soil.
Remove plants and trees and do not replant.	Conserve trees and set out plants.
Plant grass to keep the soil in place.	Pour oil on the soil.
Spill gas on the soil.	Make a compost pile.
Take care of soil.	Take soil for granted.
Waste soil.	Understand the value of soil.
Protect the soil.	Do nothing to prevent erosion.
Pollute the soil.	Grow plants to keep the soil in place.

Name _____

244

Digging Into Soil

Cut.
Match each word to its meaning.
Glue.

DIGGER

1. found in all rocks

2. wearing down and breaking apart of rock

3. number of parts soil has

4. soil that holds a lot of water

5. movement of weathered rock and soil

6. soil that holds very little water

7. part of soil, along with weathered rock, humus, and air

8. another name for soil

9. part of soil that includes decayed parts

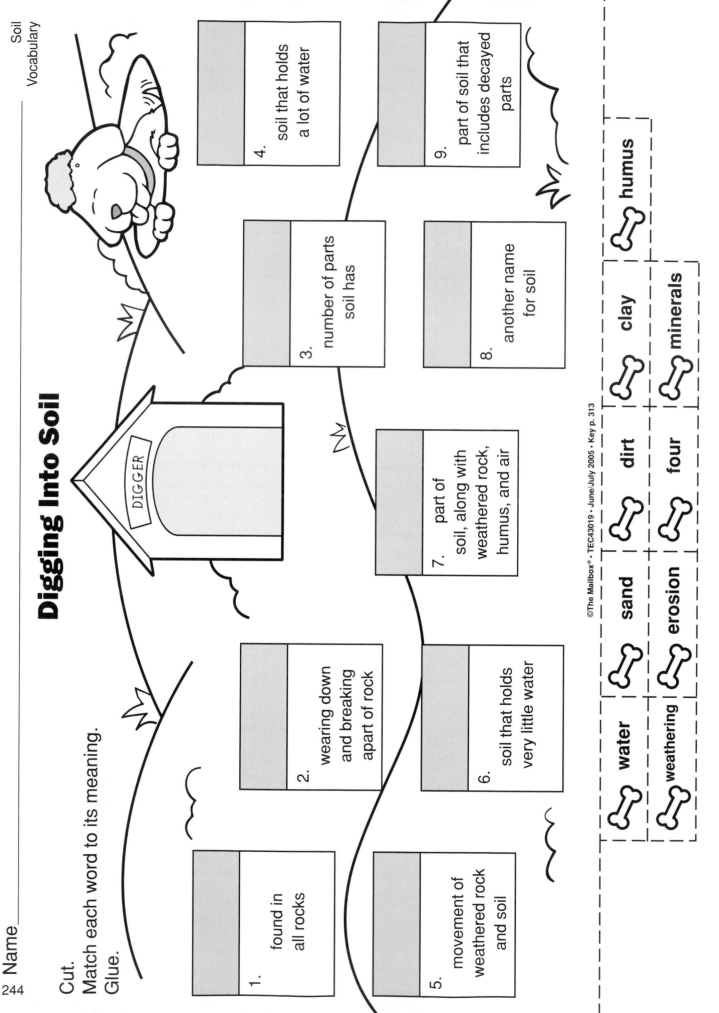

water   sand   dirt   clay   humus

weathering   erosion   four   minerals

Matter on a Platter

Serve up a meaningful review of science objectives by relating matter to something students love: food! In no time your students will be classifying, comparing, mixing, and changing matter. It's a delicious approach that's quick and easy to deliver!

ideas contributed by Liz Harrell
Sacred Heart School, Highland Falls, NY

Solids
- hamburger
- french fries
- pizza
- spaghetti
- ice cream
- grilled cheese

Liquids
- water
- orange juice
- apple juice
- root beer
- hot cocoa

Gases
- air to breath
- steam from hot cocoa
- bubbles in root beer

jennifer tipton cappoen

A Meaningful Menu
Classifying matter as solid, liquid, or gas

What does every menu list? That's right—different types of matter! However, what makes these student-made menus unique is the way in which the matter is organized! Have each child fold a sheet of blank paper in half lengthwise and then unfold the paper and write the headings "Solids," "Liquids," and "Gases" as they appear in the illustration. Ask each child to list his favorite edible matter under the headings "Solids" and "Liquids." Then provide a few hints for the types of gases that could be offered and have students complete this part of the menu. Next, have each student fold a 9" x 12" sheet of construction paper in half lengthwise, title the front cover "[Student's name]'s Matter Café," and then decorate the front and back covers to his liking. Last, have him glue his menu of matter inside. Now that brings meaning to matter!

Matter to Go
Comparing forms of matter, using the scientific process

During this hands-on activity, students are reminded that all matter takes up space, just not in the same way. Show students a zippered plastic bag and tell them that you have a hypothesis that if all matter takes up space, then a small amount of each type of matter could be stored inside the bag. Invite students to share their opinions. Then have each child form a hypothesis and write it on a copy of the recording sheet on page 247. To test the hypotheses, pair youngsters and give each twosome a zippered bag, a napkin, a drinking straw, and a small paper cup of water. Lead the students through the investigations at the right. Ask students to describe their observations on their recording sheets. Help them conclude that matter takes up space in different ways.

A. J.'s Matter Café

Investigations

Solid: Seal the napkin inside the bag. Gently press the bag and tilt it from side to side. Does the solid take up space? Does the shape of the solid change? Record your observations. Remove the napkin.

Gas: Place one end of the straw in the bag opening and partially seal the bag. Blow air through the straw. Quickly remove the straw and seal the bag. Gently press the bag and tilt it from side to side. Does the air (gas) take up space? Does the shape of the gas change?

Liquid: Open the bag. Set the cup of water inside the bag. Empty the cup, remove the cup, and seal the bag. Gently press the bag and tilt it from side to side. Does the liquid take up space? Does the shape of the liquid change?

True to Form

Naming properties of matter

This catchy tune reminds students that each form of matter has unique properties.

(sung to the tune of "Three Blind Mice")

Solid, liquid, gas.
Solid, liquid, gas.

Three forms of matter.
Three forms of matter.

A solid has texture; it keeps its shape.
A liquid is poured; it changes shape!
A gas spreads out; it has no shape!

Solid, liquid, gas.
Solid, liquid, gas.

Kathleen Morrison
St. Thomas More Cathedral School
Arlington, VA

Mix It Up

Understanding that matter can be mixed

Order up! This activity is simple—and it's definitely sweet! Each child needs a clear plastic cup, a plastic spoon, and a napkin. You also need root beer and vanilla ice cream. Pour each child a partial serving of the beverage. Draw students' attention to the bubbles that are present and explain that the beverage is a mixture of liquid and gas (the gas is carbon dioxide and is present in all carbonated beverages). Can a solid be added to the mixture as well? You bet! Add in the ice cream and the tasty result is a root beer float that contains all three forms of matter—unless the ice cream melts!

As student enjoy their combination of matter, have them brainstorm other tasty mixtures.

Ellen Closs, Oxbow Community School, White Lake, MI

Is That Reversible?

Distinguishing reversible and irreversible change

Partners serve up two kinds of change during this engaging activity. Give each twosome a paper plate, a paper napkin, and some potato chips (or a soft cookie). Next, ask students to perform different tasks and categorize each task as *reversible* (when matter can be returned to its original form) or *irreversible* (when the change is permanent). Reversible tasks include folding the paper napkin in half, holding the paper plate on its side, and turning a chip upside down. Irreversible tasks include drawing an X (in crayon) on the plate, tearing the napkin in half, and crumbling a chip. Invite students to brainstorm additional tasks for their classmates to complete and categorize. Then have each child complete a copy of page 248 to assess her knowledge of changing matter.

Name_____

Time to Investigate

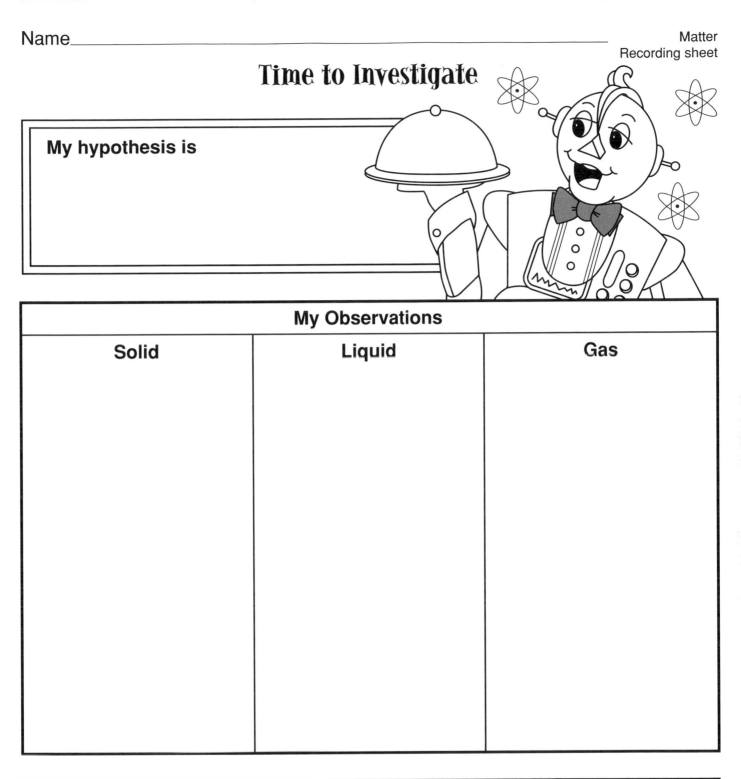

My hypothesis is

My Observations

Solid	Liquid	Gas

My Conclusion

Note to the teacher: Use with "Matter to Go" on page 245 and other matter-related investigations.

Name_____

Serving a Mixture of Matter

Choose the special of the day.
Cut it out and glue it in the box.

List five kinds of matter in it.
Tell how each changed.

Matter	Change
1. _____	_____
2. _____	_____
3. _____	_____
4. _____	_____
5. _____	_____

6. After the matter was mixed, did it change in any way? Explain. _____

_____

7. How could you make a reversible change to the matter? _____

_____

8. How could you make an irreversible change to the matter? _____

_____

©The Mailbox® • TEC43017 • Feb./Mar. 2005

fruit plate   pizza   soup

Note to the teacher: Use alone or as a follow-up to "Is That Reversible?" on page 246.

SEASONAL UNITS

Swinging Into a New School Year

Ready for a new school year? Get back into the swing of things with these ideas, which boost math skills and help students get acquainted!

First-Day Introductions
Skill: computation

Any way you slice them, these apple puzzles get to the core of computation skills! For every two students, program an apple cutout with a math problem and its answer as shown. (Include yourself if there is an odd number of students. Make sure that there are no duplicate answers.) Laminate the cutouts for durability; then use a different jigsaw cut to separate the programming on each apple cutout.

On the first day of school, hand out the puzzle pieces. Direct each child who has a math problem to find the child who has the corresponding answer. When he does, have each partner state his name and share one fact about himself. For another round of introductions, direct students to trade cutouts with different classmates and repeat the process.

Natalie Marie Fisher—Substitute teacher
Sylvania Public Schools, Sylvania, OH

13 + 5 = 18

Tasha

Glyph Garden
Skill: making and interpreting a glyph

These sunflower projects are the perfect way to cultivate glyph-making skills! Provide each child with access to the materials below. Have her cut out a green construction paper strip for a flower stem and place it on the vertically positioned sheet of blue construction paper. Direct her to use the key on page 253 to make her glyph.

Next, display students' work and a cutout copy of the key on a bulletin board titled "A Garden of Glyphs." Pose glyph-related questions, such as "How many students are eight years old?" or "Which students were born in September?" Then ask each youngster to write two or more sentences about the information displayed. Students' understanding about glyphs—and about one another—is sure to bloom!

Susan Ferguson—Gr. 2, Grandy Primary School, Camden, NC

Materials for one sunflower glyph:

copy of the glyph key (page 253)	petal template	marker
orange, brown, green, and yellow construction paper scraps	leaf template	glue
12" x 18" sheet of blue construction paper	sunflower seeds	
3" circle template (for sunflower head)	scissors	

If the Shoe Fits
Skill: measuring length

This activity is a "shoe-in" for sizing up measurement skills! To begin, each child traces her shoe onto a provided sheet of construction paper and then cuts out the resulting shape. She writes her name at the top of her cutout. Then she divides the remaining space into three sections and labels each section as shown. She measures the length of the cutout in centimeters and writes the length on the back.

Next, direct each child to trade cutouts with a classmate. Tell her to measure her partner's cutout and then flip it to check her work. Upon your signal, have each partner retrieve her own cutout. Instruct her to write her partner's name in the appropriate section to indicate whether her partner's shoe is bigger than, smaller than, or the same size as her own. Guide students to repeat this process with several different partners.

adapted from an idea by Leigh Anne Rhodes—Gr. 2
Victory Academy, Baton Rouge, LA

Melissa

Bigger than mine
Danny
Marshall

Same size
Katharine
Randy

Smaller than mine

Diane

Classy Graphs
Skills: collecting and displaying data

Begin each day with this graphing idea, which helps students get to know each other. Compile a list of questions that students would like their classmates to answer. Each morning, write a different question on the board and draw a tally table with several possible responses. (Include an open response such as "other" if appropriate.) Each morning, after a student has unpacked her things, she makes a tally mark on the table to indicate her response. After everyone has had a chance to respond, display the results on a data display such as a pictograph or bar graph. Discuss the graph as a class. Have each student complete a copy of page 254 for more graphing practice.

adapted from an idea by Diane Cirino—ESL Grs. 2–4
Coram Elementary School, Coram, NY

Which is the best place to spend a vacation?

Campgrounds Ski Resort Beach Mountains Other

Fact-Family Pictures
Skill: fact families

Give students a clear picture of the relationship between addition and subtraction! Give each child a 6" x 9" sheet of construction paper, two six-inch construction paper strips, and two nine-inch construction paper strips. Ask her to illustrate her family members on one side of the horizontally positioned paper. On the middle of the other side of the paper, tell her to illustrate two different numerals and their sum as shown. Instruct her to write a different fact from the corresponding fact family on each strip. Have her glue the strips around the fact-family portrait for a frame. Then invite each child to share her project with a classmate and tell about her family on each side!

4 + 8 = 12

12 − 8 = 4

8 + 4 = 12

12 − 4 = 8

The Perfect Day
Skill: telling time

Discover students' interests with this time-telling activity! Ask each child to imagine what his perfect day from morning to night would be like. Encourage him to think about his interests and preferred activities. Then give each child a 9" x 12" sheet of construction paper, four half sheets of drawing paper, and access to a clock stamp and stamp pad. On each page, the child stamps a clock image and writes about something he would do on his perfect day, including the time he would do it. He draws the corresponding hands on the clockface. Then he folds the sheet of construction paper in half to make a booklet cover and staples his sequenced pages inside. He titles the front cover "The Time of My Life!" and signs his name.

For additional time-telling practice, make one copy of page 255. Program the schedule so that it is similar to your class schedule. Then write each activity on a different numbered line. Have each child complete a copy of the programmed page.

adapted from an idea by Kathy Struck, Denison Elementary School, Denison, IA

Valuable Names
Skill: counting coins

This activity shows students the value of their names! Display the provided code. Give each child a set of imitation coins. Each child writes his first name on a sheet of paper. He takes a coin to represent the value of each letter. Then he counts the coins and writes the total beside his name. He repeats this process using the names of fellow students. What a rich way for students to learn money skills and their classmates' names!

Code

1¢	5¢	10¢	25¢
A	G	N	T
B	H	O	U
C	I	P	V
D	J	Q	W
E	K	R	X
F	L	S	Y
	M		Z

Kaytlin   76¢

Sunflower Glyph Key

Head

Do you have pets? _____
Yes—Cut out a **brown** circle for the head.
No—Cut out an **orange** circle for the head.
Place it at the top of the stem.

Seeds

Write the number of the month you were born. _____
Place this many seeds on the head.

Petals

How old are you? _____
Place this many petals around the head.

Leaves

How many brothers and sisters do you have? _____
Place this many leaves on the stem.

Glue the sunflower parts in place.

Lunch Choices

Follow your teacher's directions to complete the tally table.
Color the graph to show the results.

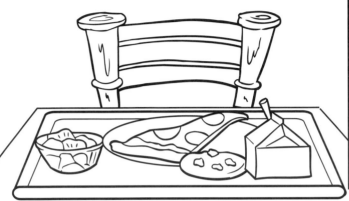

Which lunch choice is your favorite?		
Choice	Tally Marks	Number
Other		

Our Favorite Lunches

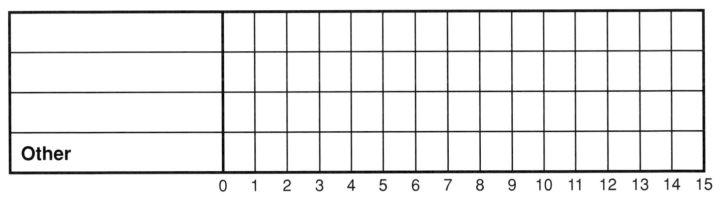

Other															

0 1 2 3 4 5 6 7 8 9 10 11 12 13 14 15

Number of Students

Write four sentences about the graph.

1. _____

2. _____

3. _____

4. _____

Note to the teacher: Make one copy of this page. Program the tally table and graph with the same school lunch choices. Give each student a copy of the programmed page. Then have students vote one at a time for their favorite lunch choices. Tell students to mark each response on the tally table.

What a Day!

Look at the list. For each activity, write the time.
Then draw hands on the clockface.

Our School Day

_____	__:__
_____	__:__
_____	__:__
_____	__:__
_____	__:__
_____	__:__
_____	__:__
_____	__:__
_____	__:__

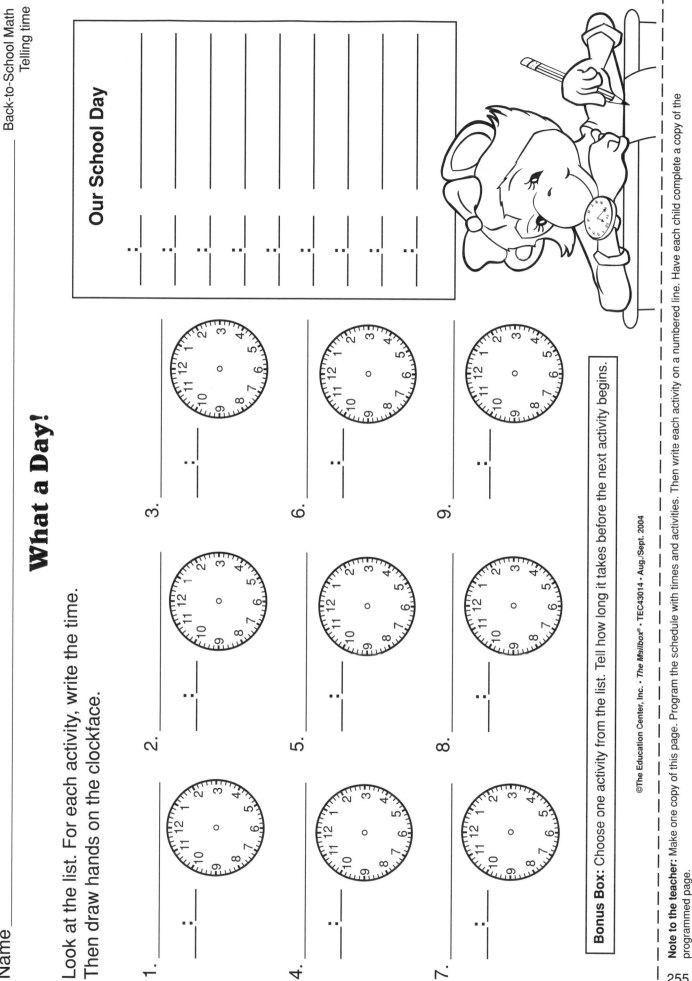

1. __:__

2. __:__

3. __:__

4. __:__

5. __:__

6. __:__

7. __:__

8. __:__

9. __:__

Bonus Box: Choose one activity from the list. Tell how long it takes before the next activity begins.

Note to the teacher: Make one copy of this page. Program the schedule with times and activities. Then write each activity on a numbered line. Have each child complete a copy of the programmed page.

'Tis the Season for... Apples!

These ready-to-pick apple ideas are sure to "a-peel" to your new crop of students!

ideas contributed by Stacie Stone Davis, Lima, NY

WRITING
Apple Announcements

It's true! Apple names can provide a bushel of writing inspiration. Write names such as "Granny Smith," "Red Rome," and "Golden Delicious" on the board. Ask students to suggest how these apples may have been named. For example, maybe Granny Smith apples were named for a grandmother who loved apples! When several explanations have been proposed, challenge each student to illustrate and write about a new variety of apple. Require that each child name his apple variety, explain the meaning of the name, and describe one or more of the apple's unique characteristics. Then plan time for students to share their apple announcements with the class over cups of apple cider.

New Apple!
My new apple is called Backyard Bounce. It grows in your backyard and it bounces like a ball! It does not have a stem. It is best to pick this apple. If it falls from a tree it bounces away.

Venn diagram:
- Fuji: smaller, smooth, streaks
- Both: red, stem, tiny spots
- Red Delicious: larger, shiny, bumpy

SCIENCE
An "A-peel-ing" Investigation

Do sweet-tasting apples look different than tart-tasting apples? That's what students investigate during this small-group activity! Give each group a Venn diagram similar to the one shown and one each of two types of apples to compare and contrast. Ask each group to study the size, shape, color, and texture of each apple as one of its members records the group's observations on the diagram. Then have each group hypothesize (based on its observations and the prior knowledge of its members) which of the two apples might be sweeter. When a group has its hypothesis, wash and slice each of its apples for taste testing. When the munching and crunching subside, invite each group to tell the class what it learned.

You're a
ood App
Congratula
Look Who's a
Good Apple!

Good Apples!

Get to the core of positive behavior with an apple-related idiom! Describe a "good apple" as a person who is considerate and respectful of others. Then, each day, set aside time to recognize your youngsters' good-apple behaviors. If desired, prepare a colorful supply of good-apple tickets (pattern on page 258) and present them to deserving students. Be sure to find an opportunity to praise each child's behavior every few days.

MATH
One Week's Worth!

You've probably heard that eating apples keeps doctors at bay. However, you may not know that eating apples can also polish up data analysis and graphing skills! Post within your students' reach a graph like the one shown. Find out who ate an apple the previous day and have each of those students draw a tally mark on the chart beside the corresponding day. Repeat the activity each school day until a week's worth of apple-eating data is collected. Ask the class several questions about the collected data. Then have each child use the data to make a bar graph that shows the apple-eating habits of the class. Very impressive!

Day	Apples Eaten
Sunday	
Monday	ⅢⅡ I
Tuesday	ⅢⅡ IIII
Wednesday	ⅢⅡ ⅢⅡ II
Thursday	ⅢⅡ III
Friday	ⅢⅡ I

Letter Sets
i, l, o, p, t
b, d, e, n, t
b, n, o, s, u
a, f, i, n, p
a, c, n, r, t

Possible Words
(it, lip, lit, lop, lot, pot, pit, tip, top)
(be, bed, bet, bent, bend, den, debt, ten)
(us, on, bus, bun, son, sun, sob, sub)
(in, an, fin, fan, pin, pan, pain, nap, nip)
(an, at, ant, can, car, cat, cart, rat, ran, tan, tar)

SPELLING
Seed by Seed

Sprout interest in word formation with an apple a day! Post a set of letters (see those provided) and hand out student copies of the apple pattern on page 258. Have each child write the letters in the seed outlines. Then challenge her to use the letters to form words. Have her write the words she makes on her apple. Clarify that a letter can only be used one time per word. Later, invite students to share the words they made. Then have each child cut out her apple shape, glue it on red construction paper, trim the red paper to make a border, and glue a construction paper stem and leaf in place.

The next day, have each child repeat the word formation activity with a different letter set. This time have each child cut out her apple and staple it to her project from the previous day. Plan to repeat the word formation activity for as many days as desired.

den
dent
be
bed
b
e
tip
top
pot
pit

Apple Pattern
Use with "Seed by Seed" on page 257.

Good-Apple Tickets
Use with "Good Apples!" on page 257.

You're a

Good Apple!
©The Education Center, Inc.

Congratulations,

Good Apple!
©The Education Center, Inc.

Look Who's a

Good Apple!
©The Education Center, Inc.

Falling Apples!

Name_____

Complete each number pattern.

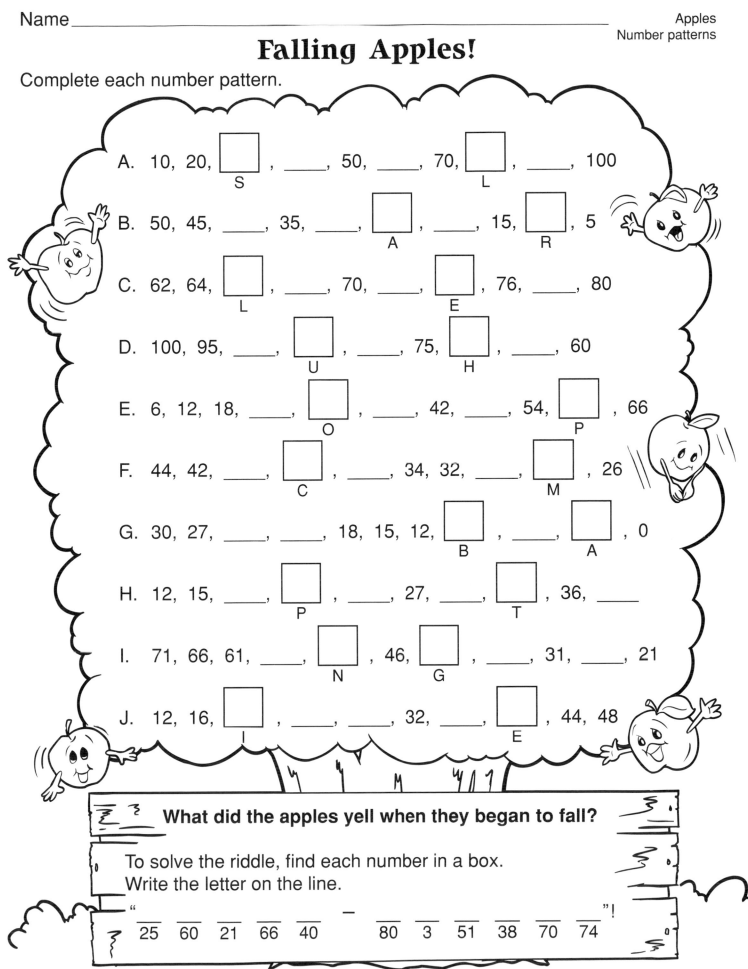

A. 10, 20, ☐S, ____, 50, ____, 70, ☐L, ____, 100

B. 50, 45, ____, 35, ____, ☐A, ____, 15, ☐R, 5

C. 62, 64, ☐L, ____, 70, ____, ☐E, 76, ____, 80

D. 100, 95, ____, ☐U, ____, 75, ☐H, ____, 60

E. 6, 12, 18, ____, ☐O, ____, 42, ____, 54, ☐P, 66

F. 44, 42, ____, ☐C, ____, 34, 32, ____, ☐M, 26

G. 30, 27, ____, ____, 18, 15, 12, ☐B, ____, ☐A, 0

H. 12, 15, ____, ☐P, ____, 27, ____, ☐T, 36, ____

I. 71, 66, 61, ____, ☐N, 46, ☐G, ____, 31, ____, 21

J. 12, 16, ☐I, ____, ____, 32, ____, ☐E, 44, 48

What did the apples yell when they began to fall?

To solve the riddle, find each number in a box.
Write the letter on the line.

" ___ ___ ___ ___ ___ — ___ ___ ___ ___ ___ ___ "!
  25 60 21 66 40   80 3 51 38 70 74

'Tis the Season for...

Use these carefully spun activities to weave a
web of cross-curricular learning for your students!

ideas contributed by Leigh Anne Rhodes
Victory Academy, Baton Rouge, LA

MATH
Flossy Draglines

Put a new spin on measurement practice by asking
students to size up spider draglines! To make this center
activity, attach a spider sticker to each of several construction
paper circles. Program each circle with a different length in
inches or centimeters. Laminate the circles for durability.
Then, using the programmed measurements, cut a dragline
from dental floss for each spider. Be sure to wrap the ends of
the floss with tape (or dip them in glue) to prevent unraveling.
Store the draglines, the cutouts, and two rulers in a seasonal
gift bag. Invite students to complete the center alone or with
a partner. Hey, this center makes measuring smooth as silk!

GRAMMAR
An Eight-Legged Helper

Encourage your spider enthusiasts to become skillful spinners
of vivid verbs, descriptive adjectives, and specific nouns. Make
a class supply of the eight-legged word web shown. Then, as a
prewriting activity, ask students to brainstorm a specific category
of words such as adjectives that describe spiders, verbs that tell
how spiders move, or nouns that name specific spider foods.
Have each child write a different word or phrase on each leg of
her spider. She'll have a ready-to-use word bank, and she'll be
reminded of the helpful nature of spiders.

Nancy Anderson, Troy, OH

run
jump
crawl
hide
creep
swing
spin
scurry

Spider Moves

Spiders!

My new and improved spider is red, purple, and yellow. It is very big, very soft, and very fuzzy. It does not bite. It smiles all the time. It has a leash so I can take it for a walk. We play too. It minds very well. It also eats all the bugs around my house!

New and Improved

Some people find spiders a bit creepy. So why not challenge students to describe how they would make spiders more appealing? First, review a spider's body parts and clarify that these cannot change. Next, ask students what they least like about spiders. List their comments on the board and agree that these characteristics could change. In a similar manner, list what students most like about spiders and agree that these characteristics could stay the same. Provide plenty of time for writing. Plan for each child to copy his final draft on web-shaped paper. Also provide arts-and-crafts supplies that students can use to fashion models of their new and improved spiders. Use a length of yarn to connect each child's spider and web. Then showcase the projects with the title "Spider Makeovers."

I think Anansi is clever because in the story he knows when to be quiet!

I'm not the one who talks to melons!

A Tricky Arachnid

Who's the trickiest spider of all? It just might be Anansi, the arachnid of folklore fame. In Eric A. Kimmel's retelling of *Anansi and the Talking Melon,* this mischievous eight-legger wiggles into trouble by squeezing inside a ripe and juicy melon. Read the story aloud. Then, after a recap of Anansi's behavior, give each child a six-inch circle of blank paper on which to illustrate Anansi and copy and complete the following prompt: "I think Anansi is _____ because in the story he…" In addition, have each child lightly sponge-paint two six-inch circles of tan construction paper with orange tempera paint. When the paint is dry, tell each child to cut a small hole in one of his painted cutouts. Then, keeping this cutout on top, have him staple his writing between his two painted cutouts. Also suggest that he cut a speech bubble from scrap paper, program it with words that Anansi might say, and glue it to the front cover of his project. No doubt Anansi will permanently change the way your youngsters look at spiders!

261

ART
No Two Alike

Every spiderweb is unique, and so is each of these student-painted ones! To render a house spider's tangled web, have a student lay a sheet of black construction paper in the bottom of a rectangular pan. Using a spoon, dip two or three marbles in white tempera paint and then drop the paint-coated marbles on the paper. Direct the child to maneuver the marbles back and forth across the paper by repeatedly lifting and tilting the pan. When a desired result is achieved, remove the artwork from the pan to dry. Later, have each child personalize his project with a glitter pen and trim it into a web shape. Then help him tape his personalized web to the front or side of his desk. Every web is unique, and so is every child!

- Mr. House Spider, is it true that you do not chew your food?
- That is right. I can't chew. I drink my food.

- Do you spin a web to catch your food?
- Yes I do. I spin a tangled web.

- Mr. House Spider, how do you hear without ears?
- The tiny hairs on my legs and body help me hear.

- How many eyes do you have, Mr. House Spider?
- I have eight eyes, and I still don't see very well!

SCIENCE
Spider Interviews

Stay tuned for the inside scoop on spiders. To prepare a spider interview sheet, have each child fold a sheet of blank paper in half lengthwise three times and then unfold her paper to reveal eight narrow sections. Next, instruct each child to alternate between two crayon colors as she draws a large colorful dot in the far left of each section. Have her write a spider-related interview question (one she can correctly answer) in the first section and then write the answer to the question in the second section, wording the response as if a spider had spoken it. Have her continue working down the page in this manner until she has four color-coded question-and-answer pairings. Provide time for students to add spider decorations to their papers. Then invite each child to air her spider interview for the class before she takes it home to share with her family.

Kelli Higgins—Gr. 3, P.L. Bolin Elementary School
East Peoria, IL

262

A Spider Slipup

In which chapter did Sammy Spider find each fact?
Use the table of contents.
Fill in the missing chapter numbers.

Table of Contents

Chapter	Fact
	All spiders spin silk.
	Not all spiders weave webs.
	A baby spider is called a spiderling.
	A spider has two body parts and eight legs.
	A crab spider moves sideways.
	Spider silk is very strong.
	Most spiders live one or two years.
	There are seven kinds of spider silk.
	A spider begins its life inside an egg.
	An ant spider looks a lot like an ant.
	There are different kinds of spider webs.
	A spider is not an insect.

Bonus Box: Figure out which chapter Sammy forgot to read. Write the name of the chapter on the back of this paper. Then write one spider fact that Sammy might find in the chapter.

Every Spider's Secret

Complete each subtraction sentence.
Then write the related addition sentence.

Please
don't tell!

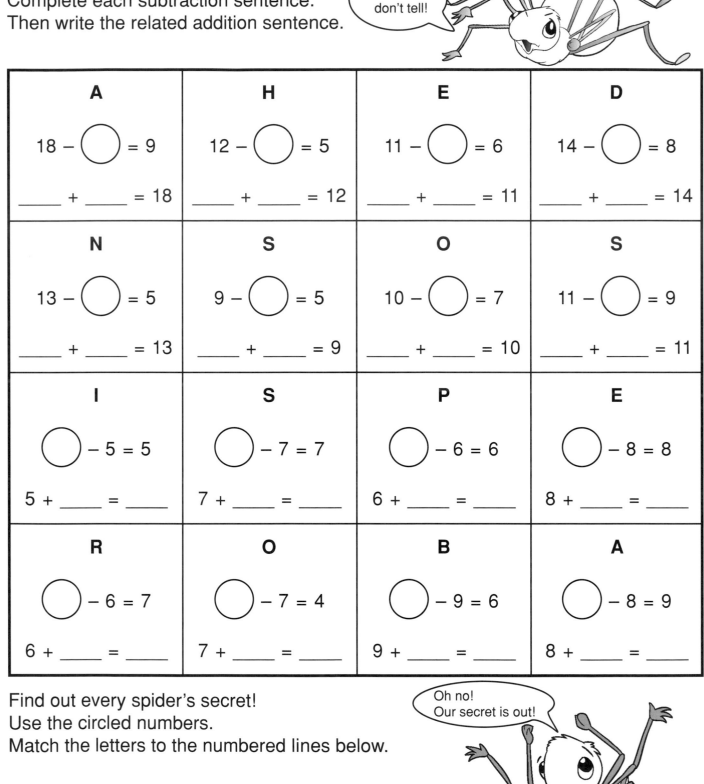

A	H	E	D
18 − ◯ = 9	12 − ◯ = 5	11 − ◯ = 6	14 − ◯ = 8
___ + ___ = 18	___ + ___ = 12	___ + ___ = 11	___ + ___ = 14
N	S	O	S
13 − ◯ = 5	9 − ◯ = 5	10 − ◯ = 7	11 − ◯ = 9
___ + ___ = 13	___ + ___ = 9	___ + ___ = 10	___ + ___ = 11
I	S	P	E
◯ − 5 = 5	◯ − 7 = 7	◯ − 6 = 6	◯ − 8 = 8
5 + ___ = ___	7 + ___ = ___	6 + ___ = ___	8 + ___ = ___
R	O	B	A
◯ − 6 = 7	◯ − 7 = 4	◯ − 9 = 6	◯ − 8 = 9
6 + ___ = ___	7 + ___ = ___	9 + ___ = ___	8 + ___ = ___

Find out every spider's secret!
Use the circled numbers.
Match the letters to the numbered lines below.

Oh no!
Our secret is out!

___   ___ ___ ___ ___ ___ ___
9   4   12   10   6   5   13

___ ___ ___   ___ ___   ___ ___ ___ ___ ___!
7   17   14   8   11   15   3   8   16   2

Skills for the Season

October Odes

Students are sure to go batty over these **poetry-writing** booklets, which provide practice with **adjectives and verbs!** To make a booklet, have each student cut an 11" x 17" sheet of black construction paper into a bat shape as shown. Then direct her to trim several sheets of white paper to fit inside the folded bat wings and staple them in place as shown. Have her use crayons to illustrate a bat's face.

Display books about bats in your classroom and brainstorm bat words and phrases. Once students have lots of rich imagery, direct them to write a poem about bats as shown. Have students copy their finished poems into their bat booklets. Then challenge students to write poems about pumpkins, spiders, scarecrows, skeletons, and other seasonal topics in their booklets.

Starin Lewis, Phoenix, AZ

Line 1 = the topic, Bats
Line 2 = two adjectives related to bats
Line 3 = three verbs about bats
Line 4 = two more adjectives about bats
Line 5 = the topic, Bats

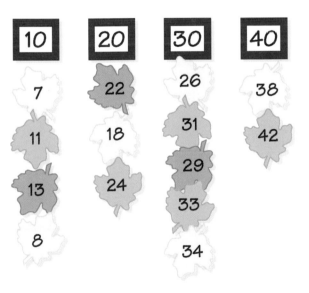

Fall Foliage Fun

Rake in heaps of practice with **rounding numbers to the nearest ten** during this "unbe-leaf-able" activity. Program a supply of laminated construction paper leaves with two-digit numbers. Then program nine paper squares by tens, from 10 to 90. Stick a self-adhesive magnet to the back of each square and leaf. Attach the squares to a magnetic surface. Each morning place a leaf on each student's desk. Direct students to round the numbers to the nearest ten and then place the leaves in the appropriate spot. As a group, check the leaves to make sure they've been rounded correctly. Between uses, store leaves in a basket. "Tree-mendous"!

Sheila Criqui-Kelley, Lebo Elementary, Lebo, KS

Gobbling Up Math Facts

Serve up a fine-feathered feast of **fact families** with this activity. Provide a copy of the patterns on page 266, a seven-inch paper plate, a marker, colored chalk, and access to tape for each student. Assign each student a different fact family and have him copy onto his plate the sentence shown, filling in his three numbers. Then, on the individual feathers, direct him to write the math sentences for that family. Next, have him color and cut out the turkey feathers, head, and feet and then tape them to the plate. To complete the project, have him color the plate to resemble a turkey's body. Wow! Those are some terrific turkeys!

Allyson Levy, Gr. 2—Middlebrook Elementary, Trumbull, CT

Turkey Patterns
Use with "Gobbling Up Math Facts" on page 265.

head

feathers

feet

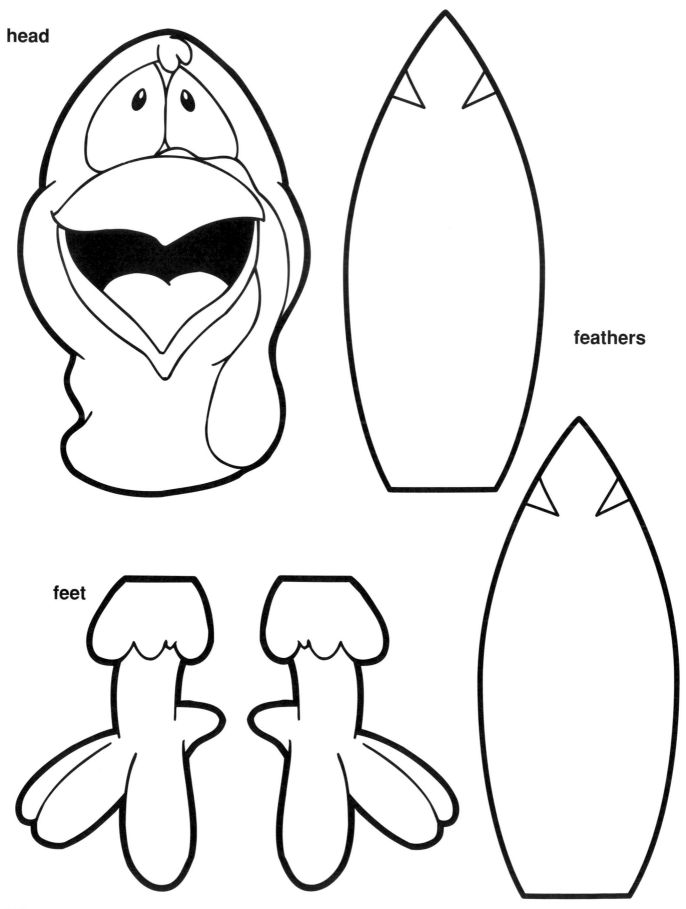

Giving!

Embrace the holiday season with skill-based activities that encourage students to give from the heart.

ideas by Laura Wagner, Raleigh, NC

WRITING
Holiday Gift List

An assortment of gift-giving options surfaces during this list-making activity. Talk with students about the joy of giving to others. Next, help youngsters brainstorm a variety of thoughtful gifts that can be given without making a purchase (such as helping with household chores). Have each child list on his paper six people to whom he would like to give a holiday gift. Then ask him to carefully consider the interests and needs of each person before he completes his gift list.

To ready each gift on his list for giving, have a student fold in half a large index card, keeping the lines to the outside. Inside the folded card have him write a brief personalized note that describes his gift. Invite him to wrap each gift in a precut 5" x 10" rectangle of holiday gift wrap and then decorate and label each wrapped gift using available supplies. If he wishes to suspend a gift from a tree, have him prepare it for hanging as shown. How nice!

To: Roger
From: Lori

Dear Grandpa,
I remember the time you took me to the planetarium and we saw the show about the stars. I loved that show! When I see stars at night I think of you and how much fun we had. Thank you for this memory!
Love,
Amelia

For Zachary

Happy Holidays

READING
Gifts of Kindness

Spotlight several gifts of kindness and reinforce comprehension skills by having each child complete a copy of page 269. This activity reminds students that gifts of kindness can be given every day of the year!

LITERATURE
Remember When...

Inspire one-of-a-kind gifts with an oral reading of Mem Fox's *Wilfrid Gordon McDonald Partridge*. In this touching tale, a young boy gives his favorite person, Miss Nancy, a gift of precious memories. At the conclusion of the story, invite a few students to share special memories of their own. Then suggest that this holiday season every student give the gift of a memory. Ask each child to select a recipient and, in a letter written to this person, recall a special time the two have shared. Ask each child to make a holiday card for this person too. When both projects are complete, have the child tuck her gift inside the card she made. Suggest that students deliver their gifts in person. When this isn't possible, help a child prepare her gift for mailing.

HEALTH
A Most Precious Gift

Gifts come in a variety of sizes and shapes, and this gift is no exception! Guide students to understand why their loved ones will be delighted to receive a collection of promises that relate to the students' health and safety. Guide students in brainstorming such promises. Then give each child six 4" x 5" paper rectangles on which to write five promises and a dedication for a loved one. Also have her decorate the blank side of a large index card to resemble holiday gift wrap. Next, instruct her to fold the decorated card in half (keeping the decorations to the outside), stack her rectangles with the dedication on top, and staple the stack inside the folded card.

For an extra special delivery, have each child fashion a self-likeness from art supplies that include a six-inch circle of skin-toned paper (face) and two construction paper strips (4½" x 12" for pants and 2" x 12" for long-sleeved top). Help each child assemble her project so it resembles the one shown. What a precious gift!

For my mom who worries about me a bunch. I love you! Bryanna

Ms. William and Ms. Martin,
We think your tacos are the best!

Leon Nigel Joseph Nia
Maria Theo
Grace Melany
Kym Alex

Happy Holidays!

SOCIAL STUDIES
Thanking Community Helpers

You don't need to look any further than your school to find a meaningful community project for the holidays. Remind the class that a school is an important part of a community. Ask students to name the roles of people who make their school a safe and happy place (such as a principal, secretary, librarian, teacher, food server, and custodian). Then engage students in brainstorming ways they can show their appreciation for the people in these roles. Ideas might include student-made office decorations for the school secretary and student-made bookmarks for the librarian. When the gifts are agreed upon, have students make and deliver the gifts. Happy holidays!

MATH
A Mystery to Solve

Here's a gift-related mystery that can only be solved using logical reasoning! Copy page 270 to make a class supply. Inform students that Papa Elf has received six very thoughtful gifts from his elf helpers, but he's forgotten which helper gave him each gift. Have each child complete a copy of page 270. Then set aside time for students to compare their results.

For Brett

Gifts of Kindness

The workshop is closed for the winter! All the elves are eager to go home. Little Ed helps his friend Ella find her missing mitten. Then he begins his hike home. On Green Street he passes Mr. Crump's house. He sees the older elf sitting in the window. Ed stops and waves. Mr. Crump smiles and waves back.

At the corner of Red Street, Ed cuts through Snowflake Park. He makes lots of fresh tracks in the snow. Then Ed spots a candy cane wrapper on the ground. He grabs the wrapper and drops it in a trash can.

Ed is almost home when he sees his friend Mrs. Finch. She has a large shopping bag in each hand. Ed offers to carry a bag upstairs to her apartment. As he leaves the apartment, Mrs. Finch hands Ed the biggest sugar cookie he has ever seen!

Elves,
Do Not
Litter!

Write a complete sentence to answer each question.

1. How does Ed help Ella? _____

   _____

2. Why does Ed pick up the candy cane wrapper? _____

   _____

3. What is Ed's gift to Mr. Crump? _____

   _____

4. Why do you think Ed offers to help Mrs. Finch? _____

   _____

5. What gift of kindness have you given today? _____

   _____

Bonus Box: Use a crayon to underline Ed's four gifts of kindness in the story.

©The Education Center, Inc. · *The Mailbox*® · TEC43016 · Dec./Jan. 2004–5 · Key p. 313

Note to the teacher: Use with "Gifts of Kindness" on page 267.

269

Name _____

Gifts for Papa Elf

Who gave Papa each gift?
Read the clues.
Use the code.
Draw an **X** or a ✓ in each empty box.

Code
X = did not give this gift
✓ = gave this gift

Clues

Sneezy sneezes around animals.
Sloppy is not allowed in the kitchen.
Shiny makes everything shine.

Sleepy loves cats.
Snoopy has a broken leg and arm.
Sweety likes to bake.

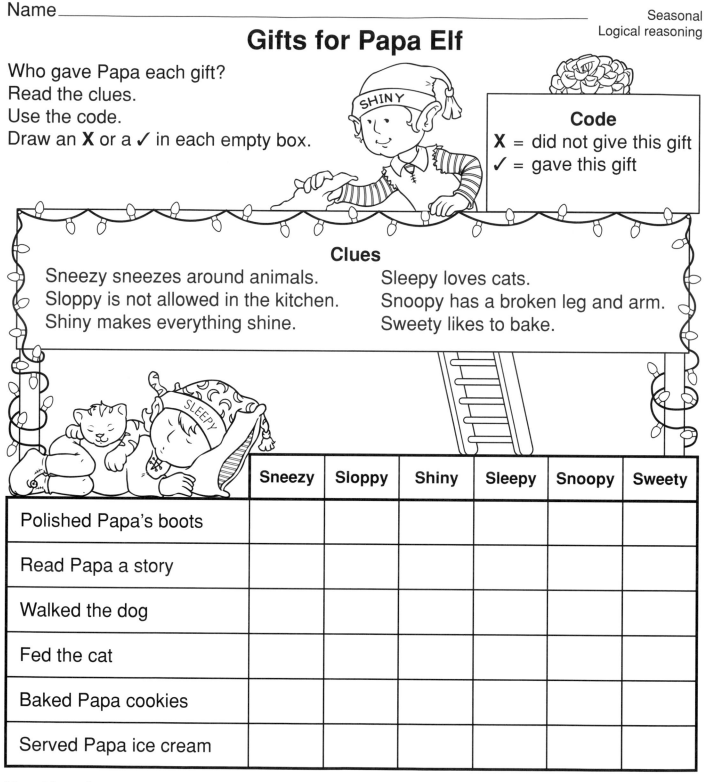

	Sneezy	Sloppy	Shiny	Sleepy	Snoopy	Sweety
Polished Papa's boots						
Read Papa a story						
Walked the dog						
Fed the cat						
Baked Papa cookies						
Served Papa ice cream						

Use the chart to answer each question.

1. Who read Papa a story? _____

2. Who baked Papa cookies? _____

3. Who helped with the pets? _____

_____

©The Education Center, Inc. • *The Mailbox* • TEC43016 • Dec./Jan. 2004–5 • Key p. 313

Note to the teacher: Use with "A Mystery to Solve" on page 268.

Skills for the Season

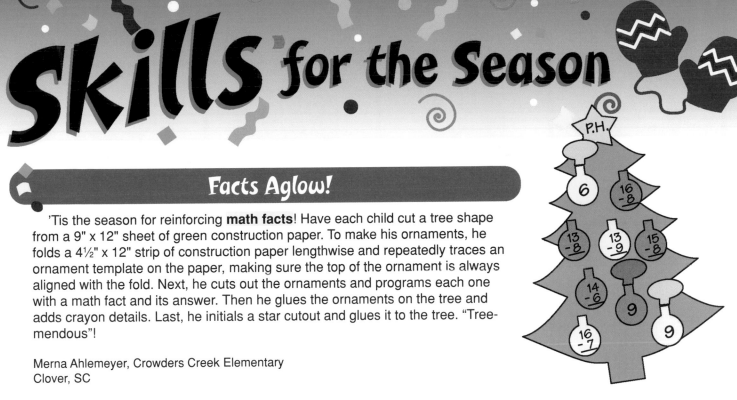

Facts Aglow!

'Tis the season for reinforcing **math facts**! Have each child cut a tree shape from a 9" x 12" sheet of green construction paper. To make his ornaments, he folds a 4½" x 12" strip of construction paper lengthwise and repeatedly traces an ornament template on the paper, making sure the top of the ornament is always aligned with the fold. Next, he cuts out the ornaments and programs each one with a math fact and its answer. Then he glues the ornaments on the tree and adds crayon details. Last, he initials a star cutout and glues it to the tree. "Tree-mendous"!

Merna Ahlemeyer, Crowders Creek Elementary
Clover, SC

Penguin Chitchat

Writing dialogue for two perky penguins is a ton of fun for students! Have each child divide a sheet of blank paper into fourths. Also have him color and cut out four poses of each penguin from a copy of page 272. To complete the project, he glues the cutouts on his paper so the two penguins appear in each quadrant. Then he writes the penguins' dialogue, enclosing each penguin's words in a speech bubble. If the penguins are especially chatty, he can flip his paper over and use the remaining cutouts to extend their conversation!

adapted from an idea by Natalie Hughes-Tanner, Ermel Elementary
Houston, TX

A Man of Words

Even as a young boy, Martin Luther King Jr. understood the importance of **word knowledge**. If possible, read aloud *Martin's Big Words: The Life of Dr. Martin Luther King, Jr.* by Doreen Rappaport. Then, once a week, introduce a new vocabulary word to students. Have students say the word, clap its syllables, share prior knowledge of the word, and predict its meaning. Then say the word in context, verify its meaning, and join students in using the word in daily language. Near the end of the week, have each child enter the word in her book of big words.

To make the book of big words, give each student one copy of the top half and several copies of the bottom half of page 273. A child cuts out the pages and personalizes the title page. Keeping this page on top, she staples the pages between two 4" x 5½" construction paper rectangles. Next, she adds her name and self-portrait to the oval, cuts it out, and glues it to the booklet cover. Dr. King would be so pleased!

adapted from an idea by Jacqueline Fraser, John F. Turner Elementary
Palm Bay, FL

Penguin Patterns
Use with "Penguin Chitchat" on page 271.

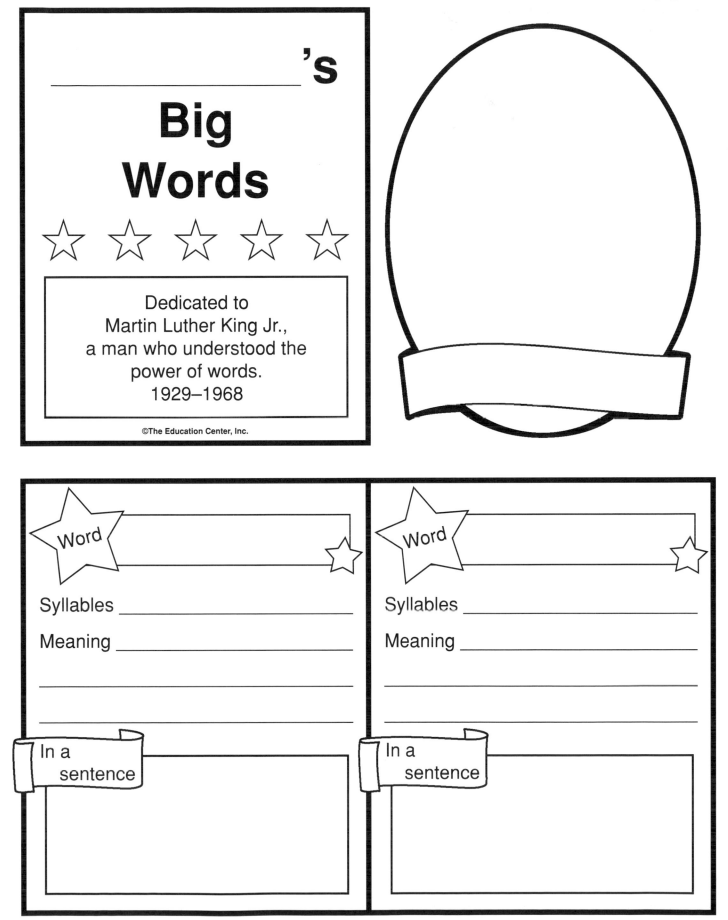

_____'s

Big Words

☆ ☆ ☆ ☆ ☆

Dedicated to
Martin Luther King Jr.,
a man who understood the
power of words.
1929–1968

©The Education Center, Inc.

Word _____

Syllables _____

Meaning _____
_____
_____

In a
sentence

Word _____

Syllables _____

Meaning _____
_____
_____

In a
sentence

Skills for the Season

More Than Just a Hat

During the month of February, pull **skill review** out of a stovepipe hat! Abraham Lincoln, who had a habit of tucking messages inside his hat, would certainly approve! Construct the hat from black tagboard or construction paper, leaving the top open. Each day before students arrive, tuck a task card and the supplies needed to complete the task inside the hat. Then, with great fanfare, have a volunteer unveil the day's task. For added fun, have students deposit their completed papers in the hat!

Lydia Hess, Providence School, Chambersburg, PA

> ★ Write the 12 months of the year in ABC order. Draw a red circle around your birth month. ★

Please Be Mine!

Designing a special valentine requires a **sense of audience,** and these valentines are no exception! Ask each student to choose a favorite nursery rhyme or fairy-tale character and write a valentine message that is made-to-order for that character. Remind her to consider the habits, needs, and wants of her character as she writes. Then have her design a valentine card that includes her written message. Be sure to set aside time for each student to share her valentine greeting and explain why she feels it's perfect for its intended receiver.

VaReane Heese, Springfield Elementary, Springfield, NE

Colorful Egg Decor

This "eggs-traordinary" review of **fractional parts of a set** doesn't look like math, but it is! First, have each child cut a large egg shape from construction paper. Next, provide colorful one-inch paper squares for decorating the eggs. Then have each student determine the fractions that describe his egg decor. To do this, he finds the denominator by counting the total number of squares on his egg. Then he labels an index card with the fractional amount of each color of square. If desired, display the eggs and cards separately and invite students to hunt for matches. It's an egg hunt!

adapted from an idea by Anna Walsh
M. B. Garvin Microsociety School
East Orange, NJ

$\frac{6}{21}$ green $\frac{6}{21}$ blue
$\frac{6}{21}$ pink $\frac{3}{21}$ purple
Decor by Trevor

An Amazing Woman

Read.
Write a word from each sentence in the puzzle.
   (Hint: Only one word will fit.)

1. My parents were slaves.
2. I was born a slave.
3. My name was Araminta.
4. My family called me Minty.
5. Being a slave was very hard work.
6. At night I listened to stories of freedom.
7. I learned about the Underground Railroad.
8. My dream was to escape.
9. I was an adult when I escaped to freedom.
10. I was so thankful to be free!
11. I helped many other slaves find freedom.
12. I kept helping people for the rest of my life.

Harriet Tubman was the first African American woman to be pictured on this.
What is it? (Hint: Study the puzzle from top to bottom.)

_ _ _ _ _ _ _   _ _ _ _ _ _

Name_____

Searching for Shamrocks

Use each clue to find a three-digit number.
Write the number on the line.
Color the shamrock.

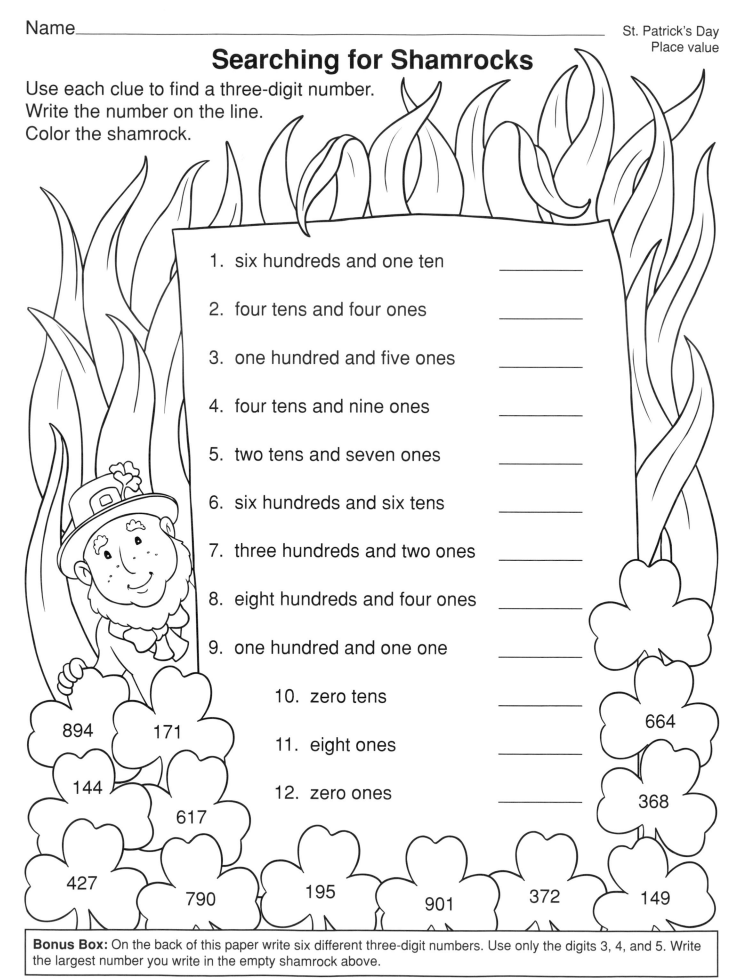

1. six hundreds and one ten _____

2. four tens and four ones _____

3. one hundred and five ones _____

4. four tens and nine ones _____

5. two tens and seven ones _____

6. six hundreds and six tens _____

7. three hundreds and two ones _____

8. eight hundreds and four ones _____

9. one hundred and one one _____

10. zero tens _____

11. eight ones _____

12. zero ones _____

894   171

144

617

427   790   195   901   372   149

664

368

Bonus Box: On the back of this paper write six different three-digit numbers. Use only the digits 3, 4, and 5. Write the largest number you write in the empty shamrock above.

'Tis the Season for... WIND!

Whoooosh! Look at what's twirling through your curriculum! It's a light and breezy collection of wind-related activities blowing in just for you!

ideas contributed by Stacie Stone Davis, Lima, NY

LITERATURE
Brother Wind

Students are sure to relate to the main character in *Mirandy and Brother Wind* by Patricia C. McKissack. After all, who wouldn't like to capture the wind for one reason or another? After an oral reading of the text, discuss Mirandy's reason(s) for wanting to catch the wind. Next, have each child imagine for a moment that he catches the wind. In what positive way will he use it? Ask each child to describe and illustrate his idea. Showcase students' creative ideas on a bulletin board titled "Watch Out, Brother Wind!"

I took the wind into my bedroom. I asked it to blow everything I stuffed under my bed back to where it is supposed to be!

Kyle

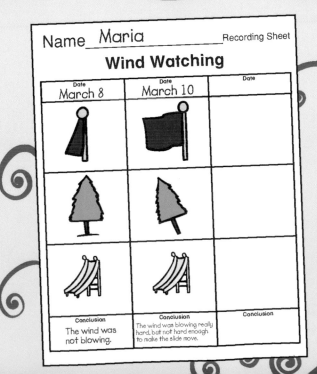

Name Maria — Recording Sheet
Wind Watching

Date March 8	Date March 10	Date
Conclusion The wind was not blowing.	Conclusion The wind was blowing really hard, but not hard enough to make the slide move.	Conclusion

SCIENCE
The Wind at Work

During this investigation youngsters get caught up in observing and drawing conclusions about the impact of the wind. Begin on a day with little or no wind. Take students outdoors to observe the position of three different objects, such as a flag, a leafy plant or tree, and a piece of heavy playground equipment. Then return to the classroom and have each child illustrate on a recording sheet what she observed. Explain that these illustrations show how the objects look when the air is calm. Have students write a similar conclusion. Plan for students to observe the same items on two different days while the wind is blowing. Each time have students record their observations, compare their most recent drawings to past drawings, and write brief conclusions. Use the students' observations and conclusions as a basis for discussing the varying effects of wind. Whoooosh!

MATH
What's Windchill?

Can reading a chart make students shiver? When it's a windchill chart, perhaps! Confirm with students that winds can lower air temperature. Explain that when it's hot outside, a cooling wind is nice. However, when it's cold outside, wind makes the air even colder! To find out how much colder, give each child a copy of page 279 to complete. Brrr! That's cold!

Starin Lewis
Phoenix, AZ

LANGUAGE ARTS
Missing Punctuation!

With a bit of imagination, you can make the wind work for you! To reinforce editing skills, write at one end of the board a set of sentences without punctuation. At the opposite end of the board, write the missing punctuation marks. Inform students that a blast of wind blew the punctuation right out of the sentences! For a large-group activity, engage students in editing the sentences on the board. For an independent activity, have students copy and edit the sentences on paper. Sometimes it's the little things that make learning the most fun.

ART
All-Season Windsock

Making this windsock reminds students that regardless of the season, wind is always on the move! To make a windsock, a student uses a ruler (or a 4" x 6" template) to divide a 6" x 18" length of white construction paper into four four-inch panels and one two-inch panel. She labels one large panel for each season of the year and then illustrates each panel to show one way the wind works during that season. Next, she rolls the strip into a cylinder and glues the overlapping edges together (keeping her illustrations to the outside). She glues several 16-inch strips of colorful crepe paper along the lower edge of the project. Then she punches two holes opposite each other at the top of the project, threads each end of a 36-inch length of yarn through a different hole, and securely ties each yarn end. Boy, the wind sure is busy!

Keeping It Cool!

Use the chart.
Find the windchill.

Wind Speed (mph)							
0	**5**	**10**	**15**	**20**	**25**	**30**	**35**
40	36	34	32	30	29	28	28
35	31	27	25	24	23	22	21
30	25	21	19	17	16	15	14
25	19	15	13	11	9	8	7
20	13	9	6	4	3	1	0
15	7	3	0	-2	-4	-5	-7
10	1	-4	-7	-9	-11	-12	-14
5	-5	-10	-13	-15	-17	-19	-21
0	-11	-16	-19	-22	-24	-26	-27
-5	-16	-22	-26	-29	-31	-33	-34
-10	-22	-28	-32	-35	-37	-39	-41

Temperature (°F)

1. The temperature is 25°F.
   The wind speed is 15 mph.
   The windchill is _____°F.

2. The temperature is 40°F.
   The wind speed is 35 mph.
   The windchill is _____°F.

3. The temperature is 10°F.
   The wind speed is 30 mph.
   The windchill is _____°F.

4. The temperature is -10°F.
   The wind speed is 15 mph.
   The windchill is _____°F.

5. The temperature is 30°F.
   The wind speed is 20 mph.
   The windchill is _____°F.

6. The temperature is 20°F.
   The wind speed is 5 mph.
   The windchill is _____°F.

7. The temperature is 0°F.
   The wind speed is 20 mph.
   The windchill is _____°F.

8. The temperature is -5°F.
   The wind speed is 25 mph.
   The windchill is _____°F.

9. The temperature is 0°F.
   There is no wind.
   The windchill is _____°F.

10. The temperature is -5°F.
    The wind speed is 10 mph.
    The windchill is _____°F.

Note to the teacher: Use with "What's Windchill?" on page 278.

279

Name _____

Blown Away!

Use each dictionary entry.
Find the meaning of the underlined word.
Write it on the line.

wind (wĭnd) *noun*
1. moving air
2. breath

wind (wīnd) *verb*
1. to wrap around
2. to twist and turn

1. The <u>wind</u> blew the door shut. _____

2. Hurricanes have very strong <u>winds</u>. _____

3. The fall knocked the <u>wind</u> out of me. _____

4. Please <u>wind</u> the kite string. _____

5. The river <u>winds</u> through the forest. _____

6. Tornado <u>winds</u> blow in a circle. _____

7. This path <u>winds</u> back and forth. _____

8. Is there enough <u>wind</u> to fly a kite? _____

9. <u>Wind</u> the string around the post. _____

10. His <u>wind</u> was gone after the race. _____

'Tis the Season for...
Butterflies

A colorful collection of student-engaging skill review is just a flutter away! And because we understand how busy you are, we're also including butterfly patterns, an incentive chart, a colorful sorting mat, and skill sheets. Perhaps it's time to unfold your wings and dance a little!

ideas contributed by Jennifer L. Kohnke,
Nature Ridge Elementary, Bartlett, IL

MATH
Designer Wings

When students complete this colorful review of **symmetry and geometric shapes,** a striking math display is born! Hand out student copies of page 284 and ask each child to find the line of symmetry on the butterfly. Then challenge her to maintain the symmetry as she colors the butterfly and decorates its wings with a variety of geometric shapes. When she's finished, ask her to cut out her fancy flyer. Next, have her name and describe the butterfly on a blank card. Finally, invite each designer to introduce the butterfly to the class. Then showcase the projects with the title "Wings of Symmetry."

This is Showy Sam. He is very colorful! The top part of each wing has a big blue circle. The bottom part of each wing has two purple triangles.

SCIENCE
From Egg to Adult

The stages of a butterfly's **life cycle** fit perfectly inside this adorable caterpillar booklet! Cut blank paper in half lengthwise and give each student three pieces to stack horizontally. Have each child slide his top two sheets to the left and then fold his papers to create six graduated layers. Staple each child's booklet near the fold. Next, have each student draw a segmented caterpillar on the front of his booklet and label the layers as shown. Provide a brief description of each life cycle stage for students to copy and illustrate on the corresponding booklet page. (See the samples shown.) Then lead students in reading their booklets from beginning to end two consecutive times to show how the last booklet page prompts a reader to begin the butterfly's life cycle again!

My life as

an egg, a larva, a pupa, an adult, and then,

A butterfly lays an egg.

an egg,

The egg hatches into a larva.

a larva,

The larva makes a case around itself and becomes a pupa.

a pupa,

The case turns clear and out comes an adult.

an adult,

In time, an adult female is ready to lay her eggs. And then...

and then,

WRITING
Butterfly Words

Your students' awareness of **word choice** is just about to soar! On the board write an overused word such as *walk*. Describe the word as being good yet plain. Then draw a caterpillar around it. Remind students that caterpillars turn into colorful, captivating butterflies. Next, ask students to suggest colorful and captivating alternatives for *walk* (such as *stomp* and *tiptoe*). Write these words on the board near the caterpillar. Repeat the activity for each of several overused words. Then copy each collection of words onto a colorful butterfly cutout (see the pattern on page 284) and display the cutouts in your writing center. Or have students customize butterfly cutouts for their writing folders.

walk
saunter
wander
hobble
amble
stroll
stomp
tiptoe

ART
Fabulous Flyers

These 3-D paper toppers foster **creativity and writing inspiration.** To make one, use crayons to color a white construction paper copy of the butterfly pattern on page 285. Do not color areas you wish to be black. Glue the pattern onto colorful paper. Then use a mixture of black tempera paint and liquid dish soap to paint the pattern. When the project is dry, cut out the pattern, fold it in half (keeping the painted surface to the outside), and make a 1½-inch cut along the center of the fold. For writing inspiration, slide the butterfly onto a top corner of a folded 9" x 12" sheet of construction paper and tape the corner to the inside of the butterfly. Students can glue their edited writing to the front of the display. Now, if I were a butterfly…

If I were a butterfly, I would fly to Hawaii. I would look for seashells. I would drink nectar from big, beautiful flowers. I might even see a volcano. Then I would fly home.

READING
Aflutter With Understanding

Keep a clear view of your students' **comprehension skills** handy! Store a transparency of page 284 near your overhead projector. Then simply use a wipe-off marker to label the outline for a review of story details (story elements, cause and effect, etc.) and write your youngsters' ideas on the resulting organizer. When the discussion is complete, wipe the transparency clean and return it to its handy location.

Who? What? When? Where?

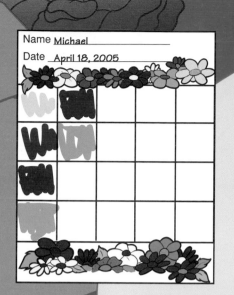

Name **Michael**

Date **April 18, 2005**

Flying Colors

Promote **student success** and avoid an outbreak of spring fever! Have each child personalize a copy of the incentive chart on page 285 and then store the chart inside his desk or work folder. Each time a child achieves a predetermined goal, such as participating appropriately in class or on the playground, have him color one box on his chart. When every box on a child's chart is colored, recognize his success with a special award or privilege. Bravo for sailing through spring with flying colors!

LITERACY CENTER
In Full Bloom!

A variety of **sorting skills** can blossom at this versatile center. Make a copy of page 286 for your files. Then cut out the colorful sorting mat on page 285, mount it on construction paper, and laminate it for durability. Program cards for word (or concept) sorts. Laminate the cards for durability, cut them out, and store each set in a zippered bag. Place the prepared materials at a center or use them with individual students.

Sort.

In Full Bloom!

shook

wood   book

roof

bloom   hoop

abdomen – feelers

scales – zoom

STUDY SKILLS
Zig and Zag

During this **guide word** activity, students zig, then zag, and then hover! In advance, label individual sentence strips with guide word pairs such as the following: *abdomen–feelers, feelers–metamorphosis, metamorphosis–scales, scales–zoom.* Post the sentence strips around the classroom. To begin, announce a broad topic or theme, such as animals or springtime, and give each child a card on which to write a related word. Collect the cards and scatter them facedown around the room. Then, on a signal from you, each child retrieves a card, reads the word, and carefully zigs and zags her way to the appropriate guide word pair. Provide time for each of the formed groups to alphabetize its cards. Repeat the activity using the prepared cards (or new card sets) as many times as you like!

Butterfly Pattern

Use with "Designer Wings" on page 281 and "Butterfly Words" and "Aflutter With Understanding" on page 282.

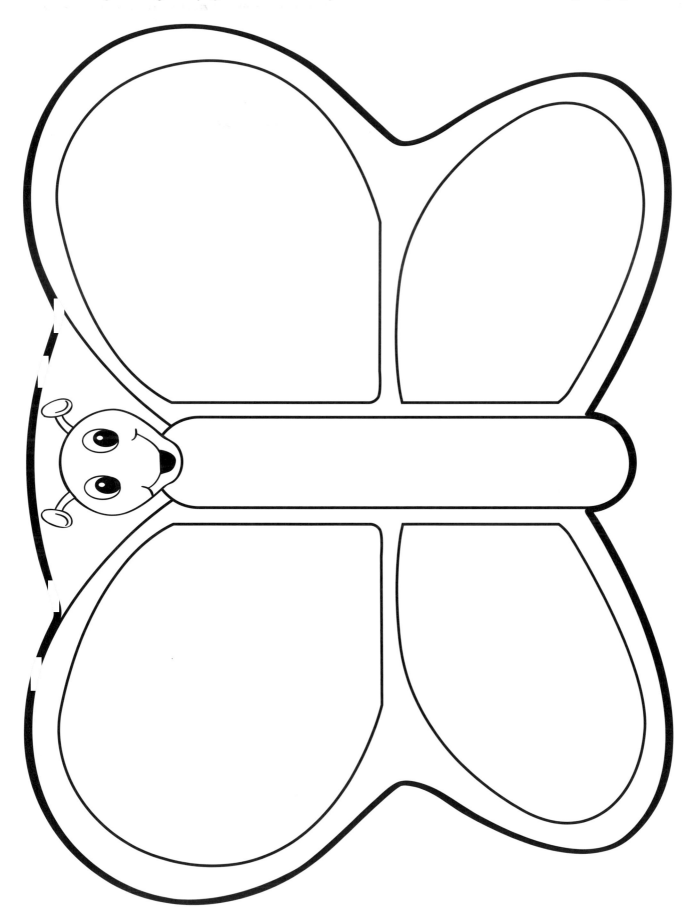

Butterfly Pattern
Use with "Fabulous Flyers" on page 282 and "Aflutter Over Facts" on page 52.

Incentive Chart
Use with "Flying Colors" on page 283.

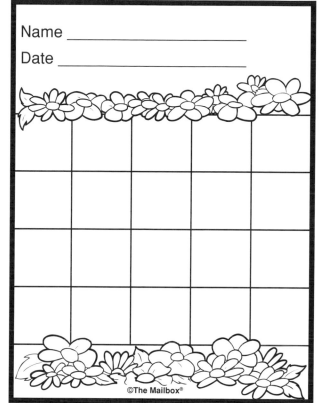

Name _____

Date _____

©The Mailbox®

Sorting Mat
Use with "In Full Bloom!" on page 283.

Sort.

In Full Bloom!

©The Mailbox®

©The Mailbox® • TEC43018 • April/May 2005

285

Name _____

All Aflutter!

Write each problem vertically.
Subtract.

475 – 254   A.

994 – 62   B.

898 – 540   C.

284 – 43   D.

728 – 526   E.

999 – 673   F.

665 – 34   G.

569 – 452   H.

193 – 51   I.

779 – 446   J.

756 – 24   K.

647 – 25   L.

Play Ball!

A Lineup of Cross-Curricular Activities

BATTER UP!
Reading

Challenge your sluggers to step up to the plate and read their way to a winning season! Have each child complete a copy of the baseball form on page 290 for a recently read book. Instruct her to rate the book by coloring one or more stars, with one star being a single and four stars being a home run. Next, ask her to trace a bat-shaped template onto a 6" x 18" construction paper rectangle and personalize the tracing. Then have her cut out the bat and ball shapes and connect them with a brad as shown. Showcase the projects with the title "Grand-Slam Readers!" Place extra copies of the baseball form nearby. For each book a student reads, she completes a form and attaches it to her bat. Plan to reward each slugger who collects five or more hits. Batter up!

adapted from an idea by Judi Lesnansky
New Hope Academy, Youngstown, OH

A Mouse Called Wolf
Dick King-Smith
This book is about a tiny mouse that has a great singing voice. He is also a hero!
I gave it a rating of 4 stars because Wolf is a really neat mouse. The book is fun to read too!

Slugger O'Neil

Knock skill review out of the park! These activities are definitely home run material!

ideas contributed by Stacie Stone Davis, Lima, NY

BALLPARK BUSINESS
Social Studies

Drive home an understanding of goods and services! For a pregame warm-up, engage students in brainstorming items sold and services provided at a baseball stadium. Next, have each student make a goods and services pennant. To do this, he folds in half a 4" x 18" construction paper strip (to 4" x 9") and, without cutting through the fold, trims the paper into the shape of a pennant. He labels one side of the folded cutout "Goods" and the other side "Services" and adds desired decorations. Then he glues together the inside surfaces, sandwiching a jumbo craft stick between them. For a few minutes each day, name a variety of goods and services found at a ballpark and have students display the appropriate sides of their pennants.

ON THE FIELD
Writing

Give your youngsters' expository-writing skills a workout. Before students begin to write, have them role-play throwing pitches, hitting home runs, and so on. Then instruct each youngster to write a paragraph that explains a baseball-related move. When the first drafts are written, pair students. Instruct each child to take a turn trying to follow the directions her partner wrote. Then have each author revise and edit her writing for clarity before publishing it in a baseball-shaped booklet like the one pictured. (Each booklet cover is the center of a paper plate.) For a tabletop display, trim away the bottom edge of each booklet to make it self-standing.

FROM THE DUGOUT
Study Skills

There's a lot of baseball lingo to alphabetize at this quick-to-prepare center! Make a copy of page 290 for your files. Next, cut out the learning center mat and answer key on page 289. Mount the cutouts on opposite sides of a sheet of construction paper and laminate the paper for durability. Place the activity at a center with a supply of the recording sheet on page 290. A student writes the words in ABC order and then flips over the learning center mat to check her work.

Slugger's Dugout

swing	mitt	walk	base
inning	out	slide	umpire
batter	tag	pitch	field
strike	hit	ball	catch

Write the words in ABC order.

©The Mailbox® • TEC43019 • June/July 2005

Answer Key

1. ball
2. base
3. batter
4. catch
5. field
6. hit
7. inning
8. mitt
9. out
10. pitch
11. slide
12. strike
13. swing
14. tag
15. umpire
16. walk

Baseball Form

Use with "Batter Up!" on page 287.

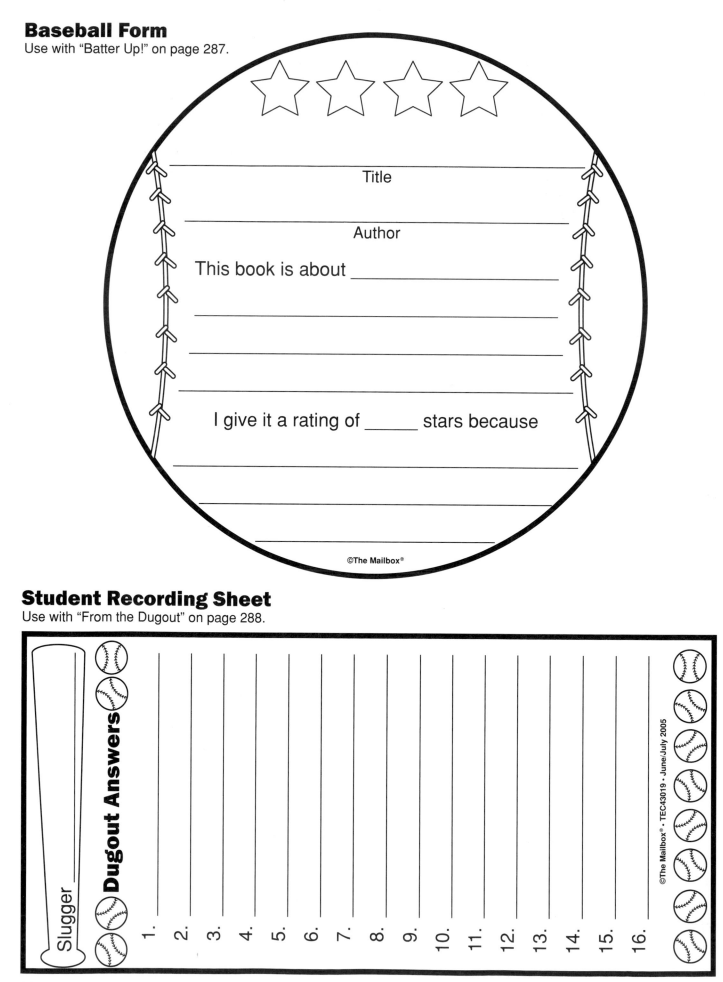

_____
Title

_____
Author

This book is about _____

_____

_____

_____

I give it a rating of _____ stars because

_____

_____

©The Mailbox®

Student Recording Sheet

Use with "From the Dugout" on page 288.

Slugger _____

Dugout Answers

1.
2.
3.
4.
5.
6.
7.
8.
9.
10.
11.
12.
13.
14.
15.
16.

©The Mailbox® • TEC43019 • June/July 2005

Baseball All-Stars

Use the chart.
Add or subtract.
Show your work.

Players	Games Played	Times at Bat	Home Runs
Sidearm Sid	140	518	15
Crush Cal	156	659	42
Speedy Petey	128	439	23
Slugger Gus	214	731	79
Slider Lex	97	399	11

1. How many games did Crush Cal and Slugger Gus play in all?

2. How many times at bat did Speedy Petey not hit a home run?

3. How many more times did Sidearm Sid bat than Slider Lex?

4. How many home runs did Slugger Gus, Sidearm Sid, and Crush Cal hit in all?

5. How many more games did Slugger Gus play than Slider Lex?

6. How many more home runs did Slugger Gus hit than Crush Cal?

7. How many times did Crush Cal and Speedy Petey bat in all?

8. How many times at bat did Slugger Gus not hit a home run?

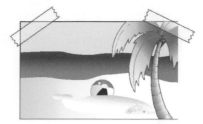

Wrapping Up

Finishing Out the School Year

WISH YOU WERE HERE!
Descriptive writing

Give students a chance to write about their dream trip with this postcard activity! To build enthusiasm, show students a variety of vacation destination pictures. Next, ask each child to choose a place he would like to visit during his summer break. Have him imagine what he will do there. Then, to create a postcard, the student draws a picture of his vacation spot on the blank side of a large index card. Next, he divides the lined side of the card into two parts as shown. In the small section he addresses the card to a family member and illustrates a postage stamp. In the large section he describes his trip. Invite students to share their cards with the class before they take them home to share with their families.

Daniela Hudock, Weston School, Manville, NJ

Hi Bobby!
I'm having lots of fun at the beach! I went surfing yesterday and rode a huge wave. I was doing great until I wiped out! Today I'm just hanging out. Wish you were here! See you soon!
Your brother,
Jeremy

Bobby Diaz
123 Main Street
Chicago, IL 60611

End the year with a finale of student memories, dreams, and smiles.

My favorite memory is our field trip to the dairy farm. I got to pet a cow! It was way cool to see how we get milk. I learned lots of interesting stuff about cows and milk. We had a picnic lunch too. Then we rode home on the bus. During the ride we played a guessing game and I won!

MEMORY QUILT
Writing a paragraph

Make a visual reminder of the school year with this class project! Set aside time for students to recall favorite memories from the past year. Next, have each student write on a 6" x 6" tagboard square a paragraph that describes her favorite memory. Invite her to illustrate the memory or decorate the square's edges. To make the quilt, punch a hole in every corner of each square. Arrange the squares into a rectangle, preparing extra squares as needed. Then use yarn lengths to connect the squares as shown. Display the completed quilt in the hallway for all to see. At the beginning of the next school year, hang the quilt in your classroom as a preview of the upcoming year for your new class.

Linda Butler, Community Therapeutic Day School
Lexington, MA

STUDENTS AS TEACHERS
Strengthening questioning skills

Try this idea as an end-of-the-year alternative to reading groups! A few weeks before summer vacation, have each child select a short picture book that he will enjoy reading to the class. Ask each child to practice reading his book, and have him complete a copy of page 294 to use as his lesson plan. Then, during the last weeks of school, invite each student to teach. To do this, he introduces his book and reads it aloud to the class. Next, he solicits answers to the three questions he prepared. Then he shares his favorite part of the book. Students will love the chance to teach their classmates, and you'll enjoy the fruits of their labor!

Bonnie Kinniff, St. Agatha School, Columbus, OH

The Worm

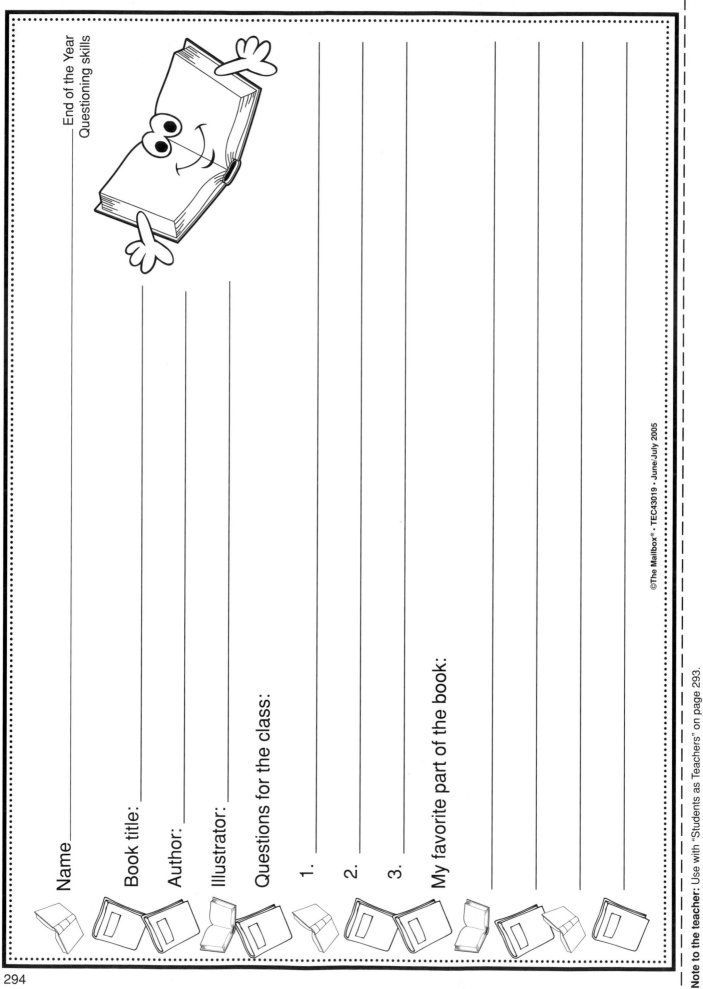

Name _____

Book title: _____

Author: _____

Illustrator: _____

Questions for the class:

1. _____

2. _____

3. _____

My favorite part of the book: _____

End of the Year
Questioning skills

Note to the teacher: Use with "Students as Teachers" on page 293.

TEACHER RESOURCE UNITS

Under the Big Top
Managing Literacy Centers

Wouldn't you agree that managing literacy centers is similar to being the ringmaster of a circus? It requires careful planning and preparation, skillful introductions, and plenty of audience participation. Use these subscriber tips and ideas to help you manage the greatest literacy centers under the big top!

some
have
their
what
very

⭐ Three Each Week ⭐

Your balancing act of preparing and maintaining centers just got easier! Set up three permanent centers in your classroom. Stock an ABC center with an alphabet strip, a spell-a-word center with magnetic letters and a magnetic surface, and a stamp-a-word center with letter stamps, colorful ink pads, and blank paper.

Each week use your computer to type a list of five or more new words for your classroom word wall. Enlarge the words to a desired size; then print the list, copy it four times onto colorful tagboard, and cut out each word. After introducing the words to students, post one set of word cutouts on your word wall and place one set in each of the described centers. Youngsters of varying abilities can step right up to these centers during literacy time!

Layla Ducote—Gr. 2
Highland Elementary, Baton Rouge, LA

⭐ What's Priority? ⭐

A prioritized list of independent literacy tasks could be just the ticket to minimizing interruptions when you're meeting with small groups. Prepare a standard list of independent activities that includes extra writing space for additional tasks. Laminate a colorful copy of the list for every child. Each day help students use wipe-off markers to list and prioritize their independent tasks. Students benefit by knowing exactly what is expected of them. They also enjoy a sense of accomplishment each time they cross an item off their lists. And you'll discover that the small amount of time you invest helping students prepare their lists is well worth the uninterrupted group time that follows.

Mary Ann Gildroy
Roundup, MT

⭐ Daily Edits ⭐

A parade of editing opportunities leads students to improved editing skills! Stock a literacy center with clipboards, colored pencils, and student copies of a paragraph or short story in need of editing. Post an edit checklist like the one provided and display the number of errors contained in the current writing sample. Challenge each child to work alone or with a partner to edit the piece of writing. Later, invite students to show off their editing expertise during a class edit of the work. Now that's an effective and easy-to-manage literacy activity!

Allison Rudback—Gr. 2
Immaculate Conception Catholic School
Port Perry, Ontario, Canada

Five-Star Edit

1. Check for complete sentences.
2. Check for capital letters.
3. Check for ending punctuation.
4. Check for correct spelling of word wall words.
5. Check for correct word spacing.

Today's writing sample contains __12__ errors.

⭐ Managing Early Finishers ⭐

This free-time choice keeps early finishers engaged in learning while their classmates complete their literacy tasks. Photocopy an assortment of skill sheets and their corresponding answer keys from a variety of educational sources, such as textbook companies, teacher magazines, and teacher resource books. Or purchase a book of skill sheets for this purpose. Laminate the skill sheets and answer keys. File the answer keys in a colorful file folder. Then sort the practice pages into skill-related groupings and file each set in a colorful folder. Store the folders in a plastic crate. Place the crate, a container of wipe-off markers, and several clean rags at a free-time center. When a child finishes his literacy work early, he selects an activity, a marker, and a rag from the center. When he finishes the activity, he finds the corresponding answer key and uses it to check his work. Then he wipes the skill sheet clean, refiles it and the answer key, and chooses another activity to complete. And the learning goes on!

Michelle Cotter—Gr 3
Anderson Elementary School, Wichita, KS

Open House Invitation
Use with "Opening Night" on page 299.

Premiere Event!
You are invited to opening night at

_____
school

Date: _____ Time: _____

Leading role: _____
student

Supporting role(s): _____
parent(s)

Director: _____
teacher

Gift Tag Pattern
Use with "X Marks the Spot!" on page 299.

You're a treasured member of our class!

Pirate's Loot

- an eraser because we all make mistakes
- Smarties candies for how smart you are
- a smiley-face sticker for happy times together

Note Pattern
Use with "On a Positive Note" on page 301.

Your child ended the day on a positive note!

_____
student

☐ worked hard

☐ helped others

☐ was cooperative

☐ followed directions

☐ had a good attitude

☐ showed improvement

☐ _____
other

☐ _____
other

_____
teacher

Getting Connected

Tips for Parent Communication

Looking for ways to connect with parents and caregivers? From open house suggestions to tips for positive parent notes, these ideas keep the lines of communication clear!

Opening Night

Boost open house interest and attendance with a movie-themed event! Program a copy of the invitation on page 298. Make a class supply and send one home with each student (or mail it if your open house is before the school year begins). Personalize a supply of star cutouts for your students and display them on your classroom door. Set a bag containing popcorn and concession candy on each child's desk. Roll a length of red bulletin board paper outside your door for a red carpet. As families arrive, invite them to explore your classroom. Then invite them to enjoy their snacks while you share pertinent information through a live presentation or prepared video. The event is sure to get rave reviews!

Anitra Elmore—Gr. 2, John Bass School, Las Vegas, NV

X Marks the Spot!

Take this treasured approach to open house! For each child, place a pencil, an eraser, a roll of Smarties candies, and a smiley-face sticker in a plastic resealable bag. Attach the gift tag from page 298. Place the treats in a large lidded box; mark the lid with an X. Place the box in a visible classroom location. Next, prepare a list of tasks that will familiarize family members with your curriculum, rules, and routines. Ensure that the last task directs readers to the marked box. Distribute the lists when families arrive and then send them off on their search for loot!

adapted from an idea by Kacie Farmer—Gr. 2 South Central Elementary, Elizabeth, IN

Ms. Farmer's Treasure Hunt

Student's name _____

Search the classroom to complete each item.

1. Find the schedule. What time is lunch?

2. How many words are on the word wall?

3. Name the student who sits next to you.

4. Write one book title from the classroom library.

5. Find the box marked with an X. Take a treat.

Quick Connection

Keep your contact information at parents' fingertips! Have an office supply store print a supply of business cards for you. (Or, for an inexpensive alternative, affix address labels with your information on card-size tagboard rectangles.) Send several cards home with each child, allowing parents to place cards in several locations, such as in a wallet and at work. As a result, parents will know that you're just a phone call or an email away!

Shannon Williams—Gr. 2
Wheat Elementary
Woodville, TX

I'd like to hear from you!

W Ms. Williams
Acornville Elementary
(323) 555-7890

I'd like to hear from you!

Ms. Williams
Acornville Elementary
(323) 555-7890

email: williams@acorn.com

Long Distance Plan

Need to keep involved parents that live far away informed about school happenings? Try this! Ask each interested parent to send or mail you a supply of stamped, self-addressed envelopes (one for each school month). Each month, mail the parent relevant papers such as field trip information, a newsletter, and samples of the child's work. If desired, include a photograph of the child or an illustration or note from the child. The parent is bound to appreciate your extra effort to keep her in the know!

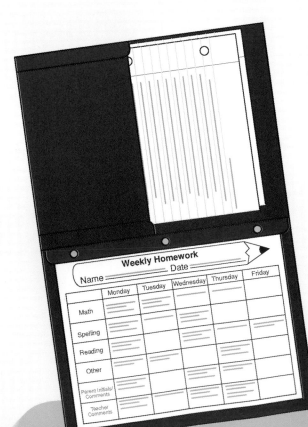

Weekly Homework

Date

Name

	Monday	Tuesday	Wednesday	Thursday	Friday
Math					
Spelling					
Reading					
Other					
Parent Initials/ Comments					
Teacher Comments					

Homework Helper

Help both students and parents stay on top of homework with this week-at-a-glance planner. Photocopy the homework sheet on page 302. On the first school day of the week, program the spaces with homework assignments. Make student copies and hole-punch the sheets. Give a copy to each child; have her place it in a provided three-prong pocket folder.

After a child completes her homework for the night, she asks a parent to check her work and jot any comments. She places her homework in the folder. The following school day, check students' work and respond to any comments in the space provided. Parents will appreciate being able to see all of the assignments for the week, and the homework sheet serves as an ongoing communication tool.

Beth Summers—Gr. 2, Holy Family School
New Albany, IN

High Five!

Here's a handy way to inform parents of their child's performance! Give each child a 12" x 18" sheet of construction paper. Have her trace her hand as many times as possible on the page and then cut out the tracings. Collect the hand cutouts for later use. When you'd like to applaud a child for her performance, jot a note on the cutout, beginning with "[Student's name] deserves a hand for…" and send the cutout home. Now that's a creative way to communicate with parents—hands down!

Amy Kurtz
Trinity Lutheran Interparish School
Council Bluffs, IA

Suzie deserves a hand for helping others today!

On a Positive Note

Tune in to this ongoing system to acknowledge positive behavior! At the beginning of the week, make a class supply of the note pattern on page 298. Program the notes with students' names. Each day, select the notes for several students who displayed exceptional behavior that day. Check off the corresponding items for each child, adding any additional behaviors as desired. Tell him to take the note home and read the checked behaviors to his family. His positive report will be music to their ears!

adapted from an idea by Gina Marinelli—Gr. 2
B. Bernice Young Elementary School
Burlington, NJ

All-in-One Communication

Keeping tabs on parent-teacher correspondence just got easier! Label a tabbed pocket divider for each child and place it in a three-ring binder. Tuck the child's emergency card or contact information sheet in the corresponding pocket. In each section, insert copies of email correspondence, notes, and parent-teacher conference forms. Also keep a log of important conversations on looseleaf paper, noting the date and what was discussed. When you need to locate information shared by or with a parent, you'll know just where to find it!

adapted from an idea by Jennifer Smith
Grs. K–3 Special Education, Sanderson Elementary
Canal Winchester, OH

Homework Planner

Use with "Homework Helper" on page 300.

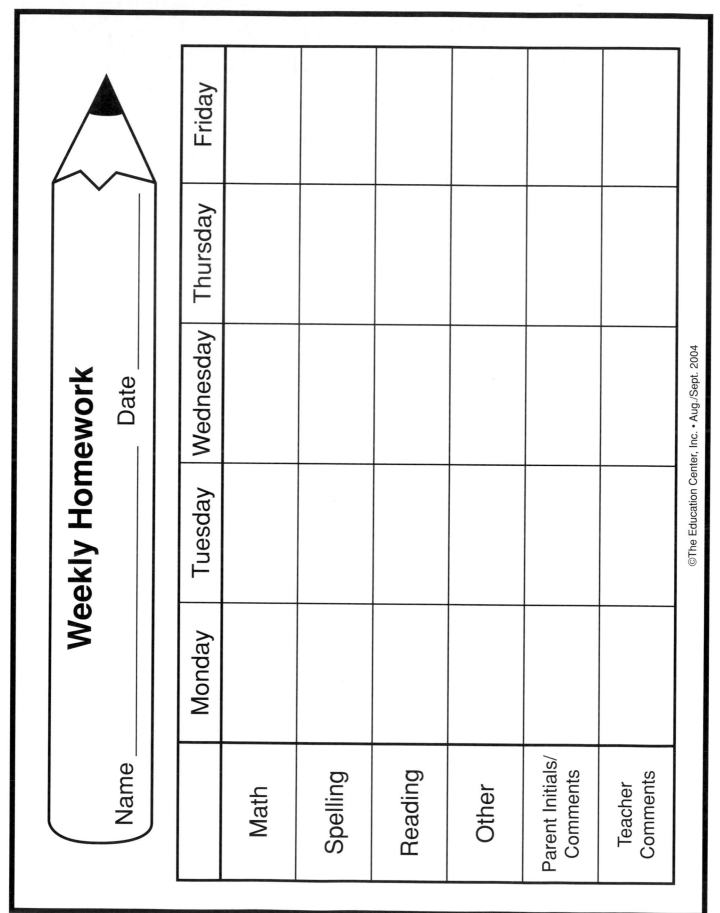

Weekly Homework

Name _____

Date _____

	Monday	Tuesday	Wednesday	Thursday	Friday
Math					
Spelling					
Reading					
Other					
Parent Initials/ Comments					
Teacher Comments					

STAYING AFLOAT!

Quick and Easy Sponge Activities

They're lifesavers during difficult-to-manage classroom routines like pre-lunch hand washing and school dismissal. They can be stress-free solutions to unexpected delays and last-minute cancellations. And they also engage students and promote learning. What are they? Sponge activities. Where can they be found? Right here!

Transparency to the Rescue

For this sponge activity, keep a container of colorful projection pens and a transparency of a coordinate grid near your overhead projector. When you face an unexpected delay, turn on the projector for a review of ordered pairs. Draw symbols on the grid and ask students to name the corresponding ordered pairs. Or supply ordered pairs and have students draw symbols on the grid in the corresponding locations. Who wants to draw a heart at (3, 6)?

Anita DeLaTorre
Hutton Elementary
Chanute, KS

In the Cards

If you have a deck of alphabet cards, you have a quick and easy sponge activity! Have two students come to the front of the room. Divide the card deck between these two card turners. Then split the class into two teams and appoint a scorekeeper for each team. For every round of play, each card turner shows the class one card. The first team to call out and correctly spell a word that includes the two letters earns one point. The first team to call out and correctly spell a word that includes the two letters and has a total of four or more letters earns two points. A team can earn all three points with one word. Keep the game moving along at a rapid pace. If no words are called out after several seconds, ask one card turner to draw a replacement card. The team with more points at the end of game time wins. Letters *m* and *h? Hamburger!*

Angela Kohl
Tappan Elementary
Ravenna, OH

303

Spy and Spell

An educational variation of the popular children's game I Spy is an instant sponge activity. Select a volunteer to be a word spy. This child selects a word in the classroom and provides his classmates with a sound-related clue and a spelling-related clue. For example, he could say, "I spy with both my eyes a word in our room. Its long *i* sound is spelled with the letters *ight*." Students offer words to the spy, who gives a thumbs-up for a correct answer or a thumbs-down for an incorrect one. The classmate who correctly guesses the mystery word becomes the word spy for the next round. Play continues for as long as desired.

Shawn Wallace-Baiza
Aerospace Academy
Moreno Valley, CA

Saved by Poetry!

Reading aloud from a book of captivating poetry is a speedy solution to a scheduling dilemma. Read aloud poems purely for your youngsters' listening pleasure or to reinforce a chosen literary skill. For example, to practice main idea, omit a poem's title when you read it aloud. Then read the poem a second time and ask students to brainstorm titles for the poem. Another option is to read aloud a poem two or three times and then ask students to illustrate it. Three cheers for poetry!

James Kellogg, Beaver River Central School
Beaver Falls, NY

Pass the Marker

The next time you need to spend a few minutes with a classroom visitor, start a game of Pass the Marker (or Pass the Chalk). Announce a category such as nouns, habitats, or things we measure. Hand a dry-erase marker (or chalk) to one student and establish a route for passing the marker to all students. When a child receives the marker, she uses it to write on the board a word that fits the named category. A child who is stumped quietly asks a classmate for help. To keep the game engaging, announce a new category every few minutes. Writing on the board? It's a student's dream come true!

Emily Furr
Mound Elementary School, Burleson, TX

Extra Edits

Students soak up editing skills during this sponge activity! On the board write two words that relate to the season. Ask a volunteer to read aloud the words. Ask another volunteer to dictate a sentence that includes both words. Write the sentence on the board so that it is in need of editing. Then have each of several volunteers make one needed edit. Silly sentences add to the fun!

Rose Welchans
Shenandoah Community Schools
Shenandoah Community, IA

sheep   rainbow

the shepe jumpt over a rainbow and broak its leg.

Scrambled Letters

Rather than scramble for an activity when your schedule unexpectedly changes, scramble some letters! Secretly identify a classroom item. Then, on the board, write the letters of its name in scrambled order. Students study the letters, scan the room, and guess what word the letters spell. A correct guess entitles a student to choose the next word and scramble its letters on the board. The popularity of this game may make it a free-time favorite for partners!

Michelle McCormick
Holdrege, NE

dske = ?

The big fluffy orange cat ran down the stairs after a little gray mouse.

Details, Please!

All you need for this sponge activity is a three-word sentence and a beanbag (or another soft object suitable for tossing). State a sentence, such as "The cat ran," and gently toss the beanbag to a child. The child holding the beanbag repeats the sentence. Next, he adds a detail to the sentence and says the revised sentence out loud. Then he gently tosses the beanbag to a classmate. This child follows the same procedure. Continue until several different students have added details to the sentence. Then introduce a new three-word sentence. Wow! Where did the time go?

Leslie Wilmes
Cypress Ridge Elementary
Clermont, FL

A Change of Scenery

Taking Skill Review Outdoors

Make the most of beautiful spring days by heading outdoors for selected learning activities like the ones that follow. It's amazing how a change of scenery and some fresh air can revitalize a child's enthusiasm for learning!

Up or Down?
Rounding numbers

For this upbeat review of rounding, march students right out onto the playground. Lead the class in the provided chant one or more times. Then keep the cadence as you sound off each of several two-digit numbers. Pause between the numbers so students can chant in unison a reply of "Round up!" or "Round down!" Sure, you'll make a ruckus, but you'll also march students to a better understanding of rounding!

Rounding Chant
(chanted to the marching cadence of "Sound Off")

Leader	Class
Rounding's not that hard to do.	(Repeat.)
Let me tell the rules to you.	(Repeat.)
For the digits five through nine,	(Repeat.)
Round that number *up* the line.	(Repeat.)
For the digits four and less,	(Repeat.)
Round that number *down,* oh yes!	(Repeat.)

Chorus: Chant twice.

Leader	Class
Round *up!*	Five through nine!
Round *down!*	Four and less!

Dorothy Cook, West Chester, PA

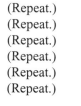

A Horse for a Night

Beginning
Emily sees a puffy white cloud in the sky that looks just like a horse. She wishes it were a real horse.

Middle
Emily dreams that the cloud horse comes to see her that night. They go for a ride. She feeds it an apple and a sugar cube.

Ending
The next day the cloud horse is gone. Emily is happy that she had a horse for a little while.

Trish

In the Clouds
Writing a story

A sky filled with intriguing cloud shapes is ready-made writing inspiration. For a prewriting activity, head outdoors with your class. Ask students to observe the clouds and name adjectives that describe them, such as *fluffy, puffy, weightless,* and *low.* Also challenge youngsters to find familiar shapes in the clouds. Then return to the classroom and have each child make a graphic organizer like the one shown and use it to plan a cloud-related story. Creativity is a breeze with the right writing motivation!

Stephanie Affinito
Craig Elementary School
Niskayuna, NY

twirl

waddle

Lights, Camera, Action!
Identifying action verbs

There's no need to compete with springtime wiggles and giggles when you can incorporate them into a parts-of-speech review! Label each of several large index cards with a different action verb. Write nouns or adjectives on a few more cards and add them to your collection. When you take students outdoors, bring along the prepared cards and a portable audio player that contains a desired musical recording. Start the music and show the class a card. If a verb is displayed, the students act it out to the music. If a noun or an adjective is shown, the students stand still. Continue displaying individual cards at a relatively rapid pace until the music runs out. Then head back indoors. To keep future reviews fresh and fun, make additions (or substitutions) to your card deck and vary your music selections.

Dawn Thurlow
Kemp Elementary
Powder Springs, GA

Hop to It!
Skip-counting and multiplication

Gather students around a hopscotch grid and exercise their bodies and their brains! Use chalk to label each grid box for a multiplication factor your students are working to memorize. Have half of your class line up at each end of the grid, and hand a beanbag (or eraser) to the first student in one line. This child tosses the beanbag on the grid. Where it lands determines his counting pattern. Then he simultaneously hops and counts his way to the opposite end of the grid, pausing to retrieve the beanbag. He hands the beanbag to the first child in the other line and then walks to the end of that line. The child holding the beanbag tosses it on the grid and takes his turn in the same manner but in the opposite direction. Play continues until every child has taken one or more turns.

adapted from an idea by Cheryl Escritt
Gibbon Elementary
Gibbon, NE

3
4   3
6
5   3
4
6   3
3
6
4

NAVIGATING THE WRITING PROCESS

Help your students chart a course for writing with these top-notch management ideas. Smooth sailing is guaranteed!

Pleasing Portfolios

This monthly approach to **portfolios** makes it easy for students to log their writing progress. Ask each student to bring in a three-ring binder to use for his portfolio. (Arrange to provide a binder for any student who does not bring one.) Have each youngster create a title page that includes his name and grade level. Then help him secure the page in his binder.

At the beginning of each month, ask each youngster to create a seasonal or holiday illustration on a blank sheet of paper and then label it with the month and year. Have him hole-punch the resulting divider page and secure it in his binder behind any other pages already in place. Throughout each month, instruct him to add selected writing samples in chronological order behind the appropriate divider page. The result will be a treasured record of his work!

Virginia Conrad, Bunker Elementary School
Bunker, MO

The "Write" Route

Keep your crew of young writers headed in the right direction with a picture-perfect **display.** Label a construction paper pencil for each stage of the writing process used in your classroom. Laminate the pencils for durability; attach a strip of magnetic tape to the back of each one. Mount a small photo of each student on a separate tagboard square and then secure a piece of magnetic tape to the back of it. Sequence the pencils in a column on a magnetic board.

Review the stages with students, pointing out that sometimes writers move back and forth among the different tasks. Ask each youngster to indicate her current stage of writing by displaying her photo beside the corresponding pencil. To keep the display up-to-date, encourage her to move her photo whenever she enters a different stage of writing.

Sheila Criqui-Kelley
Lebo Elementary
Lebo, KS

Prewriting

Writing

Revising

Editing

Publishing

Writers' Blocks

With this **management** plan, a writer's block doesn't stop the writing process—it keeps it moving! Obtain several blank wooden blocks (or cover several small boxes with light-colored paper). Use colorful markers to label the blocks with question marks. Stack the prepared blocks in an easily accessible location. Whenever a student would like a student-teacher conference, he quietly takes a block and places it in clear view on a corner of his desk. He continues working until he receives teacher assistance; then he returns the block. What a simple way to make the most of students' writing time!

adapted from an idea by Jennifer Nelson
Advantage Tutoring
Jacksonville, FL

Student __Cinder__   Date __1-11-05__

Classmate __Rex__

Revising Form

Is the writing easy to understand?   _____

Is any information missing?   _____

Does the writing stay on topic?   _____

Does it have good details?   _____

Suggestions: _____

_____

_____

See Three!

What's a surefire strategy to get writing shipshape? Promote **peer conferences!** Prepare a revising form, similar to the one shown, that is appropriate for your students' abilities. Place copies of the form in a designated classroom area. Ask each student to get feedback from three peers before she presents her writing for your review. During a youngster's first peer conference, she has a classmate complete a revising form and then staples the form to her work. After she revises her work as desired, she arranges two more peer conferences for proofreading assistance. Not only will the conferences increase students' sense of responsibility, but they'll also decrease the need for teacher assistance!

Julie Lewis, J. O. Davis Elementary, Irving, TX

Tag Time

When it comes to managing **peer conferences,** this idea is a lifesaver! Pair students and have each youngster use the TAG process with his partner. To do this, a youngster listens carefully as his partner reads aloud a sample of his unfinished writing. Then he makes three comments about the writing that correspond with the acronym TAG as shown. After the writer responds to the feedback, the partners trade roles. As students share their work, circulate to observe the discussions, and join in as desired.

Jennifer Singleton
Read School
Bridgeport, CT

Tell the writer one thing that you like.
Ask a question.
Give a suggestion.

Writing Buddies

All hands on deck for **revising and editing help!** Label a blank card "Revising" and a different-colored blank card "Editing." Place the revising card in the top row of a pocket chart and the editing card a few rows below it. Then designate each student a revising buddy or an editing buddy, depending on her skills. To do this, write each youngster's name on a blank card that is the same color as her assigned role. Then place her card in the corresponding section of the pocket chart.

When a student needs revising or editing help, she takes an appropriate name card and then shares her writing with the designated youngster. Afterward, she returns the card so that the blank side faces outward. To ensure that each student has a turn, ask students to remove only the cards with names displayed. Now that's putting collaboration to wise use!

Julie Lewis
J. O. Davis Elementary
Irving, TX

Time to Share!

Line up this idea to set students' sights on **sharing their completed work.** List each student's name on a vertically positioned sentence strip, beginning each name near the left edge. Use a magnetic clip to secure the list to the board or another magnetic surface. Clip a clothespin beside the first name. At a scheduled time, invite the corresponding youngster to read a chosen sample of his writing to the class. After he shares his work, move the clothespin to the following name to show who will share next time.

Beverly Wells
Hopkins Road Elementary
Richmond, VA

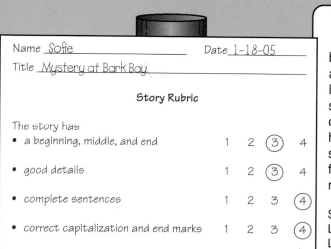

Assessment Plus!

What better way to help young writers learn the ropes than by giving them feedback? Prepare an **assessment** form with a desired writing rubric. Also prepare a chart with space for listing the titles, dates, and rubric scores of completed writing samples. After reviewing a student's writing, complete a copy of the assessment form and then staple it to her work. Have her make a corresponding entry on a copy of the chart that she stores in her writing folder. The feedback will help her focus on specific goals. Plus, her growing list of samples will remind her of her writing accomplishments!

Sheila Criqui-Kelley
Lebo Elementary
Lebo, KS

Answer Keys

Page 40

1. Dear
2. son
3. creek
4. our
5. berry
6. so
7. wood
8. one
9. for
10. aunt
11. fur
12. read
13. new
14. eight
15. not
16. do

Bonus Box: Illustrations and descriptions will vary.

Page 41

Order of answers will vary.

not	will
didn't	it'll
doesn't	he'll
haven't	we'll
isn't	I'll
don't	they'll
aren't	you'll
hasn't	she'll

Page 42

1. today
2. starfish
3. snowball
4. maybe
5. sunrise
6. cookbook
7. outside
8. birthday
9. touchdown
10. baseball
11. lifeboat
12. mailbox
13. into
14. toenail
15. keyboard
16. campground
17. indoor
18. dugout
19. homemade
20. airplane

Page 73

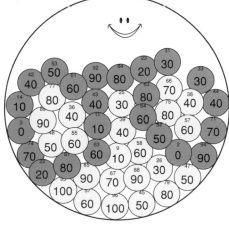

Bonus Box: Answers will vary, but each should explain that when there are fewer than five ones, you round down to the nearest ten. When there are five or more ones, you round up to the nearest ten.

Page 75

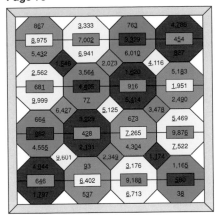

Page 77

Sunday	🪰 🪰
Monday	🪰 🪰 🪰
Tuesday	🪰 🪰 🪰 🪰
Wednesday	🪰 🪰
Thursday	🪰 🪰
Friday	🪰
Saturday	🪰 🪰 🪰 🪰 🪰 🪰

1. Friday
2. Saturday
3. 6; Answers may vary.
4. 60
5. more; 18

Page 78

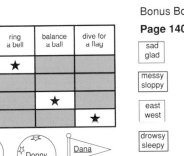

	jump through a hoop	ring a bell	balance a ball	dive for a flag
Dotty		★		
Dexter	★			
Donny			★	
Dana				★

Page 111

1. three
2. sleep
3. sheep
4. team
5. streak
6. beat
7. seats
8. treat
9. leave
10. meet
11. see
12. dream

Bonus Box: Each pair of letters stands for one vowel sound.

Page 116

Answers may vary.
1. huge elephant
2. striped zebra
3. hairy gorilla
4. tall giraffe
5. noisy lion
6. spotted leopard
7. fast cheetah
8. blue sky
9. puffy clouds
10. scaly snake
11. clear water
12. tiny flea

Page 117

1. Rex walks toward a sleeping lion.
2. He firmly holds his camera.
3. Lex hides behind Rex.
4. Yesterday, Lex scared a rhinoceros.
5. Today Lex remembers to be quiet!
6. Rex steps over a tree trunk.
7. The lion quietly moves one eye.
8. Now Rex takes a picture.
9. The lion roars loudly.
10. Lex and Rex stand still.
11. Soon the lion falls asleep.
12. Lex and Rex sneak away.

How?	When?	Where?
firmly	Yesterday	toward
quietly	Today	behind
loudly	Now	over
still	Soon	away

Page 125

Bonus Box: Details will vary.

Page 140

sad / glad	enemy / friend	dry / wet	mistake / error
messy / sloppy	gift / present	narrow / wide	alike / same
east / west	relax / rest	fast / quick	question / answer
drowsy / sleepy	neat / tidy	tame / wild	add / subtract
short / tall	shout / whisper	sad / unhappy	buddy / pal

Page 144

Sentences may vary but should include the underlined idioms.
1. Finding our picnic spot was a piece of cake.
2. We were all ears while the directions were read.
3. But we were in a pickle because we forgot a blanket!
4. Ellie was on the ball and found a good place for us to sit.
5. The food was out of this world!

Page 152

Order of answers will vary.

Miss Nelson
talks with a sweet voice
cannot make students behave
wears bright clothes
reads to students

Miss Swamp
gives a lot of homework
makes students behave
wears dark clothes
snaps at students

Page 159

The following statements should be crossed out. Completed sentences will vary.

Marvin Redpost
says mean things to his classmates
remembers everything

Mrs. North
never gets excited
takes up a lot of the president's time

The President
is very quiet
tries to hurry people

Page 162

The sentences each child writes about himself will vary. The
sentences about Little Gopher should be completed as follows:
Little Gopher likes to make <u>toys</u> to play with.
Little Gopher wants people to <u>remember</u>.
He wants to know how to paint bright <u>colors/paintings</u>.
He makes people happy with his <u>paintings/colors</u>.

Page 165

Cause	Effect
Tacky slapped a penguin on the back.	The penguin nearly fell.
Tacky made a splashy dive.	The other penguins got very wet.
The hunters came with traps.	The other penguins ran and hid.
Tacky did not run from the hunters.	The hunters walked up to Tacky.
Tacky marched and flopped down.	The hunters were puzzled.
Tacky sang to the hunters.	The hunters ran away.
Tacky made the hunters leave.	The other penguins hugged Tacky.

Page 171

The Lorax's Point of View

I thought Thneeds wouldn't sell.
I was mad that the Bar-ba-loots were hungry for tree fruit.
I hated that the factory's smoke stopped the birds from singing.
I was mad that machine goo went into the pond.
I was sad the trees were all gone.

[Child]'s Point of View: Answers will vary.

Page 182

1. <u>ramona</u> lives on <u>klickitat</u> <u>street</u>.
   S   R   E   K
2. <u>klickitat</u> <u>street</u> is in the state of <u>oregon</u>.
   O   W   S   K
3. <u>ramona</u> <u>quimby</u> finished second grade in <u>june</u>.
   U   Q   J   R
4. <u>this</u> year, <u>ramona</u> <u>quimby</u> is in the third grade.
   R   T   S   Q
5. <u>she</u> goes to <u>cedarhurst</u> <u>primary</u> <u>school</u>.
   S   S   P   C   I
6. <u>her</u> teacher is <u>mrs.</u> <u>whaley</u>.
   M   S   W   H
7. <u>ramona</u> has a sister named <u>beezus</u> <u>quimby</u>.
   Q   B   Y   R
8. <u>beezus</u> goes to <u>rosemont</u> <u>junior</u> <u>high</u> <u>school</u>.
   T   J   B   R   H   S
9. <u>there</u> is no school on <u>saturday</u> or <u>sunday</u>.
   S   T   M   S
10. <u>no</u> school means no <u>willa</u> <u>jean</u>!
    W   N   O   J
WE MISS YOU!

Page 187

318—Bedroom   165—Bathroom
224—Kitchen   419—Family room
153—Living room   361—Dining room
240—Guest room   507—Playroom

Bonus Box:

312

Page 191

38 > 25	41 < 46	76 > 72	19 > 18	59 > 49
27 > 11	82 < 88	92 > 86	33 < 35	74 > 69
54 > 50	75 > 63	28 > 21	91 < 92	44 > 28
90 < 99	46 < 49	71 < 84	16 < 61	32 > 15
43 < 62	33 > 32	84 > 58	13 > 11	56 > 23
17 < 71	58 > 47	23 < 39	89 < 98	29 < 39
82 < 97	64 > 60	75 > 59	57 > 49	73 > 65

Page 192

994	1,420
155	4,620
672	815
2,210	2,047
1,301	9,800
434	4,515
935	695

<u>ANYTHING YOU WANT.</u>
<u>THEY CAN'T HEAR YOU</u>!

Page 193

100 — eggs in a dozen
12 — days in a month
30 — pennies in a dollar

6 — speed of a car
25 — puppies in a litter
65 — students in a classroom

5 — sunrise each day
1 — seeds in an apple
64 — pages in a book

30 — degrees on a hot day
4 — degrees on a cool day
80 — quarters in a dollar

12 — mittens in a pair
4 — cups in a quart
2 — months in a year

24 — hours in a day
96 — passengers in a car
6 — pages in a book

Bonus Box: Answers will vary. Accept reasonable responses.

Page 196

1. 44
   + 23
    67 minutes

2. 26
   − 12
    14 songs

3. 16
   + 12
    28 hats

4. 56
   − 33
    23 times

5. 47
   − 25
    22 dances

6. 54
   + 15
    69 chairs

7. 37
   − 20
    17 minutes

8. 31
   + 38
    69 taps

Page 197

Order of addends may vary.

		44	87		
		+ 19	− 24		
		63	63		

33	75	26	53	23	56
+ 25	− 17	+ 15	− 12	+ 16	− 17
58	58	41	41	39	39

56	84	29	68	61	99
+ 19	− 9	+ 19	− 20	+ 25	− 13
75	75	48	48	86	86

19	47	18	81	37	90
+ 7	− 21	+ 34	− 29	+ 26	− 27
26	26	52	52	63	63

Page 201
Order of coins may vary. Written amounts should correspond with coin placement.

Page 209
Order of answers will vary.

one inch	one foot	one yard
nail	paintbrush	shovel
paper clip	lunchbox	umbrella
safety pin	screwdriver	ladder
thumbtack	bucket	broom
key	hammer	mop
button	ruler	rug

Page 214

Hit 1	Hit 2	Hit 3
_6_ inches	_3_ inches	_4½_ inches
_420_ feet	_210_ feet	_315_ feet

Hit 4	Hit 5	Hit 6
_5_ inches	_5½_ inches	_4_ inches
_350_ feet	_385_ feet	_280_ feet

Page 215

68 +23 = 91 **I**	25 +79 = 104 **A**	92 −41 = 51 **P**	32 +56 = 88 **L**	83 −47 = 36 **E**
54 −19 = 35 **R**	85 −16 = 69 **T**	17 +43 = 60 **S**	75 −28 = 47 **M**	44 +54 = 98 **F**
			68 +22 = 90 **C**	57 −26 = 31 **G**

AMERICA'S FIRST PILGRIMS

Page 221
A. 4
B. 2
C. 2
D. 2
E. 8
F. 12
G. 4
H. 3
I. 10
J. 16

Page 222
1. gallons, blue
2. cups, green
3. pints, yellow
4. quarts, purple
5. pints, yellow
6. quarts, purple
7. gallons, blue
8. pints, yellow
9. gallons, blue
10. gallons, blue
11. cups, green
12. gallons, blue

Page 226
E. 14 D. 36 G. 64 K. 35 Y. 54 U. 8
W. 15 N. 48 Q. 49 I. 12 A. 18 P. 40
T. 16 S. 30 H. 63 V. 20

HIDE-AND-SQUEAK!

Page 240
1. false
2. true
3. false
4. false
5. true
6. false
7. true
8. false
Bonus Box: The following words should be circled:
1. east
3. Adélie
4. Atlantic
6. north
8. no or south

Page 244
1. minerals
2. weathering
3. four
4. clay
5. erosion
6. sand
7. water
8. dirt
9. humus

Page 259
A. 10, 20, _30_, _40_, 50, _60_, 70, _80_, _90_, 100
B. 50, 45, _40_, 35, _30_, 25, 20, 15, _10_, 5
C. 62, 64, _66_, _68_, 70, _72_, _74_, 76, _78_, 80
D. 100, 95, _90_, _85_, 80, 75, _70_, _65_, 60
E. 6, 12, 18, _24_, _30_, _36_, 42, _48_, _60_, 66
F. 44, 42, _40_, _38_, _36_, 34, 32, _30_, _28_, 26
G. 30, 27, _24_, _21_, 18, 15, 12, _9_, _6_, _3_, 0
H. 12, 15, _18_, _21_, _24_, 27, _30_, _33_, 36, _39_
I. 71, 66, 61, _56_, _51_, 46, _41_, _36_, 31, _26_, 21
J. 12, 16, _20_, _24_, _28_, 32, _36_, _40_, 44, 48

"APPLE-LANCHE"!

Page 263
Chapter
3
4
6
1
2
3
6
3
6
2
4
1
Bonus Box: "What's for Dinner?"

Page 264
Order of addends will vary.

A	H	E	D
18 − (9) = 9	12 − (7) = 5	11 − (5) = 6	14 − (6) = 8
9 + 9 = 18	7 + 5 = 12	6 + 5 = 11	6 + 8 = 14
N	**S**	**O**	**S**
13 − (8) = 5	9 − (4) = 5	10 − (3) = 7	11 − (2) = 9
8 + 5 = 13	4 + 5 = 9	3 + 7 = 10	2 + 9 = 11
I	**S**	**P**	**E**
(10) − 5 = 5	(14) − 7 = 7	(12) − 6 = 6	(16) − 8 = 8
5 + 5 = 10	7 + 7 = 14	6 + 6 = 12	8 + 8 = 16
R	**O**	**B**	**A**
(13) − 6 = 7	(11) − 7 = 4	(15) − 6 = 9	(17) − 8 = 9
6 + 7 = 13	7 + 4 = 11	9 + 6 = 15	8 + 9 = 17

A SPIDER HAS NO BONES!

Page 269
Each answer should be a complete sentence. Sentences will vary.
1. He helps Ella find her missing mitten.
2. It is litter.
3. He stops and waves at Mr. Crump.
4. She looks as though she could use some help.
5. Answers will vary.
Bonus Box: Ed's four gifts should be underlined in the passage. The four gifts are the following: helping Ella find her missing mitten, waving to Mr. Crump, putting the wrapper in the trash can, helping Mrs. Finch.

Page 270
The gift givers are as follows:
Sneezy served ice cream.   Sleepy fed the cat.
Sloppy walked the dog.   Snoopy read a story.
Shiny polished boots.   Sweety baked cookies.
1. Snoopy
2. Sweety
3. Sloppy, Sleepy

Page 275

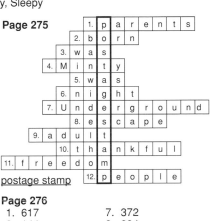

postage stamp

1. parents
2. born
3. was
4. Minty
5. was
6. night
7. Underground
8. escape
9. adult
10. thankful
11. freedom
12. people

Page 276
1. 617
2. 144
3. 195
4. 149
5. 427
6. 664
7. 372
8. 894
9. 171
10. 901
11. 368
12. 790

Bonus Box: Order of the following numbers may vary: 345, 354, 435, 453, 534, 543. The number 543 should be written in the shamrock.

Page 279
1. 13
2. 28
3. −12
4. −32
5. 17
6. 13
7. −22
8. −31
9. 0
10. −22

Page 280
1. moving air
2. moving air
3. breath
4. to wrap around
5. to twist and turn
6. moving air
7. to twist and turn
8. moving air
9. to wrap around
10. breath

Page 286

A.	B.	C.	D.
475 −254 = 221	994 −62 = 932	898 −540 = 358	284 −43 = 241
E.	**F.**	**G.**	**H.**
728 −526 = 202	999 −673 = 326	665 −34 = 631	569 −452 = 117
I.	**J.**	**K.**	**L.**
193 −51 = 142	779 −446 = 333	756 −24 = 732	647 −25 = 622

Page 291
1. 370 games
2. 416 times
3. 119 more times
4. 136 home runs
5. 117 more games
6. 37 more home runs
7. 1,098 times
8. 652 times

Index

314